KING
OF THE
GRILL

Ross Dobson's passion for food began when he was young, influenced by the cuisines of his neighbours from Hong Kong and Italy. He threw himself into the sizzling hot world of barbecue cookery after writing several other cookbooks (including *Chinatown* and *Three Ways with Stale Bread*). Now, with a couple of successful cafés and a career writing for some of Australia's top food magazines, Ross celebrates cooking outdoors with his take on no frills, flavoursome, fun-to-cook barbecued food.

ROSS DOBSON

KING
OF THE
GRILL

MURDOCH BOOKS

CONTENTS

INTRODUCTION

In a fast-paced world, there is great comfort to be had in the very thought of a barbecue. This is cooking by the most elemental means. Raw food on hot metal. This is about simple, stressless, tasty, no nonsense food. Well, at least for me it is.

To save confusion early on in the piece, let's use the word barbecue to broadly cover food that is cooked by applying dry heat to the surface of food – grilling, barbecue-braise, broil, char-broil or griddle. Whatever term you use to describe this method of cooking probably depends on where you are from. As an Australian, barbecue is my word of choice.

Where I come from, we do like to think we have a unique take on barbecuing. But don't we all? Having a barbecue is foremost a social event. It is the very socialness of the activity that defines it. This itself makes barbecues special and often memorable.

One such memory for me is being on a rooftop in Camden, London, enjoying the best that British summer had on offer; a fitted-like-a-glove heat made even more special because you knew the blue sky wouldn't last. Before the clouds inevitably gathered, we enjoyed barbecued mackerel spotted with lemon and bay leaves and sweet grilled Dublin Bay prawns. Not a bad spread, London Town.

Potrero Hill, San Francisco, is where I experienced my first all-American barbecue, high on a warehouse rooftop overlooking the city that looks even more pristine and enchanting from a distance. Over friendly discourse with relative strangers, we bonded over grilled ribs and the view. We ate these with potato salad, washed down with a Bud beer before we raced off into the fog to the ball park.

There is something magical about the hiss of food on the grill and the irresistible aromas that accompany it. This is quick, simple cooking at its sizzling best. In a large medieval square in Marrakesh, the marketplace by day sells everything from orange juice to leather backpacks, with snake charmers, charlatans and magicians vying for attention. At night, the market transforms into the world's largest barbecue. Hundreds of food stalls are lit by blurred fairy lights, made even more romantic by the thick shroud of wood-fire smoke in the air. People share long trestle tables. Strangers come together over barbecued lamb kebabs and the ubiquitous chilli condiment, harissa.

Marketplaces in Bangkok, Thailand, are similarly famous for their smoking hotplates and grills, sizzling with barbecued treats. Here, the metal skewers of the Middle Eastern kebab give way to bamboo skewers of spiced beef and pork satay.

My food travels have made an indelible impact on how and what I barbecue. I can bring back home my experiences and relive the flavours on my own grill in my backyard, on my verandah, balcony, patio or rooftop; under a tree, by the beach or on the river bank.

The versatility of grilling allows us to cook wherever we choose. This has to make it the most sociable way to cook food, right?

In barbecuing I could never deny my roots. I am Australian with a unique attitude towards barbecuing. I relish our cultural diversity, which brings to us food, flavours and influences from afar. Combine our style of cooking and access to such fine ingredients and you have really tasty food that can be made with ease. And fancy barbecue or not, I think this is how most of us like to cook. With a handful of flavours and a hot grill, you have made something that you can't wait to cook again.

In a sense, grilling allows us to be masters, or mistresses, of flavour. It really is up to you how the food will taste. It really is up to you how tender the meat is, in terms of cooking time and utilising different cuts of meat. I think we have become slightly overly concerned with food hygiene these days. Having said that, I am not saying it should not be a concern. Keep chicken and seafood refrigerated. On a warm day I would not leave chicken or fish sitting out too long. We should not eat rare cooked chicken – it must be cooked all the way through. Beef and lamb, on the other hand, can benefit from being allowed to sit at room temperature. And just because we might like our meat cooked rare doesn't mean we want our steak or lamb fillet to be fridge cold in the centre. Get the meat out of the fridge an hour or two before cooking. You will notice the difference. Aside from getting your food ready before barbecuing remember a few other tips: season well just before cooking; don't continuously (and mindlessly) turn the meat on the barbecue; and always allow the meat to rest after being cooked.

I am lucky enough to have a front verandah with room to spare for my barbecue and me. It is one of those old-world over-sized verandahs with no logical explanation as to exactly why it need be so big. But who's complaining? It's a beauty. Sun drenched and north facing, with just the right amount of shade. Rain, hail or shine, summer or winter, I can grill to my heart's content on the front verandah, waving at neighbours and passers-by. Sounds sociable? It is!

Barbecuing is as much about having fun as it is about anything else. Relax, enjoy, and you are halfway there to really good food and a lingering memory.

TYPES OF BARBECUES

Before talking about types of barbecues, let's establish exactly what a barbecue does. A barbecue cooks food on a metal hotplate or grill, conducting the heat from underneath. The food can be cooked by either direct or indirect heat. Closing the lid of a barbecue creates an oven-like effect, so that the heat circulates around the food, cooking it evenly.

ELECTRIC
These are ideal for apartment living. Even better if you have a balcony so you feel like you are barbecuing outdoors. They are a mobile and convenient way of cooking. But they do have downsides. Electric barbecues and grills often have built-in thermostats that cut off the heat, meaning you have less control when cooking. Not ideal for a barbecue.

GAS
The thing here is making sure you actually have gas to burn. Some outdoor barbecues have the luxury of town or natural gas piped directly into them. Certain stove tops have built-in hotplates and grills, which means you can cook many barbecue recipes indoors. But you probably will need an exhaust fan of some sort. Topping up the LPG is not always convenient and can be expensive – but note that you can never cook indoors using LPG. Inside or out, cooking with gas gives you greater control over heat, which is what a good barbecue is all about.

WOOD
Cooking over a wood fire requires attention, but it produces a barbecued result like no other. Maintaining consistent heat is tricky, and it will take time to master a wood-fired barbecue. Ideal in the great outdoors and in a great big yard, but because they are generally constructed of brick they aren't mobile, which is an obvious limitation.

COAL
These are designed as compact, mobile units, which equates to convenience. They range in size and function, with many of the larger charcoal barbecues made to slow-cook big cuts of meat. These obviously cannot be used indoors but are great if you have a yard or a balcony. In Japan, what we know as an hibachi was actually designed to heat homes, not to cook food. In America, the hibachi grill has become synonymous with quick, efficient and healthy grilling. Some smaller coal barbecues can actually be placed in the centre of the table so diners can cook their own food, making the act of barbecuing very interactive.

FINE FEATHERED FRIENDS

CHILLI **CHICKEN BLT**

LEMON, BALSAMIC AND
GINGER WINGS

FRAGRANT **CHICKEN PARCELS**

HONEY HOI SIN CHICKEN WINGS

QUAILS WITH PEANUTS AND
THAI HERBS

BUCCANEER **CHICKEN SKEWERS**

CHIMICHURRI CHOOK

CHICKEN THIGHS WITH GARLIC CREAM

CHICKEN WITH **BACON AND WITLOF**

AMELIA'S **QUAIL**

BLACKENED BIRD

TERIYAKI AND BEER CHICKEN

TANDOORI CHICKEN

LEMONGRASS AND **LIME
LEAF CHICKEN**

LEMON CHICKEN, FETA AND
HERB **INVOLTINI**

PIRI PIRI SPATCHCOCK

FESTIVE TURKEY WITH CRANBERRY
AND CHERRY SAUCE

CHILLI CARAMEL CHICKEN

BARBECUE CHICKEN WITH
GREEN OLIVE SALSA VERDE

BEER CAN ROASTED CHICKEN

FIERY THIGHS

CHINATOWN DUCK SHANKS

DUCK WITH SAFFRON RICE
STUFFING AND ROASTED VEGETABLES

SLOW-COOKED **SHANTUNG CHICKEN**

CHILLI YOGHURT CHICKEN

CHICKEN WITH **JALAPEÑO BUTTER**

CHICKEN WITH **TARRAGON, OLIVES
AND GARLIC**

SPICED QUAIL WITH VIETNAMESE LIME
AND PEPPER DIPPING SAUCE

VERDANT CHOOK

HARISSA CHICKEN

COCONUT **CHICKEN TENDERLOINS**

GREEN CURRY CHICKEN

CREOLE CHICKEN

KERALAN CHICKEN

MEXICAN PESTO CHICKEN

THAI BARBECUED CHICKEN

SPECIAL **BRINED ROAST CHICKEN**
WITH AÏOLI

**SWEET CHILLI AND
GINGER** CHICKEN

CHILLI **CHICKEN BLT**

This chicken is perfect as a spin on the old bacon, lettuce, tomato – BLT. I am cooking the breast on a low–medium heat so the meat doesn't dry out too much, which chicken breast meat is prone to.

SERVES 4

2 large red chillies,
    seeded and chopped
2 garlic cloves, chopped
1 handful flat-leaf (Italian) parsley
    leaves, roughly chopped
3 tablespoons olive oil
2 large boneless chicken breasts,
    cut in half
4 rashers streaky bacon
4 soft bread rolls
mayonnaise
2 large handfuls baby rocket (arugula)
2 tomatoes, finely sliced

Put the chillies, garlic and parsley in a small food processor and whiz to combine. Add the oil and whiz until all the ingredients are finely chopped and flecked throughout the oil. Put the chicken in a snug-fitting non-metallic dish and pour over the marinade. Cover and then refrigerate for 3–6 hours, or you could do this the day before.

Remove the chicken from the fridge 20 minutes before cooking. Put the chicken breasts on a chopping board and wrap each with a rasher of bacon.

Preheat the barbecue hotplate to low–medium and drizzle with a little olive oil to lightly grease. Put the chicken breasts on the hotplate and cook for 10 minutes. You may need to adjust the heat so the breasts gently sizzle the entire cooking time, watching that the bacon doesn't burn. Press down on the thickest part of the breast with a flat metal spatula a few times. Turn over and cook for another 10 minutes. Remove and rest on a plate for 5 minutes.

Serve the chicken as a BLT-type burger on the roll spread with mayonnaise and topped with rocket and tomato.

LEMON BALSAMIC
AND **GINGER WINGS**

Okay, now this will sound odd. You are putting the chicken on a cold barbecue hotplate. This means your hotplate should be clean. But this is a good way to cook chicken wings. They are a thick, bony mass and often are overcooked on the outside before cooking all the way through. This method ensures even cooking.

SERVES 4

12 chicken wings
125 ml (4 fl oz/½ cup)
    balsamic vinegar
125 ml (4 fl oz/½ cup) lemon juice
2 tablespoons light olive oil
2 tablespoons finely grated ginger
2 garlic cloves, crushed
¼ teaspoon cayenne pepper
lemon cheeks, to serve

Chop the wing tip off each wing and discard. Cut between the joint to get two bits of chicken from each wing. Put the chicken into a large non-metallic bowl or dish. Combine the vinegar, lemon juice, olive oil, ginger, garlic and cayenne pepper and pour over the chicken. Use your hands to toss it all together, cover and refrigerate for 3–6 hours or overnight.

Remove from the fridge 30 minutes before cooking. Do not turn the barbecue on, but lay your wings onto the clean, cold hotplate. Sprinkle sea salt generously all over the chicken. Now turn the heat on to high, close the lid and cook for 12–15 minutes, or until golden. After several minutes you will hear the chicken start to sizzle. Turn the chicken over and cook for another 5 minutes, or until cooked through. Serve with the lemon cheeks, extra salt and freshly ground black pepper.

FRAGRANT **CHICKEN PARCELS**

Where would we be without Chinese food? Here we have some classic Chinese flavours, sweet and salty with intense aromatics. Tenderloins are great. They often don't need any cutting or chopping. I like their shape and size and use them all the time in curries, not even browned off, just thrown into the hot curry and left to poach. Here, the tenderloins are wrapped and steamed on the hotplate.

SERVES 4

12 chicken tenderloins
8 garlic cloves, peeled
3 tablespoons light soy sauce
50 g (1¾ oz) unsalted butter, melted
2 tablespoons honey
4 star anise
2 cinnamon sticks, broken in half
fresh coriander (cilantro) leaves,
    to serve

Put all the ingredients in a bowl, tossing to combine. Set aside at room temperature for 30 minutes, or cover and refrigerate for up to 6 hours. Remove from the fridge 30 minutes before you begin cooking.

Tear off four large sheets of foil and lay on a work surface. Tear off four large sheets of baking paper and lay each one on top of the foil.

Put 3 tenderloins in the centre of each sheet of baking paper. Use the foil to form a cup shape around the chicken. Spoon equal amounts of the marinade over each portion of chicken. Twist the foil to secure and enclose to make a parcel.

Preheat the barbecue hotplate to medium. Sit the parcels on the hotplate, close the lid and cook for 5–6 minutes, or until cooked through. Put the parcels on a platter to unwrap at the table. Garnish with fresh coriander leaves and serve with barbecued corn, if desired.

HONEY HOI SIN CHICKEN WINGS

A favourite for both kiddies and adults alike, these wings are a sweet and sticky easy-to-eat treat, just as good as a cold snack as they are straight off the grill. The Asian sauces here are a must-have, but this isn't too much of an ask as these ingredients can be picked up in just about any supermarket if you aren't near an Asian specialty store. They have good shelf life but once opened do keep them in the fridge. I say to marinate these overnight and if you do, remember to turn them often.

SERVES 4

12 chicken wings

HONEY HOI SIN MARINADE
2 tablespoons light soy sauce
3 tablespoons hoi sin sauce
3 tablespoons tomato sauce (ketchup)
3 tablespoons honey
1 tablespoon sesame oil

Cut the wing tips off the chicken wings, then cut the wings between the centre joint to give two pieces – one of them looking like a little drumstick. Put the chicken in a steamer lined with baking paper (a Chinese bamboo steamer is perfect), cover with the lid and sit the steamer over a saucepan of boiling water for 10 minutes. Remove the chicken wings and allow to cool.

Combine the honey hoi sin marinade ingredients.

Put the chicken wings in a non-metallic dish, pour over the marinade and toss to coat. Cover and put in the refrigerator for 3 hours or overnight, turning often.

Remove the chicken wings from the fridge 20 minutes before you begin cooking.

Preheat the barbecue grill to low and brush with a little olive oil to grease. (The cooking is easy but you do have to keep your eyes and ears alert that the wings are gently sizzling.) Shake the excess marinade off the chicken into the dish, put the chicken wings on the grill, reserving the marinade, and cook for 2 minutes on each side until they begin to turn golden, then start to baste. Baste, turn and cook for 2 minutes, then repeat. Keep doing this for 10–12 minutes until wings become deep reddish-brown, glazed and just starting to char.

QUAILS WITH PEANUTS AND THAI HERBS

If you haven't noticed I am a big fan of Asian flavours, and I find that the fresh Thai ingredients work well in barbecuing. These flavours also very much typify modern Australian cooking. This recipe uses lots of exotic herbs, that thrive in our climate, combined with Thai staples that can be bought easily at any local Asian specialty stores and most supermarkets.

SERVES 4

8 jumbo quails, about 200 g
   (7 oz) each
1 lime, cut in half
1 handful coriander (cilantro),
   roughly chopped
1 teaspoon white pepper, to serve

THAI PESTO
40 g (1½ oz/¼ cup) crushed peanuts
2 garlic cloves, chopped
¼ teaspoon white pepper
1 large green chilli, chopped
1 small bunch Thai basil leaves
1 small bunch coriander (cilantro),
   leaves only
1 small bunch mint leaves,
   roughly chopped
1 tablespoon fish sauce
1 teaspoon sugar
1 tablespoon lime juice
1 tablespoon olive oil

For the Thai pesto, put all the ingredients in a food processor and whiz to a chunky paste. Put in a container and refrigerate until ready to use.

To prepare the quails, put one on a chopping board, breast side up. Hold the bird with one hand and insert a heavy, sharp knife into the cavity, firmly cutting either side of the backbone all the way through. Throw the backbone away and spread the quail open on the chopping board with the skin side up. Press firmly down on the breast with the palm of your hand to flatten the bird. Repeat with the other quails. Wash the quails and pat dry. Now gently separate the skin from the flesh, being careful not to tear the skin. Reserve 60 g (2¼ oz/¼ cup) of the pesto and put aside. Spoon some of the remaining pesto under the skin and gently spread over the breast and as far down towards the leg as you can, without tearing the skin. Put the quail on a baking tray lined with baking paper, cover and refrigerate until needed.

Remove the quail from the fridge, squeeze the lime over the skin of each and set aside for 20 minutes.

Preheat the barbecue hotplate to medium and drizzle with a little olive oil to grease. Put the quail on the hotplate and cook, skin side down, for 5 minutes with the lid on until the skin is crispy and dark golden. Reduce the heat to low, turn the quail over and cook for another 10 minutes. Remove to a plate, lightly cover with foil and rest for 5 minutes. Serve with the reserved pesto spooned over and with coriander and white pepper.

BUCCANEER **CHICKEN SKEWERS**

Not too sure why I decided to title this one buccaneer, considering a buccaneer is someone who robs and plunders from the sea. I think it stems from an obsession with Caribbean food, which to me means lots of hot cayenne pepper and tropical lime – which brings buccaneers to mind!

SERVES 4

6 boneless, skinless chicken thighs,
    each cut into 4 pieces
2 spring onions (scallions), chopped
1 handful flat-leaf (Italian) parsley
2 garlic cloves, chopped
¼ teaspoon cayenne pepper
2 tablespoons lime juice
2 tablespoons olive oil

LIME CHILLI SAUCE
3 tablespoons lime juice
2 tablespoons olive oil
3 tablespoons finely chopped flat-leaf
    (Italian) parsley
2 teaspoons finely chopped rosemary
1 large red chilli, finely chopped
4 spring onions (scallions),
    thinly sliced

Put the chicken in a ceramic dish or bowl. Put the spring onions, parsley, garlic, cayenne pepper, lime juice and olive oil in a food processor and process to a paste. Rub all over the chicken. Cover and refrigerate for 6 hours or overnight.

To make the lime chilli sauce, combine all the ingredients in a bowl. Pour over 125 ml (4 fl oz/½ cup) boiling water, stir to combine. Set aside. Soak some wooden skewers for 30 minutes.

Remove the chicken from the fridge 30 minutes before cooking. Thread the chicken onto skewers, three pieces on each.

Preheat the barbecue hotplate or grill to high. Cook the skewers for 8–10 minutes, or until cooked through, turning often. Spoon the sauce over to serve.

CHIMICHURRI CHOOK

This is the stuff of folklore and urban myth – the famous Argentinean/Uruguayan steak condiment. I've come across many tales. I do like the one ditty that claims for the sauce to be authentic the meat you marinate it in must taste like it has been dragged through the garden! Another tale goes, it was named after an Irishman by the name of Jimmy Curry. (Say it quickly enough, after a few drinks on a warm day, and you may end up saying something like chimichurri.) But this tale sounds like a bit of a stretch.

SERVES 4

4 boneless chicken breasts, skin on
1 lemon, cut in half

CHIMICHURRI
2 garlic cloves, coarsely chopped
½ teaspoon sea salt
1 small handful flat-leaf (Italian)
    parsley, coarsely chopped
1 tablespoon chopped oregano leaves
1 small handful coriander (cilantro)
    leaves and some stems,
    coarsely chopped
¼ teaspoon cayenne pepper,
    or a big pinch
¼ teaspoon Hungarian paprika
3 tablespoons olive oil
3 tablespoons red wine vinegar

For the chimichurri, put the garlic and sea salt in a pestle and pound to a chunky paste. Add the herbs, spices and olive oil and pound to combine, then stir through the red wine vinegar. Set aside for the flavours to develop. Soak some bamboo skewers in water for 30 minutes.

Cut each chicken breast into 4–6 large chunky pieces and put in a non-metallic dish. Pour over the chimichurri marinade and toss to coat the chicken pieces. Cover and refrigerate for no longer than 3 hours, otherwise the vinegar will start to 'cook' the chicken.

Remove the chicken from the fridge 20 minutes before cooking and thread 3–4 pieces of meat onto the skewers. Put the skewers on a plate and reserve the marinade.

Preheat the barbecue hotplate to medium. Put the chicken skewers on the hotplate and cook for about 12 minutes, brushing over the marinade and turning so each side cooks for 3 minutes. When the skewers are golden brown, remove, squeeze over the fresh lemon, season to taste and then serve.

CHICKEN THIGHS
WITH GARLIC CREAM

Trim the fat off the chicken thighs if you must, but I would encourage you to leave it on. Most of it will render off and sizzle away. It acts as a buffer between the thigh meat and the intense heat of the barbecue, leaving the thigh tender and very tasty. But the real star here is the toum, or garlic cream. This is the toothsome stuff you most definitely would find at any good Lebanese restaurant. Think of it as similar to but also very different from aïoli. It has no yolks just egg whites and tastes so bloody good.

SERVES 6

6 large boneless, skinless
   chicken thighs
125 ml (4 fl oz/½ cup) lemon juice
125 ml (4 fl oz/½ cup) white wine
2 teaspoons sea salt
1 teaspoon sugar
1 teaspoon dried oregano
flat-leaf (Italian) parsley leaves,
   to serve

GARLIC CREAM
4 garlic cloves, chopped
2 egg whites
185 ml (6 fl oz/¾ cup) olive oil

To make the garlic cream, put the garlic and egg whites into the bowl of a food processor and whiz to combine. With the motor running, slowly add the olive oil until the mixture is fluffy, white and creamy. Transfer to a bowl.

Combine the chicken, lemon juice, white wine, sea salt, sugar and oregano in a non-metallic dish. Set aside at room temperature for 30 minutes, or cover and refrigerate for 3–6 hours. Remove the chicken from the fridge 30 minutes before you begin cooking.

Preheat the barbecue grill to high. Cook the thighs for 8 minutes. Turn over and then cook for another 5 minutes. Sprinkle with parsley leaves and serve with the garlic cream.

CHICKEN WITH
BACON AND WITLOF

Witlof loses some of its bitter intensity when cooked, and this isn't a bad thing.
You could throw the ingredients of this recipe between a lovely, soft burger bun
with some aïoli. Or even sprinkle some grated parmesan cheese over the top —
a bit like a chicken Caesar salad.

SERVES 6

6 large boneless, skinless
  chicken thighs
12 rashers streaky bacon
3 tablespoons olive oil
1 tablespoon red wine vinegar
1 garlic clove, finely chopped
2 tablespoons roughly chopped
  flat-leaf (Italian) parsley, plus
  extra sprigs, to serve
4 large witlof (chicory/Belgian
  endive), quartered
lemon cheeks, to serve

Cut each chicken thigh in half. Wrap a rasher of bacon around the middle of each thigh and sit in a flat dish.

Mix together the olive oil, vinegar, garlic and parsley in a bowl, pour over the chicken and toss to coat. Set aside at room temperature for 30 minutes, or cover and refrigerate for 3–6 hours.

Remove the chicken from the fridge 30 minutes before you begin cooking.

Season the chicken well with sea salt and ground white pepper. Preheat the barbecue grill and hotplate to high.

Cut the witlof in half lengthways. Put the cut side of the witlof down on the grill. Put the chicken on the hotplate and close the lid. Cook for 8–10 minutes, so the witlof is well browned and the bacon and chicken golden. Turn both witlof and chicken over, close the lid and cook for another 5 minutes.

Arrange the witlof and chicken randomly on a serving platter and scatter over the extra parsley. Serve with the lemon cheeks on the side.

AMELIA'S **QUAIL**

Most of these are typical Asian flavourings so you may be wondering why the use of olive oil? That's what I asked myself one summer when a friend suggested I try these flavours as a marinade for tasty little quail. The fruity olive oil really enhances the simple yet distinctive flavours here. Nice one, Amelia.

SERVES 4

8 quails
3 tablespoons olive oil
2 tablespoons light soy sauce
4 garlic cloves, roughly chopped
1 tablespoon lightly grated ginger

To prepare the quails, put on a chopping board, breast side up. Insert a heavy, sharp knife into the cavity. Firmly cut either side of the backbone, all the way through. Discard the backbone and spread the quail open on the chopping board with the skin side up. Press down firmly to flatten the bird. Cut off each of the wing tips and throw away. Cut in half through the breastbone. Now cut each of the halves in half again, so the legs and thighs are separated from the breast. Wash and pat dry with paper towel and put the quails in a snug-fitting non-metallic dish.

Combine the other ingredients in a bowl and pour over the quails, tossing the quail pieces around so they are evenly coated in the marinade. Cover and set aside for 30 minutes or put in the refrigerator for 3–6 hours, turning them often. If you do refrigerate the quails just remember to take them out of the fridge 1 hour before cooking. The cooking time is short so you don't want them to still be cold in the centre.

Preheat the barbecue hotplate to medium. Shake any excess marinade off the quails and reserve for later use. Put the quails on the hotplate and cook, skin side down for 2 minutes. Reduce the heat to low and cook for another 4 minutes, pressing down occasionally with a flat metal spatula on the thicker breast pieces. The skin should be golden brown. Turn the quails over, cover the barbecue with the lid and cook for 5 minutes, again pressing down a couple of times on the thicker pieces. Working quickly, stir the reserved marinade and pour evenly over the quail, turning the birds a couple of times to coat in the sauce. Remove to a platter, cover lightly with foil and let the quails rest for 5 minutes before serving.

BLACKENED BIRD

This is Cajun cooking at its finest, nothing more or less. Let the classic spice rub weave its spell as it defies the sum of its parts. On their own these are really full throttle flavours – but combined they become voodoo magic!

SERVES 4

2 spatchcock (small chickens), about
    500 g (1 lb 2 oz) each

CAJUN RUB
2 tablespoons smoked paprika
1 teaspoon dried oregano
1 teaspoon dried thyme
¼ teaspoon cayenne pepper
2 teaspoons sea salt flakes
2 garlic cloves, crushed
2 tablespoons light olive oil

Combine the cajun rub ingredients in a small bowl and set aside.

Cut the spatchcock in half through the breastbone to give four portions of bird. Remove the cartilage in the breastbone and cut off the wing tips. Wash and pat dry with paper towel.

Rub spice blend all over the birds and put in a snug-fitting non-metallic dish. Cover and then refrigerate for at least 3 hours or overnight if you like.

Preheat the barbecue hotplate to medium. Sit a rack on the hotplate – this will keep the birds lifted up from the direct heat, preventing them from burning.

Sit the birds on the rack, skin side up. Cover the barbecue with the lid and cook for 35–40 minutes. They should be darkened with a reddish tone from the paprika. Remove to a plate and gently cover with foil for about 15 minutes, not too tightly. You don't want them to sweat and the skin to lose its crispiness under there. Serve whole.

NEXT TIME Cut a large chicken, about 1.8 kg (4 lb), in half like the smaller birds and then cut the halves across to give four portions from the one large chicken. Rub with the spice blend and refrigerate overnight. Cook on a hotplate preheated to medium for 15 minutes skin side down, turn over and cook for another 15–20 minutes, until the juices are no longer pink when pierced with a skewer.

TERIYAKI AND BEER CHICKEN

The Japanese are one of the masters of really tasty grilled food. Yet the flavourings are pretty much always the same, just used in different ratios. The beer is not a traditional Japanese marinade ingredient, but I couldn't resist using it to add extra flavour to my favourite cut of chicken, the tender thigh.

SERVES 4

8 chicken thigh fillets

TERIYAKI AND BEER SAUCE
3 tablespoons beer (a light ale is good
    here, preferably Japanese)
3 tablespoons Japanese soy sauce
1 tablespoon sugar
1 teaspoon mustard powder

Combine the teriyaki and beer sauce ingredients in a small bowl and stir until the sugar has dissolved. Put the chicken fillets in a flat non-metallic dish and pour over the marinade. Cover and refrigerate for no more than 3 hours, turning the chicken often.

Remove the chicken from the fridge 20 minutes before you begin cooking.

Preheat the barbecue grill to medium and brush with a little vegetable oil to grease. Put the chicken thighs on the grill, reserving the marinade, and cook for 5 minutes, then turn over and cook for a further 3 minutes. Now start basting with the teriyaki and beer sauce, turning the chicken over every minute. Continue this process for about 4 minutes, until the edges of the thighs are starting to look slightly charred and the rest of the chicken is a dark amber, golden colour. Remove to a plate, lightly cover with foil and allow to rest for 5 minutes before eating.

TANDOORI CHICKEN

I cannot claim to have invented the technique of sitting the chicken on a beer can. However, I just love the idea and the results. It is also the most ideal way to barbecue a whole bird, when many of us do not have a rotisserie built in to our barbecue. This chicken is so good on grilled Indian naan bread, with some shredded lettuce and lemon squeezed over.

SERVES 4

1 teaspoon saffron threads
2 small chickens, about 1.2 kg
   (2 lb 10 oz) each
125 ml (4 fl oz/½ cup) lemon juice
3 teaspoons sea salt
2 onions, chopped
260 g (9¼ oz/1 cup) plain yoghurt
2 tablespoons ghee
2 garlic cloves, chopped
1 tablespoon finely grated ginger
2 teaspoons ground cumin
1 teaspoon ground coriander
½ teaspoon ground turmeric
½ teaspoon chilli powder

Soak the saffron threads in 2 tablespoons of hot water for 10 minutes.

Wash the chickens and pat dry with paper towel. Cut two deep slashes into the breasts and legs of each bird and put into a large bowl. Combine the lemon juice, sea salt and saffron mixture in a small bowl and pour over the chicken. Toss to coat and rub the mixture into the slashes. Set aside at room temperature for 30 minutes.

Put the onions, yoghurt, ghee, garlic, ginger, cumin, coriander, turmeric and chilli powder in a food processor and blend to a paste. Rub all over the chicken. Cover and refrigerate for 6 hours or overnight, turning the chicken every now and then.

Remove chicken from the fridge 30 minutes before cooking.

Preheat the barbecue burners to high and close the lid to create a hot-oven effect. Sit the cavity of each chicken on an empty beer can.

Reduce the heat to medium and sit the chicken upright on the hotplate so the can and the ends of the chicken drumsticks form a tripod. Close the lid and cook for 1 hour 10 minutes, or until golden and cooked through. The juices should run clear when the thigh is pierced with a skewer. Serve half a chicken per person.

LEMONGRASS AND
LIME LEAF CHICKEN

You may have guessed that lemongrass is a grass. The top, green part is more fibrous and less flavoursome, so use the soft white part of the grass, close to the bottom, for the best results. If you live somewhere temperate it is easy to grow lemongrass and it is much better when picked and used fresh. This is something I often serve in summer, with boiled rice and greens, and some Chinese chilli sauce on the side.

SERVES 4

8 chicken thigh fillets

**LEMONGRASS AND LIME
LEAF MARINADE**
2 lemongrass stalks, white part only,
    finely sliced
4 small makrut (kaffir lime) lime
    leaves, very finely shredded
3 garlic cloves, chopped
1 tablespoon grated ginger
2 spring onions (scallions), chopped
1 tablespoon olive oil
1 tablespoon fish sauce

For the marinade, put the lemongrass, makrut leaves, garlic, ginger and spring onions in a food processor and whiz until the mixture looks like a fibrous and chunky paste. Put in a bowl and stir through the oil and fish sauce.

Put the chicken in a snug-fitting non-metallic dish. (Chicken thighs often have a little fat which is okay to leave on. You can trim the fat if you really want to, but they are cooked so well here that the fat will only render off and give a little extra flavour, and keep the meat moist as it cooks.) Pour on the marinade and rub all over the chicken. Cover and refrigerate for 3–6 hours or overnight, turning often.

Remove the chicken from the fridge 20 minutes before you begin cooking.

Preheat the barbecue grill to high. When it is hot, brush just a little vegetable oil onto the grill. Put the chicken on the grill and cook for 5 minutes, pressing down occasionally on the thickest part of the thigh with a flat metal spatula. This is the part that is often left under-cooked, which is what you don't want with chook. There should be a golden crust formed on the cooked side. Turn the chicken over and cook for another 5 minutes. Remove to a plate, lightly cover with foil and allow to rest for 5 minutes before eating.

LEMON CHICKEN, FETA AND HERB **INVOLTINI**

This is an Italian thing – rolling a flattened piece of meat, usually veal, into a log and flavouring it with anything you like, really. I had to have an excuse to include soft marinated feta in a recipe in this book, so here it is. These involtini are thick buggers, so don't rush them, let them sizzle gently and slowly and you will be rewarded.

SERVES 4

4 large chicken thigh fillets
35 g (1¼ oz/¼ cup) soft feta cheese
     (marinated or Persian feta)
4 short rosemary sprigs
2 tablespoons olive oil
2 tablespoons lemon juice
1 handful flat-leaf (Italian) parsley
     leaves, roughly chopped
2 tablespoons chopped
     oregano leaves

Put a chicken thigh between two layers of plastic food wrap and gently pound so it is an even thickness all over, about 5 mm (¼ in). Repeat with the remaining chicken thighs. Spread 1 tablespoon of feta over each flattened thigh and put a sprig of rosemary across. Sprinkle a little sea salt (but not too much as the feta could be salty enough) and some freshly ground black pepper over the meat and gently roll up the thigh, from one short end to the next, enclosing the feta and rosemary so it sticks out either end. Tie the involtini with kitchen string and put in a non-metallic dish. Repeat to make four involtini. Combine the olive oil, lemon juice and remaining herbs in a bowl and pour over the chicken. Cover and refrigerate for at least 3 hours.

Remove the involtini from the fridge 20 minutes before you begin cooking.

Preheat the barbecue hotplate to low. Put the involtini on the hotplate and cook for 16 –18 minutes, turning often so they sizzle the whole time and are golden brown all over. Put the involtini on a heatproof plate, cover with foil and sit on the lid of the warm barbecue for 10 minutes to rest before serving.

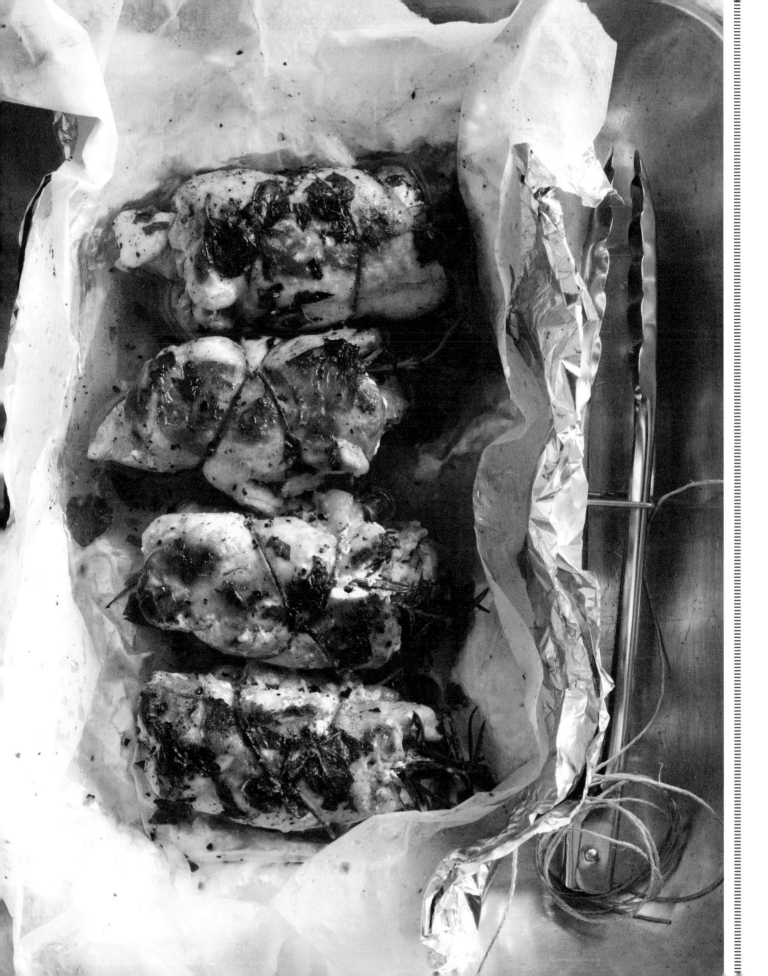

PIRI PIRI SPATCHCOCK

We have seen many fast-food franchises claiming to provide Portuguese flavoured grilled chicken. Some of it is good. According to the recipe title, my version makes a similar claim. It is not traditional, with the inclusion of Chinese chilli garlic sauce and shop-bought roasted red capsicum in the ingredient list. But I think it is very tasty and extremely easy. For a more traditional piri piri recipe, check out page 208.

SERVES 4

4 spatchcock (small chickens), about 500 g (1 lb 2 oz) each

PIRI PIRI MARINADE

300 g (10½ oz/1½ cups) chopped roasted red capsicum

4 tablespoons Chinese chilli garlic sauce

1½ tablespoons olive oil

1½ teaspoons ground cumin

1½ teaspoons fresh marjoram, plus extra, for serving

To make the piri piri marinade, put all the ingredients in a food processor and blend until smooth. Set aside.

Sit each chicken, breast side up, on a chopping board. Lay the palm of your hand on the top of the chicken to make stable. Insert a large knife into the cavity of the chicken and cut either side of the backbone. Remove and discard the backbone.

Flatten the chickens on the chopping board by firmly pressing down on the breastbone with the palm of your hand.

Put the chickens in a large dish or bowl and rub all over with two-thirds of the marinade. Put the remaining marinade in a bowl and refrigerate until needed. Cover the chicken and refrigerate for 3–6 hours or overnight, turning often.

Remove the chicken from the fridge 30 minutes before you begin cooking.

Preheat the barbecue hotplate and grill to high and close the lid to create a hot-oven effect.

Sprinkle sea salt over the skin of the chicken. Lay the chicken, skin side down, on the hotplate, close the lid and cook for 5 minutes. Reduce the heat to medium–low and cook for another 10–15 minutes, until aromatic and the skin is dark golden. Turn over and cook for another 15 minutes, or until the chicken is cooked through. Allow to rest for 10–15 minutes.

Scatter with fresh marjoram leaves and serve with the reserved marinade as a sauce.

FESTIVE TURKEY WITH CRANBERRY AND CHERRY SAUCE

Marinating turkey breast is a good start to a tasty cooked bird. Leaving the skin on will also help prevent the meat from drying out. Cook the turkey until just done, wrap in foil and allow to rest.

SERVES 4

1 boneless turkey breast, about 800 g
    (1 lb 12 oz), skin on
1 handful sage leaves, to serve

CRANBERRY AND CHERRY SAUCE
170 ml (5½ fl oz/⅔ cup) port
4 tablespoons crème de cassis
2 tablespoons chicken stock
1 tablespoon cornflour (cornstarch)
125 g (4½ oz/¾ cup) fresh or frozen
    halved and pitted cherries
100 g (3½ oz/1 cup) fresh or
    frozen cranberries
½ teaspoon ground cinnamon
2 teaspoons sugar

To make the cranberry and cherry sauce, combine the port, crème de cassis, chicken stock and cornflour in a small saucepan, stirring so the mixture is lump-free. Add the cherries, cranberries, cinnamon and sugar and simmer over medium heat for 4–5 minutes, until the liquid has thickened and the fruit is just tender. Set aside.

Preheat the barbecue hotplate and grill to high and cover with the lid to create a hot-oven effect. Reduce the heat to medium. Sprinkle sea salt over the skin of the turkey and lay the turkey, skin side down, on the hotplate. You will want to hear a gentle sizzle as the turkey hits the hotplate – if it is too hot, or sizzling too loudly, turn the heat down a little. Close the lid and cook for 15–20 minutes so the skin is golden and crisp. Turn over, close the lid and cook for another 10 minutes. Loosely wrap the turkey in foil and sit on the warm barbecue lid for 15 minutes, allowing the turkey to rest.

Carve the turkey, arrange on a serving plate and spoon over the cranberry and cherry sauce. Scatter over the sage leaves and serve.

CHILLI CARAMEL CHICKEN

When you use sugar or sweet sauces and honeys in a marinade you have to watch out that it doesn't burn the meat when cooking. I try to avoid this by using any overly sweet concoction as a baste, not a marinade. So basically, cook the meat first then patiently baste on any sweet sauce for the desired result. This recipe calls for chicken breast fillets with skin on, but skinless breast fillets can also be used.

SERVES 4

4 chicken breasts with wing attached, skin on
1 teaspoon white pepper

CHILLI CARAMEL BASTE
3 tablespoons rice vinegar
3 tablespoons light soy sauce
1 tablespoon fish sauce
2 tablespoons white sugar
1 teaspoon dried chilli flakes
2 garlic cloves, finely chopped

Combine the basting ingredients in a small jug or bowl and set aside.

Remove the chicken from the fridge 20 minutes before cooking and sprinkle the white pepper and some sea salt over the skin.

Preheat the barbecue hotplate to high and drizzle with a little vegetable oil to grease. Put the chicken on the hotplate and cook, skin side down, for 4–5 minutes, until the skin begins to turn golden and crispy. Turn over and cook for another 3 minutes.

Turn the barbecue down to medium. Baste the skin side of the chicken, turn over and cook for 1 minute. Repeat this process until all the baste has been used up and the chicken has a dark caramel glaze all over – this should take a further 8–10 minutes. Remove to a plate, lightly cover with foil and allow to rest for 5 minutes before serving.

BARBECUE CHICKEN WITH GREEN OLIVE SALSA VERDE

I use a procedure here called 'brining'. This is really nothing more than the most basic marinating method – soaking the meat in salt, sugar and spices – but the flavour is something else!

SERVES 4

2 x 1.25 kg (2 lb 12 oz)
    free-range chickens
140 g (5 oz/½ cup) table salt
60 g (2¼ oz/⅓ cup) brown sugar
3 bay leaves
3 tablespoons olive oil
3 tablespoons lemon juice

GREEN OLIVE SALSA VERDE
1 thick slice white bread,
    crusts removed
60 g (2¼ oz/½ cup) pitted
    green olives
1 large handful flat-leaf (Italian)
    parsley leaves, roughly chopped
1 large handful mint leaves,
    roughly chopped
1 large handful celery leaves,
    roughly chopped
1 tablespoon salted capers, well rinsed
2 garlic cloves, chopped
2 anchovy fillets
2 tablespoons lemon juice
3 tablespoons olive oil

Cut the chickens in half through the breastbone, remove the cartilage and backbone, cut off the wing tips, then wash and pat dry with paper towel. Put the chickens in a snug-fitting non-metallic dish, cover and refrigerate.

Bring a large saucepan of water to the boil and add the table salt, sugar and bay leaves. Return to the boil, stir until the salt and sugar have dissolved, then remove from the heat and cool completely. Pour enough of the brine liquid over the chickens so they are well immersed and refrigerate for 3–6 hours or overnight.

For the salsa verde, tear the bread and put in a food processor with the olives, herbs, celery leaves, capers, garlic, anchovies and lemon juice. Pulse to combine, leaving the mixture a little chunky. Put into a bowl and stir through the olive oil, and add some freshly ground black pepper.

Remove the chickens from the brine and pat dry with paper towel. Put in a bowl and add the olive oil and lemon juice, rubbing the mixture all over the chickens. Season with sea salt and black pepper and set aside for 20 minutes.

Preheat the barbecue hotplate to low–medium. Put the chickens on the hotplate, skin side down. Put the lid on the barbecue and cook for 15–20 minutes, pressing down occasionally with a flat metal spatula, until the skin is dark golden and crispy. Turn the chicken over and cook for a further 15 minutes, until cooked through. You can test if it is ready by making a small, deep incision between the end of the drumstick and the breast. Any liquid that runs out should be clear, not bloody. Remove the chicken to a plate and lightly cover with foil for 10 minutes to rest. Serve half a chicken per person with the salsa verde spooned over.

BEER CAN ROASTED CHICKEN

In cooking this you could be excused for thinking you have reinvented the wheel. You see, there has always been a problem in roasting a chicken on the barbecue if you don't have a fancy-pants rotisserie. If you do, good on you! But if you don't, then what do you do? Well, there is something right under our noses at a barbecue that can solve this problem – a half-full can of beer. The obvious advantages of beer-can chook are twofold: sitting the chicken on the beer can keeps the bird up off the hotplate; and, meanwhile, the beer itself slowly boils, steaming the inside of the chicken. The result is a perfectly roasted, moist and tender chicken.

SERVES 4

2 x 1.5 kg (3 lb 5 oz)
   free-range chickens
1 lemon
1 tablespoon Cajun seasoning
1 tablespoon olive oil
1 tablespoon finely chopped tarragon
1 tablespoon finely chopped flat-leaf
   (Italian) parsley
2 tablespoons finely chopped
   coriander (cilantro)
2 tablespoons lemon juice
2 x 375 ml (13 fl oz/1½ cups)
   can of beer
coriander (cilantro), extra,
   roughly chopped
1 lemon (or lime), cut in half

Wash the chickens inside and out with cold water, pat dry with paper towel, then rub all over with lemon.

Combine the Cajun seasoning in a little bowl with the oil and herbs to form a paste. Brush over the skin of the birds, then sprinkle with a good amount of sea salt.

Preheat the barbecue to hot. If you have an average three-burner barbecue (one hotplate and two grills, or vice versa) put them all on as you really want to crank the heat up so it acts like an oven. And you will need a barbecue with a lid for this.

Drink some of the beer, not too much, no more than a couple of big sips. Now sit the chickens on the beer cans so the cans fit snugly in the chickens' cloaca (technical term for the cavity, AKA 'the clacka').

Sit the cans on the barbecue, making sure the end of the drumsticks are at the same level as the bottom of the beer cans (so they sit balanced on the hotplate). Close the lid and cook for 1 hour. (If the chooks are a bit bigger, say 1.8 kg/4 lb, give them 10 minutes more.) Test if the chickens are cooked by piercing the skin and flesh where the leg meets the thigh. If the juices are clear, they are ready. Remove the chickens to a plate and lightly cover with foil for 15 minutes before cutting each into 10–12 small pieces. Sprinkle over the extra coriander and serve with the fresh lemon or lime to squeeze over.

FIERY THIGHS

A tip here for flavour success – use dried Greek oregano. You will find this at delis, hung in dry bushes in a plastic bag. It is much more flavoursome than most supermarket varieties and I reckon it even smells very different. Although I don't use many dried herbs, and there are some I will never use, this one I use more like a spice and I would even go so far as to say it is better than fresh oregano.

SERVES 4

6 boneless, skinless chicken thighs
1 teaspoon dried Greek oregano
1 teaspoon chilli flakes
1 teaspoon sea salt, plus extra,
    to serve
2 tablespoons finely chopped
    flat-leaf (Italian) parsley
3 tablespoons lemon juice
3 tablespoons olive oil
lemon wedges, to serve

As one end of the thigh is thicker than the other, pound the thicker end with a meat mallet so it is all the same thickness. Cut each thigh in half and put into a bowl with the oregano, chilli, sea salt, parsley, lemon juice and olive oil. Toss the chicken to coat in the marinade. Cover and set aside at room temperature for 30 minutes, or refrigerate for up to 6 hours or even overnight. Turn the chicken often if it is in the fridge and remove from the fridge 30 minutes before you begin cooking.

Preheat the barbecue hotplate to high. Put the chicken on the hotplate, leaving the excess marinade in the bowl. Cook for 7–8 minutes. Pour over about half of the reserved marinade and then turn the chicken over and cook for 5–6 minutes. Pour the remaining marinade over the chicken. Turn the chicken over on the hotplate a few times until the marinade is cooked off. Season with extra sea salt and serve with the lemon wedges.

CHINATOWN DUCK SHANKS

When I first saw the words duck and shank together I thought it must be a mistake, or a joke. After all isn't a shank part of the leg of a four-legged creature? I was thinking lamb. But, no. A shank is the part of the leg of any vertebrate. Anyway, lucky for me I live but 20 minutes from Australia's largest free-range duck farm. This means lots of whole ducks, livers, marylands and shanks.

SERVES 4

12 duck shanks
2 tablespoons hoisin sauce
2 tablespoons light soy sauce
2 tablespoons Chinese rice wine
2 star anise
2 drops cochineal (optional)
2 tablespoons honey
2 spring onions (scallions), thinly
   sliced on an angle
Chinese barbecue sauce (char siu),
   to serve

Put the duck shanks into a dish with the hoisin sauce, soy sauce, rice wine, star anise and cochineal, if using, tossing the shanks around in the marinade. Cover and refrigerate for 24 hours, turning the duck every now and then.

Remove duck from the fridge 30 minutes before cooking.

Preheat the barbecue hotplate and grill to medium and close the lid to create a hot-oven effect.

Remove the duck from the marinade. Sit the duck on a rack and sit the rack over a deep baking tray. Half-fill the baking tray with water and sit on the barbecue, close the lid and cook for 30 minutes. Turn the duck shanks over and cook for another 30 minutes, or until golden. Brush the honey over the shanks and cook for another 10 minutes, turning the shanks and brushing each side with the honey until they are glistening and crisp.

Arrange the shanks on a serving platter and scatter over the spring onions. Serve with Chinese barbecue sauce on the side.

DUCK WITH SAFFRON RICE STUFFING AND ROASTED VEGETABLES

Duck is a funny one. To be honest, there was a time when I was a little reluctant to cook with it as many recipes seemed like too much work for too little pleasure. Save confit for eating out. Then two things happened. Duck became less expensive and I threw away the recipe book for cooking it. When I mastered a simple roast duck in my oven it then became all too easy to take it outside to the barbecue and with all that hot fat around, the outside seems like the best place. Up there with the glazed ham, this could be served up as a regular Christmas treat.

SERVES 4

2.5 kg (5 lb 8 oz) roasting duck
2 tablespoons sea salt
8 small new potatoes
2 carrots, cut into long pieces
2 parsnips, cut into long pieces

SAFFRON RICE STUFFING
1 small white onion, finely chopped
1 garlic clove, chopped
½ teaspoon saffron threads
2 bay leaves
100 g (3½ oz/½ cup) long-grain rice
1 teaspoon ground ginger
250 ml (9 fl oz/1 cup) chicken stock

Trim the excess fat from around the duck cavity and cut off the neck, leaving 2–3 cm (¾–1¼ in) of neck intact. Wash the duck thoroughly and pat dry with paper towel, inside and out. Set aside for 1 hour.

For the stuffing, put the onion, garlic, saffron and bay leaves in a small saucepan with 125 ml (4½ fl oz/½ cup) of water and cook on high heat for 5 minutes, so the onion softens and the water has evaporated. Add the rice and ginger and cook for 1 minute, stirring so the rice looks shiny. Add the chicken stock, bring to the boil then cover tightly. Cook on low heat for 10 minutes, so the rice is partially cooked and the stock is absorbed.

Preheat all the barbecue burners to low, with the lid on. This will create a hot-oven type effect in which to roast the duck. Loosen the skin and pierce with a skewer all over. This will help the fat drain out as it cooks. Spoon the rice stuffing into the cavity and seal the cavity with a skewer. Rub the sea salt all over the duck and sit on a cooking rack over a deep baking tray. Sit the tray on the hotplate of the barbecue, cover with the lid and cook for 1 hour. Check after 30 minutes. The skin will have just started to shrink and look slightly golden. If the side of the duck facing the grills is cooking quicker you may need to turn off the grill burner, or one of them, as heat flows vary from barbecue to barbecue.

Carefully lift the rack to one side and pour off all the fat, and as much sediment as possible, from the roasting tray into a heatproof dish. Arrange the vegetables in a single layer on the roasting tray then spoon over 2 tablespoons of the hot duck fat. Sit the rack back on the tray and spoon 1 tablespoon of the fat over the duck breasts. Cover and then cook for 30 minutes.

Again, remove the duck to one side. Carefully pour off any excess fat in the roasting tray, leaving about 2 tablespoons. Turn the vegetables over and return the rack to the tray. Baste the duck with 1 tablespoon of the fat, cover and cook for another 30 minutes.

By this time the duck will be dark golden and the vegetables cooked. Remove the vegies to a heatproof plate and cover lightly with foil. Leaving the duck over the roasting tray, turn all the barbecue burners to high, cover and cook for 10–15 minutes, so the duck skin is crispy and dark golden all over. Sit the tray of vegies on the hot hood of the barbecue to keep warm.

Remove the duck, cover lightly with foil to keep warm and rest for 15 minutes. Cut the duck into quarters and serve with the stuffing and roasted vegies.

SLOW-COOKED
SHANTUNG CHICKEN

If you're a fan of barbecued chicken from the local takeaway you are bound to love this. The sauce here is a classic balance of salt, sour, sweet and spice. It takes the humble chook to another level.

SERVES 4

1 large chicken, about 1.8 kg (4 lb)
2 tablespoons sesame oil
2 tablespoons light soy sauce
1 tablespoon lemon juice

SHANTUNG SAUCE
2 tablespoons light soy sauce
2 tablespoons rice vinegar
2 teaspoons caster (superfine) sugar
½ teaspoon sea salt
2 large red chillies, thinly sliced
1 small bunch coriander (cilantro),
   roughly chopped

Sit the chicken, breast side up, on a chopping board. Use a long, sharp knife to reach into the cavity of the chicken and cut either side of the backbone. Remove and discard the backbone.

Flatten the chicken on the chopping board and press down on the breastbone with the palm of your hand to butterfly.

Put the chicken in a large dish. Combine the sesame oil, light soy sauce and lemon juice in a small bowl. Pour over the chicken, cover and refrigerate for 3 hours.

Remove the chicken from the fridge 1 hour before cooking.

Preheat the barbecue hotplate and grill to low and close the lid to create a hot-oven effect.

Take a 'V'-shaped barbecue rack and turn it over so it is now an upside down 'V'. Put the chicken on the grill rack, with the breast bone in the centre, and reserve the marinade. Sit the grill rack on the hotplate, close the lid and cook on low heat for 1½–2¼ hours, basting every 15 minutes with the reserved marinade, or until the chicken is golden brown and tender enough to remove the flesh with a fork. Remove the chicken to a serving platter.

To make the shantung sauce, combine all the ingredients in a bowl and pour over the warm chicken. Serve with steamed Asian greens, if desired.

CHILLI YOGHURT CHICKEN

Don't you just love a good food memory? I remember my first banana fritter — yum. My first taste of coriander — odd and challenging. Then there is this combination of yoghurt and chicken I had at a cutting-edge café in the Blue Mountains, west of Sydney, in the early 1980s. I say cutting edge because the gals who ran this place were exploring flavours and ingredients ten years ahead of everyone else. At a time when much of the food scene was haute, teensy and uptight, they were doing big, bold and tasty food from Asia and the Middle East. They passed on this recipe to me.

SERVES 6

130 g (4½ oz/½ cup) plain yoghurt
2 garlic cloves, crushed
½ teaspoon ground ginger
¼ teaspoon chilli powder
2 tablespoons lemon juice
6 boneless, skinless chicken thighs
light olive oil, for cooking
lemon cheeks, to serve
rocket (arugula) leaves, to serve

Combine the yoghurt, garlic, ginger, chilli powder and lemon juice in a large non-metallic bowl or dish. Add the chicken and toss to coat. Cover and then refrigerate for 6 hours or overnight.

Remove from the fridge 30 minutes before cooking.

Preheat the barbecue hotplate to high. Drizzle a little of the olive oil onto the hotplate to grease. Put the chicken onto the hotplate and cook for 7–8 minutes, or until golden. Make sure the chicken sizzles the whole time. Turn over and cook for another 7–8 minutes, or until cooked through. Serve with the lemon cheeks and rocket.

CHICKEN WITH **JALAPEÑO BUTTER**

A couple of my fave things here – jalapeños in brine and chicken breast with skin. There seemed a time when we all obsessed about skinless chicken breasts. And what an odd obsession, don't you think? Leaving the skin on makes all the difference when it comes to flavour. Even if you don't like the skin (you can always put it aside – someone else at the table is bound to snap it up) leaving it on during cooking will make the breast lovely and tender. As for jalapeños, I use them all the time in salsas with corn, in mayonnaise and even Chinese stir-fries with pork or duck.

SERVES 4

4 chicken breasts, with wings
    attached and skin on
lime halves, to serve
fresh coriander (cilantro) leaves,
    to serve

JALAPEÑO BUTTER
2 tablespoons sliced jalapeños
    in brine, drained
1 garlic clove, chopped
1 large handful coriander
    (cilantro) leaves
2 anchovy fillets in oil, drained
125 g (4½ oz) unsalted butter,
    softened to room temperature

To make the jalapeño butter, put all the ingredients in a food processor and whiz until well combined. Transfer to a bowl.

Rub as much of the butter mixture as you can under the skin of the chicken breasts, being careful not to break the skin. Rub any remaining butter over the skin and sprinkle with a little sea salt. You can secure the skin with toothpicks. This will help prevent the skin from retracting when cooked.

Preheat the barbecue hotplate to high and close the lid to create a hot-oven effect. Sit the chicken on a rack and sit the rack over a deep baking tray. Half-fill the baking tray with water and sit it on the barbecue. Close the lid and cook for 35–40 minutes, until the skin is golden. Remove from the barbecue and allow to rest for 10–15 minutes.

Serve with the lime halves and coriander sprinkled over.

CHICKEN WITH **TARRAGON, OLIVES AND GARLIC**

This is about as close as my barbecuing gets to fine dining. I feel like fresh tarragon has taken a back seat to the more trendy herbs like coriander, Thai basil and lemongrass. But who can forget the first time they had a creamy tarragon chicken vol-au-vent? (If you haven't, dig out a '70s cookbook and give it a go.) The trick with tarragon is to use it sparingly and it does love being with chicken.

SERVES 4

4 chicken breasts, with wings
    attached and skin on
24 tarragon leaves
2 garlic cloves
2 tablespoons small black olives
    (in oil, not kalamata)

Carefully separate (but don't remove) the skin from the flesh of the chicken breasts, without tearing the skin, and set aside.

Put the tarragon leaves on a chopping board and roughly chop. Add the garlic and a good sprinkle of sea salt and chop the tarragon, garlic and salt together until they are finely chopped. Add the olives to the mix and finely chop. Spoon the mixture under the skin of the chicken breasts and rub evenly over the breast meat. Use a couple of toothpicks to secure the skin either side of the breast. (This will stop the skin from retracting too much when cooking.) Put on a plate, cover and refrigerate until needed.

Remove chicken from the fridge 20 minutes before cooking. Preheat the barbecue hotplate to medium. Drizzle a little olive oil over the skin of the chicken and sprinkle with some sea salt. Put on the hotplate and cook, skin side down, for 5 minutes, pressing down occasionally on the thickest part of the breast with a flat metal spatula. Reduce the heat to low, turn over and cook for a further 10 minutes, with the barbecue lid on. Again, press down a couple of times on the chicken with a spatula. Put the chicken on a heatproof plate, cover with foil and sit the plate on the hot barbecue lid for 5 minutes. Remove from the barbecue and let the chicken rest for a further 5 minutes before serving.

SPICED QUAIL WITH VIETNAMESE LIME AND PEPPER DIPPING SAUCE

Every Vietnamese restaurant seems to have its own version of this quail. It is probably marinated, then deep-fried. Here, I am going for grilling. The dipping sauce is zesty and peppery with a sherbety feel on the tongue.

SERVES 4

8 quail
1 tablespoon rice bran oil
½ teaspoon Chinese five-spice
1 teaspoon sea salt
lime wedges, to serve

LIME AND PEPPER SAUCE
3 tablespoons lime juice
½ teaspoon ground white pepper
½ teaspoon caster (superfine) sugar

To make the lime and pepper sauce, combine all the ingredients in a small bowl and set aside.

Sit a quail on a chopping board, breast side up. Use a small sharp knife to insert into the cavity of the quail and cut either side of the backbone. Remove and discard the backbone. Open the quail to flatten on the chopping board, so it is butterflied. With the palm of your hand, press down on the breastbone to flatten. Repeat for the remaining seven quails. Cut each quail lengthways in half to give 16 pieces. Put the quail into a large bowl or dish with the rice bran oil, five-spice and sea salt, tossing the quail around to coat in the mixture. Set aside for 1 hour.

Preheat the barbecue hotplate to medium. Cover the hotplate with a sheet of baking paper. Lay the quail, skin side down, on the paper, close the lid and cook for 10 minutes, until the quail is aromatic and the skin crispy. Turn the quail over and cook for another 4–5 minutes, until the quail is golden, aromatic and cooked through.

Serve the quail with the lime and pepper sauce in a bowl on the side, and the lime wedges.

VERDANT CHOOK

Similar to a salsa verde, but without the bread. All the fresh herbs make this chicken dish a very fresh-tasting number, and the versatile sauce could be served up with any cuts of simple barbecued chicken or lamb. If you happen to have any left over, or maybe cook extra, then this chicken is ideal eaten cold, thinly sliced and added to a salad the next day.

SERVES 4

4 chicken breasts, with wings
   attached and skin on

HERB MARINADE
3 tablespoons olive oil
2 garlic cloves
4 anchovies plus 2 teaspoons oil
   from the jar
2 tablespoons salted capers,
   well rinsed
1 tablespoon Dijon mustard
1 handful parsley leaves
1 handful basil leaves
1 handful mint leaves
2 tablespoons lemon juice

Put all the herb marinade ingredients in a food processor and process for just a few seconds until you have a herby, green and chunky sauce. Add some freshly ground black pepper to taste.

Carefully separate (but don't remove) the skin from the flesh of the chicken breasts, without tearing the skin, and put in a snug-fitting non-metallic dish. Rub the marinade under the skin, then cover and refrigerate for at least 3 hours or overnight.

Remove chicken from the fridge 20 minutes before cooking.

Preheat the barbecue hotplate to medium. Put the chicken on the hotplate, skin side down, and cook for 5 minutes, pressing down occasionally on the thickest part of the breast with a flat metal spatula. When the skin develops a golden crust turn the chicken over, turn the heat down to low and cook for another 10 minutes, again pressing down a few times on the thickest part. Make sure the chicken has a low and even sizzle for the cooking time – you may need to adjust the heat on your barbecue. Remove to a plate and lightly cover with foil for 10 minutes before serving.

HARISSA CHICKEN

Harissa takes many forms. It is a spice blend originating in Africa and you may have seen it in a paste or sauce, flavoured intensely with chillies and made wet and saucy with a mixture of fresh chillies and red peppers. Garlic and other combinations of spices are thrown in.

SERVES 4

12 chicken drumsticks
1 handful coriander (cilantro) leaves,
   coarsely chopped
1 handful flat-leaf (Italian) parsley,
   coarsely chopped

HARISSA
10–12 dried chillies
4 large red chillies, seeded and
   chopped
3 garlic cloves, chopped
1 teaspoon caraway seeds
3 tablespoons olive oil

For the harissa, seed the dried chillies if you want less heat (I don't generally), then put them in a heatproof bowl and cover with boiling water. Soak the chillies for 30 minutes, drain and roughly chop. Put the chopped chillies into a spice mill or pestle with the fresh chillies, garlic, caraway seeds, olive oil and a generous pinch of sea salt, and grind until you have a rough paste. Set aside.

Cut a couple of deep incisions across the skin side of the drumsticks and put them in a snug-fitting non-metallic dish. Pour over the harissa and stir well so the drumsticks are evenly covered. Cover and refrigerate for 3–6 hours or overnight if you have the time.

Preheat the barbecue hotplate to medium.

You will notice your average chicken leg is shaped roughly like an oval sphere but with two wider sides and two more narrow sides. Put the chicken on the hotplate, on one of the broader skin sides, and let them gently sizzle without turning or moving for 8 minutes. Turn over and cook for another 8 minutes, again without turning or moving the chicken. Now turn and cook on one narrow side for 3 minutes, then finally turn and cook on the other narrow side for a further 3 minutes. The chicken should be a golden rusty brown colour. Put the chicken in a large bowl, cover with foil and allow to rest for 5 minutes. Add the chopped herbs to the bowl, toss to coat the chicken and serve.

COCONUT **CHICKEN TENDERLOINS**

This is kind of Indian, but then again the flavours are more typical of the Caribbean – lots of fragrant spice, coconut and tropical lime. Tenderloins are great as they don't have the fat of the thigh but don't tend to dry out either.

SERVES 4

800 g (1 lb 12 oz) chicken tenderloins
1 onion, chopped
1 handful flat-leaf (Italian) parsley
1 handful coriander (cilantro) leaves
¼ teaspoon ground cloves
¼ teaspoon ground cinnamon
1 tablespoon lime juice
250 ml (9 fl oz/1 cup) coconut milk
2 tablespoons light olive oil
lime cheeks, to serve
½ teaspoon sweet paprika,
    to serve (optional)
coriander (cilantro) sprigs,
    to serve (optional)

Place the chicken tenderloins in a large non-metallic dish.

Put the onion, parsley, coriander, cloves, cinnamon, lime juice and coconut milk in a food processor and process to a paste. Pour the marinade over the chicken and toss to cover the chicken in the marinade. Cover and then refrigerate for 3–6 hours.

Remove the chicken from the fridge 30 minutes before cooking. Preheat the barbecue hotplate to high. Drizzle the olive oil onto the hotplate to grease. Shake any excess marinade off the chicken and put the tenderloins on the hotplate, making sure there is some space between each one. Cook for 8–10 minutes, turning often, until cooked through and the chicken is golden, tender and aromatic.

Arrange on a serving platter with the lime cheeks on the side. Sprinkle with the paprika and scatter over the coriander, if using.

GREEN CURRY CHICKEN

This really isn't an authentic 'curry' but has all the great flavours of a Thai green curry. Again, when cooking chicken on the bone do be patient and remove it from the fridge about 20 minutes before cooking. I raise an eyebrow, and so should you, if you see a recipe asking for chicken on the bone to be cooked for a mere 5 minutes each side. It will be raw and pink — raw chicken is not a good thing.

SERVES 4

8 chicken leg quarters

GREEN CURRY PASTE
1 teaspoon coriander seeds
1 teaspoon cumin seeds
1 teaspoon white peppercorns
2 large green chillies, seeded
    and chopped
1 lemongrass stalk, chopped
2 garlic cloves, chopped
3 spring onions (scallions),
    roughly chopped
4 small makrut (kaffir lime)
    leaves, shredded
1 tablespoon grated ginger
4 coriander roots
4–5 cm (1¾–2 in) coriander (cilantro)
    stem, washed and chopped
1 tablespoon fish sauce
1 tablespoon sugar
3 tablespoons coconut cream

To make the curry paste, put the coriander and cumin seeds and peppercorns in a small frying pan over high heat, shaking the pan, until they start to smoke and darken. Remove from the pan and allow to cool. Put them in a small food processor or spice mill and grind. Add the remaining curry paste ingredients and process, stopping and starting the food processor a few times, scraping down the sides of the bowl until you have a chunky, pale green paste.

Cut the chicken between the drumstick and thigh joint. Gently separate the skin from the meat and put the chicken pieces in a non-metallic dish. Rub the paste all over the chicken pieces, including under the skin. Cover and refrigerate for 3–6 hours or overnight, but remember to remove from the fridge 20 minutes before cooking.

Preheat the barbecue hotplate to low and drizzle with a little vegetable oil to lightly grease. Put the chicken on the hotplate, and cook, skin side down, for 10 minutes with the lid on, pressing down occasionally with a flat metal spatula. They should gently sizzle until the spices cook, turning the skin into a golden crust. Turn over and continue to cook for another 15 minutes, with the lid on. Remove the chicken to a heatproof serving plate, lightly cover with foil and sit the chicken on the warm barbecue lid for 10 minutes to rest.

CREOLE CHICKEN

This is a versatile one. The marinade and sauce would work really nicely with pork fillet or pork chop, rump steak or flank steak. I can even imagine it working beautifully with lamb.

SERVES 4

4 boneless chicken breasts,
    skin on
1 onion, chopped
2 garlic cloves, chopped
1 tablespoon finely chopped
    coriander (cilantro) stems
2 tablespoons olive oil
2 tablespoons white wine vinegar

SAUCE
2 tablespoons olive oil
2 tablespoons lime juice
2 teaspoons ground cumin
2 garlic cloves, crushed
3 tablespoons chopped
    coriander (cilantro) leaves

Put the chicken in a non-metallic dish or bowl. Put the onion, garlic, coriander stems, olive oil and vinegar in a food processor and process to a paste. Rub all over the chicken. Cover and refrigerate for 6 hours or overnight.

Remove chicken from the fridge 30 minutes before cooking.

To make the sauce, put all the sauce ingredients in a small bowl, stirring to combine.

Preheat the barbecue grill or hotplate to high. Cook the chicken, skin side down, for 8–10 minutes. Turn over and cook for another 5 minutes, or until cooked through. Remove and allow to rest for 10 minutes.

Spoon the sauce over the hot chicken and serve with grilled corn and vine-ripened tomatoes, if desired.

KERALAN CHICKEN

Keralan cuisine is much less complex and full-on than in other parts of India. And by full-on I mean heavy and rich. This is a very simple barbecued chicken dish. It would also work really well with a maryland (drumstick and thigh on the bone), but do remember it would need a longer cooking time.

SERVES 4

4 boneless chicken breasts,
　skin on
3 tablespoons lemon juice
2 garlic cloves, finely chopped
1 tablespoon finely grated ginger
1 small onion, chopped
¼ teaspoon ground turmeric
1 teaspoon ground cumin
1 teaspoon paprika
¼ teaspoon chilli powder
vegetable oil, for cooking
4 slices of flat bread or naan bread,
　sliced tomato, sliced red onion,
　coriander (cilantro) sprigs, plain
　yoghurt and lemon wedges,
　to serve

Put the chicken in a ceramic dish. Put the lemon juice, garlic, ginger, onion, turmeric, cumin, paprika and chilli powder in a food processor and process to a smooth paste. Pour over the chicken. Roll the chicken around to coat in the marinade. Cover and refrigerate for 6 hours or overnight.

Remove the chicken from the fridge 30 minutes before you begin cooking.

Preheat the barbecue hotplate to high. Drizzle a little vegetable oil over the hotplate to lightly grease.

Put the chicken, skin side down, on the hotplate and cook for 8–10 minutes, or until the skin is golden. Turn the heat to low and turn the chicken over. Close the lid and cook for 10 minutes, or until the chicken is cooked through. Remove the chicken and cover loosely with foil to rest for 10 minutes before carving.

Cook the flat bread on the barbecue until warmed through and a little charred. Serve slices of the chicken on the flat bread and top with the tomato, red onion and coriander sprigs, with the yoghurt and lemon wedges on the side.

MEXICAN PESTO CHICKEN

Pesto or the French 'pistou' is a classic side to grilled chicken and fish. This Mexican-style pesto includes chilli for a bit of kick.

SERVES 4

1.6 kg (3 lb 8 oz) free-range chicken
1 lime, cut in half

CHILLI PESTO
2 large green chillies
25 g (1 oz/¼ cup) pepitas (pumpkin seeds), lightly toasted until golden
40 g (1½ oz/¼ cup) pine nuts, lightly toasted until golden
1 small bunch coriander (cilantro), chopped
1 tablespoon olive oil
2 tablespoons lime juice
2 tablespoons finely grated parmesan cheese

Put the chillies over a naked gas flame, or on the grill of your barbecue, and cook until charred all over, turning often with tongs. Remove to a plastic bag to help them sweat and allow to cool. Roughly peel the chillies then put in a food processor with the pepitas, pine nuts, coriander, olive oil and lime juice. Process to a chunky paste. Put in a non-metallic bowl, stir through the parmesan and set aside. This can be made the day before if you like.

Cut the chicken in half through the breastbone, remove the cartilage and backbone, cut off the wing tips, then wash and pat dry with paper towel. Gently separate the skin from the meat, being careful not to tear the skin. Spoon the pesto under the skin, smothering it over the leg and breast meat. Secure the meat to the skin using toothpicks. (This will stop the skin from pulling back when cooking.) Rub the lime halves over the skin of the chicken, squeezing the lime as you do so. Cover and set aside at room temperature for 20 minutes.

Preheat the barbecue hotplate to high and the grill to low–medium. You will need a cooking or cake rack for this.

Drizzle a little vegetable oil over the hotplate to grease. Put the chicken on the hotplate and cook, skin side down, for 3 minutes with the lid on until the skin is golden brown and crispy. Now put the chicken, skin side up, on the rack and sit the rack over the grill so the chicken is not sitting directly on the grill. Close the lid and cook for another 20 minutes. The skin of the chicken will look split in some places and the tasty pesto will have oozed out a bit. Test if the chicken is cooked by piercing the skin and flesh where the leg meets the thigh. If the juices are clear, it is ready. Remove the chicken to a plate and lightly cover with foil for 10 minutes to rest. To serve, cut each half in half again to make four pieces.

THAI BARBECUED CHICKEN

If you look at the ingredients in the coriander rub you could be excused for thinking that it all sounds a bit full on. But that is the nature of Thai cooking. It is all in the balance. A good Thai meal is like a roller coaster of flavour in your mouth – challenging, scary to some and quite addictive. I actually like using this same rub on chicken thigh fillets, which have been gently pounded to flatten, and cooking them on a hot grill.

SERVES 4

1.5 kg (3 lb 5 oz) free-range chicken
coriander (cilantro) sprigs, to serve

CORIANDER AND PEPPER RUB
6 coriander (cilantro) roots and 4–5 cm
    (1¾–2 in) of the stem, washed
    and chopped
6 garlic cloves, chopped
½ teaspoon black peppercorns
½ teaspoon white peppercorns
3 tablespoons fish sauce
4 spring onions (scallions), chopped

Put the coriander into a mortar with a generous pinch of sea salt. Pound with a pestle for a couple of minutes until pulpy, then add the garlic. Pound again until the garlic is also pulpy, then add the remaining marinade ingredients. Pound until you have a chunky paste.

Put the chicken on a chopping board, breast side down. Use a sharp knife or cleaver to cut either side of the backbone and throw away. Open up the chicken to reveal the inside of the rib cage. Cut the chicken down the middle and carefully remove the cartilage. Turn over and cut several diagonal slashes across the skin of the chicken. Make the incisions deeper across the legs. Put into a flat non-metallic dish, skin side up, and rub the paste over the chicken. Cover and refrigerate for 3–6 hours.

Remove the chicken from the fridge 1 hour before cooking.

Preheat all the barbecue burners to low–medium. Drizzle a little olive oil on the hotplate to lightly grease. Put the chicken on the hotplate, skin side down, and cook for 10 minutes with the lid on. Reserve any marinade in the dish. The skin should really sizzle the entire cooking time. Spoon the reserved marinade over the chicken. Reduce the heat, turn the chicken over and cook for 15–20 minutes with the lid on, pressing down a few times on the legs with a flat metal spatula, until the chicken is cooked through. Put the chicken on a tray, cover with foil and leave to rest on a warm part of the barbecue (away from direct heat) for 10 minutes. Cut each half into several pieces and serve with coriander sprigs scattered over.

SPECIAL **BRINED ROAST CHICKEN** WITH AÏOLI

Brining is not something you want to do every day, or every time you barbecue, but the resulting flavour of a brined chicken (or turkey for that matter) is very special indeed. Brining is pure science. It's osmosis. It's about getting flavour from one place to another. It does require some planning but is well worth the effort.

SERVES 4

520 g (1 lb 2 oz/2 cups) cooking salt
250 ml (9 fl oz/1 cup) white
    wine vinegar
1 tablespoon fennel seeds
2 bay leaves
2 small chickens, about 1.2 kg
    (2 lb 10 oz) each

AÏOLI
2 egg yolks
2 garlic cloves, crushed
pinch white pepper
1 tablespoon lemon juice
185 ml (6 fl oz/¾ cup) rice bran oil

Put the salt, vinegar, fennel seeds and bay leaves in a very large saucepan with 10–12 litres (340–405 fl oz/42–51 cups) of cold water. Bring to the boil, then reduce the heat and simmer for 30 minutes. Remove from the heat and allow to cool to room temperature.

Cut the chickens in half lengthways between the breasts, immerse them in the brining solution and refrigerate for 6 hours or overnight. Remove the chicken, discard the solution and place the chicken, skin side up, on a baking tray or a few large plates. Refrigerate for another 3–6 hours. Remove them from the fridge 30 minutes before cooking.

To make the aïoli, put the egg yolks, garlic, white pepper and lemon juice in the bowl of a small food processor and whiz to combine. With the motor running very slowly, add the rice bran oil in a steady stream. Continue adding the oil until you have a creamy custard- or mayonnaise-like consistency. Transfer to a bowl.

Preheat the barbecue hotplate and grill to high and close the lid to create a hot-oven effect. Sit the chicken skin side up on a rack and sit the rack over a deep baking tray. Half-fill the baking tray with water and place it on the barbecue. Close the lid and cook for 40–45 minutes, until the skin is golden. Remove from barbecue and allow to rest for 10–15 minutes.

Serve the chicken with the aïoli on the side, and chargrilled baby carrots, if desired.

SWEET CHILLI AND GINGER CHICKEN

In recent years sweet chilli sauce has come to sit proudly next to tomato sauce as a kitchen staple, a true sign of the culinary times. I personally find it too sweet and sticky as a sauce, but these qualities make it perfect as a sweet marinade base – with all its hidden ingredients – making cooking easy.

SERVES 4

8 chicken thigh fillets

SWEET CHILLI MARINADE
150 g (5½ oz/½ cup) Thai sweet
    chilli sauce
2 tablespoons Chinese rice wine
    (or dry white wine)
1 tablespoon fish sauce
1 tablespoon finely grated ginger
1 small bunch coriander
    (cilantro), chopped

Put a chicken thigh between two layers of plastic food wrap and gently pound so it is an even thickness all over, about 5 mm (¼ in). I like to leave on the little fat that is on the thigh – it will keep the meat really moist while it cooks. Repeat with the remaining chicken thighs.

Put the chicken in a flat non-metallic dish. Combine the marinade ingredients in a bowl, pour over the chicken and rub all over the meat. Cover and refrigerate for 3–6 hours.

Remove chicken from the fridge 20 minutes before cooking.

Preheat the barbecue grill to high and brush with a little vegetable oil to grease. Put the chicken on the grill and cook for 2 minutes, gently pressing down occasionally with a flat metal spatula. Turn over and cook for another 2 minutes, again pressing down on the meat. Remove to a platter, lightly cover with foil and then leave to stand for 5 minutes before serving.

WHERE'S THE BEEF?
AND THE PORK, LAMB AND VEAL?

PENANG **BEEF SATAY**

VEAL AND PROVOLONE INVOLTINI

LAMB KEBABS WITH SPICED YOGHURT

PORK AND VEAL **MEATBALLS**

FRAGRANT **BEEF KEFTA**

CHEESEBURGERS

LEMONGRASS, PEPPER AND CORIANDER
  PORK SKEWERS

SPICY **BEEF KEBABS**

HOT DOGS WITH BEER-BRAISED ONIONS

SHEFTALIA

MERGUEZ **SAUSAGES**

SMOKY **PORK KEBABS**

VEAL CUTLETS WITH ROSEMARY,
  ANCHOVIES AND RED WINE

BEEF RIBS WITH BARBECUE SAUCE

TOPSIDE **STEAK SANDWICHES**

LAMB CHOPS WITH ANCHOVY BUTTER

FAJITA **RUMP STEAK**
  WITH MASHED AVOCADO

HAND-MADE PORK AND
  FENNEL **SAUSAGES**

ROAST **BEEF FILLET** WITH
  PAPRIKA MAYONNAISE

CHINATOWN **PORK**

T-BONE WITH BERCY SAUCE

MINTY SALMORIGLIO **LAMB STEAKS**

BEEF RISSOLES WITH HARISSA

VIETNAMESE GARLIC, BLACK PEPPER
  AND LIME **STEAKS**

PERSIAN **LAMB CUTLETS**

SIRLOIN STEAKS WITH
  CHIMICHURRI BUTTER

MIXED MEAT GRILL

RUMP STEAK WITH GINGER,

BUTTERFLIED LAMB MASALA

FILLET STEAK WITH
  CAFÉ DE PARIS BUTTER

ROAST **BEEF**

MARRAKESH **CHOPS**

SPANISH **RUMP STEAK**

PORK SHOULDER
  WITH FENNEL AND GARLIC

T-BONE FLORENTINE

LAMB WITH GREEN OLIVE SALSA

PEPPER **BEEF FILLET**

STOUT **BEEF BURGERS**

RUMP STEAK WITH TABASCO BUTTER

NEW YORK **COWBOY**

LAMB SHOULDER WITH
  ROSEMARY AND GARLIC

ORANGE AND SPICE **PORK MEDALLIONS**

FILET MIGNON WITH
  ROAST GARLIC BUTTER

SEARED **CALVES' LIVER**

CHRISTMAS BARBECUED
  GLAZED HAM

BEEF RIB EYE FILLET
  WITH HORSERADISH BUTTER

CHUNKY **LAMB LEG STEAKS**

FILLET STEAK WITH GREEN
  PEPPERCORN SAUCE

CURRIED **LEG OF LAMB**

SIRLOIN STEAK WITH BÉARNAISE

PORK SHOULDER WITH
  VINEGAR, GARLIC AND SPICE

CHAR SIU **LAMB** WRAPS

VEAL CUTLETS WITH
  HERBS AND PROSCIUTTO

ROAST SIRLOIN WITH ROOT VEGIES
  AND GARLIC CRÈME

PENANG **BEEF SATAY**

Some recipes stand out. For me they can do this in two ways. Some recipes, when you read them, sound a bit odd and others, when you make them, really taste good. This is both. I first made this some time ago while researching traditional southern Thai and northern Malay satay sauces. Several recipes had condensed milk listed in the ingredients. My initial reaction was very much 'what the ... ?' until I made this. The sweetness of the milk caramelises, making this a rich affair so I think it really needs the home-made chilli sauce, spiked with lots of vinegar, drizzled over. Possibly, maybe, the best beef satay ever.

SERVES 4 AS A SNACKY STARTER

400 g (14 oz) beef rump steak

PENANG SATAY MARINADE
4 spring onions (scallions), white part
   only, chopped
80 g (2¾ oz/½ cup) crushed peanuts
2 tablespoons good-quality
   curry powder
125 ml (4 fl oz/½ cup) condensed milk
125 ml (4 fl oz/½ cup) coconut cream
2 tablespoons fish sauce
½ teaspoon turmeric
2 tablespoons brown sugar

Put all the ingredients for the satay marinade in a food processor and whiz until you have a quite runny, yellow-curry-coloured marinade. Pour into a non-metallic dish.

Put the beef on a chopping board and slice on an angle going across the grain into thin 10–12 cm (4–4½ in) strips. Put the beef into the satay marinade, separate the pieces and massage the marinade into the meat. Cover and refrigerate for 3–6 hours or overnight if you have the time.

Remove the beef from the fridge 1 hour before cooking and soak 16 wooden skewers. Thread 2–3 pieces of meat onto each skewer, reserving the marinade.

Preheat the barbecue hotplate to high and drizzle with a little olive oil to grease. Put the satay sticks on the hotplate and cook for 4 minutes, brushing a little remaining marinade onto the beef. The cooked side should develop a dark golden crust. Turn over and cook for another 3–4 minutes.

Remove to a platter and serve with home-made sweet chilli sauce (see page 365) for a delicious combination of flavours.

VEAL AND PROVOLONE INVOLTINI

Think of involtini as a roll or a log. Provolone is a very tasty, firm Italian cheese that melts to a very gooey goodness. This, with the pancetta, really complements the mildly flavoured, yet tender, veal.

SERVES 4

400 g (14 oz) veal backstrap fillet
1 egg, lightly beaten
1 tablespoon finely chopped flat-leaf (Italian) parsley
1 tablespoon finely chopped rosemary
4 slices pancetta
75 g (2½ oz) provolone cheese, thinly sliced
2 tablespoons olive oil

Cut the veal into four equal-sized portions. Put the veal between two layers of plastic wrap or baking paper and pound until very thin.

Combine the egg, parsley and rosemary in a bowl then brush over the top side of each slice of veal. Top each piece of veal with a slice of pancetta and a layer of provolone.

Firmly roll up the veal into a log and tie with cooking string. Lay the veal rolls in a tray and rub all over with the olive oil. Season with salt and freshly ground black pepper and set aside for 30 minutes.

Preheat the barbecue grill to high. Cook the rolls for 8 minutes, turning every 2 minutes, until golden. Remove and rest for 5 minutes. Slice each roll into 3–4 pieces to serve. Serve with a simple rocket and parmesan salad, if desired.

LAMB KEBABS
WITH SPICED YOGHURT

Lamb meat is made for barbecuing. But keep in mind the lamb leg, like rump in beef, is made up of several different muscles so it will vary in texture and tenderness.

SERVES 3

1 small boned leg of lamb,
    about 1.25 kg (2 lb 12 oz)
3 tablespoons plain yoghurt
1 teaspoon ground cumin
1 teaspoon ground turmeric
½ teaspoon garam masala
2 teaspoons sea salt
1 white onion, chopped
2 garlic cloves, chopped
1 tablespoon finely grated ginger
1 large handful chopped coriander
    (cilantro) leaves
olive oil, for brushing
lemon wedges, to serve

Cut the lamb into large chunks, about 4 cm (1½ in) long. Put the chunks into a large non-metallic bowl.

Put all the other ingredients, except the olive oil and lemon wedges, in a food proceesor and process to make a finely chopped paste. Spoon over the lamb and toss the lamb pieces so they are evenly coated in the marinade.

Cover and set aside at room temperature for 2–4 hours.

Preheat the barbecue grill to medium. Skewer pieces of lamb onto six long metal skewers and brush with the olive oil. Cook on the grill for 10 minutes, turning every 2 minutes. Serve with the lemon wedges and a tomato salad, if desired.

PORK AND VEAL **MEATBALLS**

We make heaps of these at our tapas restaurant. They are so good for a few reasons. They can be made a day in advance, and the flavour will actually benefit from doing so. You can eat these 'dry' as in this recipe or serve them in a very simple tomato-based sauce with some bread on the side.

SERVES 6–8

500 g (1 lb 2 oz) minced (ground) pork
500 g (1 lb 2 oz) minced (ground) veal
60 g (2¼ oz/1 cup) fresh breadcrumbs
1 red onion, grated
1 garlic clove, crushed
1 teaspoon ground cinnamon
1 teaspoon ground cumin
½ teaspoon chilli flakes
1 teaspoon dried oregano
2 teaspoons smoked paprika
1 egg
light olive oil, for cooking

Combine all the ingredients except the olive oil in a bowl, using your hands to mix really well. Pick up handfuls of the mixture and firmly throw back into the bowl or onto a clean work surface. This helps to tenderise the meat and remove any air. Use wet hands to roll the mixture into golf ball sizes and flatten each ball slightly to make a disc.

Preheat the barbecue hotplate or grill to medium and drizzle with the olive oil to lightly grease. Cook the meatballs for 8 minutes, turning every minute and gently pressing down with a spatula, until golden and aromatic.

FRAGRANT **BEEF KEFTA**

Kefta is a meatball in Morocco. They can be cooked in a tomato-based sauce and baked in a pot, which could be called a tagine. Ras-el-hanout is a blend of spices, and can vary greatly, somewhat like garam masala in Indian cooking.

SERVES 4

750 g (1 lb 10 oz) minced (ground) beef
1 red onion, finely chopped
2 garlic cloves, crushed
1 teaspoon ground ginger
2 teaspoons ground cinnamon
2 teaspoons ras-el-hanout (Moroccan
　spice blend)
1 teaspoon sea salt, plus extra,
　for seasoning
3 tablespoons finely chopped
　coriander (cilantro) leaves
3 tablespoons finely chopped flat-leaf
　(Italian) parsley
3 tablespoons olive oil

Put the beef, onion, garlic, ginger, cinnamon, ras-el-hanout, salt, coriander and parsley in a large bowl. Use your hands to combine. Pick the mince up and firmly throw it back into the bowl or onto a clean work surface to remove any air and to tenderise the meat. Cover and refrigerate for 2–6 hours.

Using wet hands, divide the mixture in half. Keep dividing in half until you have 16 portions, roughly about the same size. Again, with wet hands, form each portion into a torpedo shape, tapering at each end.

Preheat the barbecue grill to high. Brush the olive oil over the meat. Put the kefta on the grill, sprinkle over some extra sea salt, and cook for 5 minutes, without turning or moving. This allows the kefta to form a golden crust so they can then be turned without breaking up. Turn over and cook for another 3–4 minutes. Serve with toasted pitta bread, and a tomato, cucumber and onion salad, if desired.

CHEESEBURGERS

Use these tasty mince patties between a couple of buns with tomato, onions, lettuce and beetroot for the ultimate Aussie hamburger experience (sorry, I draw the line at pineapple). The kids will love these cooked on the barbecue and finished off with a slice of tasty cheddar melted on top. And they'll be great for the adults too!

SERVES 4

1 tablespoon olive oil
1 small onion, finely chopped
1 bacon slice, finely chopped
1 garlic clove, crushed
1 teaspoon dried mixed herbs
500 g (1 lb 2 oz) minced (ground) beef
1 egg
4 slices cheddar cheese

Heat the oil in a small frying pan over medium heat and cook the onion and bacon for about 2–3 minutes until the onions are soft. Add the garlic and dried herbs, cook for another minute then remove from the heat. Put in a bowl and allow to cool to room temperature. Add the beef and egg, and season well with sea salt and freshly ground black pepper. Use your hands to combine all the ingredients. Divide into four and firmly roll each into a ball. Flatten each ball into a burger-like patty and put on a plate lined with baking paper, cover and refrigerate until needed. These can be prepared the day before.

Remove the patties from the fridge 30 minutes before you begin cooking.

Preheat the barbecue hotplate to medium and drizzle with a little olive oil to grease. Put the patties on the hotplate and cook for 6 minutes, letting them gently sizzle. Turn over and cook for another 5 minutes, until they are evenly brown all over. Cook for another 2 minutes on each side for a well-done patty. Put a slice of cheese on each patty, close the lid and cook for another 2 minutes, until the cheese has melted.

Put the patty on buns and top with a combination of fillings and sauces.

LEMONGRASS, PEPPER AND CORIANDER **PORK SKEWERS**

In Vietnam and much of the cooking of South-East Asia, pork is often used with sweet, salty and sour flavours. Here, barbecued pork mince cooks to a charred sweetness complemented by the fragrant lemongrass. Nuoc cham is the ubiquitous Vietnamese dipping sauce.

SERVES 4

500 g (1 lb 2 oz) minced (ground) pork
2 lemongrass stalks, white part only, finely chopped
1 teaspoon caster (superfine) sugar
1 tablespoon fish sauce
2 tablespoons chopped coriander (cilantro) roots
1 teaspoon freshly ground black pepper
8 lemongrass stalks, about 15 cm (6 in) long
lettuce leaves, to serve

NUOC CHAM
4 small red chillies, finely chopped
2 garlic cloves, finely chopped
2 teaspoons sugar
1 tablespoon rice vinegar
125 ml (4 fl oz/½ cup) fish sauce

To make the nuoc cham, combine all the ingredients in a bowl. Set aside.

Put the pork, chopped lemongrass, sugar, fish sauce, coriander and black pepper in a food processor and process until well combined. Scrape into a bowl. Pick the mince up and firmly throw it back into the bowl or onto a clean work surface to remove any air.

Divide mixture into eight equal portions. Using wet hands, wrap a ball of the mixture around a stalk of lemongrass. Repeat with the remaining lemongrass and pork. The pork mixture can be made to this stage up to a day in advance.

Preheat the barbecue grill to high. Brush oil over the pork mixture and cook on the barbecue for 8–10 minutes, turning every minute until golden and cooked through.

To serve, wrap the pork in the lettuce leaves and spoon over the nuoc cham.

SPICY **BEEF KEBABS**

Don't you find that many skewered meats (kebabs) are tough? And try not to be tempted by those premade ones you see at the butchers. Here, the acid in the grated onion tenderises the meat in this Moroccan-inspired recipe.

SERVES 4

1 small onion
2 garlic cloves, crushed
2 teaspoons ground cumin
1 teaspoon paprika
1 teaspoon dried chilli flakes
1 handful coriander (cilantro) leaves
    and stems
1 handful flat-leaf (Italian) parsley
    leaves and stems
2 tablespoons lemon juice
600 g (1 lb 5 oz) thick cut beef rump
    steak, cut into chunky 2–3 cm
    (¾–1¼ in) cubes
fresh lemon, to serve

Finely grate the onion so you have 2 tablespoons. Put the onion pulp into a small bowl with the garlic, cumin, paprika, chilli flakes, coriander, parsley and lemon juice, and stir to combine. Soak some bamboo skewers.

Put the steak cubes in a non-metallic dish and add the spicy onion mix. Stir well so the meat is evenly covered in the spices or cover firmly with plastic food wrap and shake the bowl to combine the ingredients. Refrigerate for 3–6 hours, shaking the bowl from time to time.

Thread 3–4 pieces of meat onto a wooden skewer. Season each skewer well with sea salt and freshly ground black pepper. Set aside for 30 minutes.

Preheat the barbecue hotplate to high and drizzle with just enough olive oil to grease. Put the kebabs on the hotplate and cook for 8 minutes, turning every 2 minutes, until all the sides of the beef are brown. Remove, place on a serving plate and cover with foil to rest for 5 minutes. Squeeze over fresh lemon to serve.

HOT DOGS WITH
BEER-BRAISED ONIONS

I will admit, the idea of cooking a hot dog, or a hamburger for that matter, on the barbecue is very American. The frankfurters are of course already cooked, you are just heating them through. So do try and get your hands on some good veal frankfurters from a European deli. The recipe here is really all about the onions which can be used on many other barbecue occasions.

SERVES 4

4 veal frankfurters
3 large white onions
125 ml (4 fl oz/½ cup) beer
1 tablespoon butter, plus extra,
    to serve
4 hot dog buns, to serve
German mustard, to serve

Preheat the barbecue burners to high and brush the hotplate and grill with a little vegetable oil to grease.

Prick your frankfurters all over with a fork. Put them on the grill and the onions on the hotplate. Push the pile of onions around with your barbecue tongs to spread them out in a single layer. Keep turning your frankfurters every 2 minutes, until they are starting to just get little char marks, and keep tossing the onions on the hotplate. Put the frankfurters in among the onions and pour a couple of tablespoons of beer over the frankfurters and onions causing the hotplate to sizzle. When the beer has evaporated keep adding a little more at a time to the hotplate until all the beer has been used up. When the onions are golden add the butter and cook for a few more minutes until the onions turn an amber ale colour.

To serve, butter the hot dog buns and spread with the mustard. Add the frankfurters and onions.

SHEFTALIA

Sheftalia is a traditional Greek and Cypriot grilled meat recipe – lamb mince with a few other simple seasonings thrown in. It's lovely wrapped in warm pitta bread with a Mediterranean salad (see page 288) and some extra feta dressing dolloped all over.

SERVES 4

700 g (1 lb 9 oz) minced (ground) lamb
4 garlic cloves, crushed
2 tablespoons finely chopped flat-leaf
    (Italian) parsley
1 tablespoon finely chopped oregano
plain yoghurt, to serve
mint, to serve
cayenne pepper, to serve
4 soft pitta breads, to serve

Put the lamb in a large bowl with the garlic, parsley, oregano, 1 teaspoon of sea salt and some freshly ground black pepper. Use your hands to combine the meat with the other flavourings, throwing the meat against the side of the bowl so the meat begins to look like a paste. Lightly wet your hands with water and divide the mixture into 16 equal parts, then roll each into a ball, about the size of a golf ball. Put on a tray, cover and refrigerate for 3 hours or overnight.

Remove the meatballs from the fridge 30 minutes before you begin cooking.

Preheat the barbecue hotplate to medium and drizzle with a little olive oil to grease. Put the meatballs on the grill and cook for 5 minutes, gently pressing down with a flat metal spatula so they look more like a disc or a small burger patty. Turn over and cook for 5 minutes. Remove to a plate and top with the yoghurt and mint, and sprinkle the cayenne over. Serve in warm pitta rolls with salad.

MERGUEZ **SAUSAGES**

Made with beef or lamb, these are little home-made sausages with a history originating in north Africa. The paprika gives them their unique redness. The tomato and honey jam can be made a day or two in advance, kept in the fridge and served on the side with many of the other red meat recipes.

SERVES 4

750 g (1 lb 10 oz) minced (ground) beef
2 garlic cloves, finely chopped
1 tablespoon ground cumin
2 teaspoons ground coriander
1 tablespoon za'atar mix (optional),
    plus extra, to serve
1 tablespoon paprika
1 teaspoon cayenne pepper
1 teaspoon dried thyme
1 teaspoon sea salt

SPICY TOMATO AND HONEY JAM
4 ripe tomatoes, cut in half
1 large red chilli (seeded if it is
    a really hot one), sliced
1 tablespoon olive oil
1 garlic clove, crushed
½ teaspoon sugar
1 large pinch sea salt
90 g (3¼ oz/¼ cup) honey

To make the sausages, put the meat, spices and salt in a large bowl. Use your hands to combine, throwing the meat against the side of the bowl. Lightly grease your hands with olive oil and form the meat into 16 balls about the size of a large walnut. Form them into small sausages 5–6 cm (2–2½ in) long. Put them on a tray lined with baking paper. Cover and refrigerate overnight.

For the jam, preheat the barbecue hotplate to high. Put the tomatoes in a bowl with the chilli and olive oil and toss around. Put the tomatoes, cut side down, and chilli on the hotplate and cook for about 3–4 minutes, until they just start to develop a golden crust. Turn over and cook for another 3–4 minutes, pressing down with a flat metal spatula. Remove and put the tomatoes and chilli in a food processor while they are still hot with the garlic, sugar and a large pinch of sea salt. Pulse until really mushed up. Transfer to a small saucepan and boil until the mixture has reduced by about half, stirring often. This will take about 8–10 minutes. Add the honey and boil for another 2–3 minutes, until you have a red sauce the colour of a rich chutney. Put in a bowl and allow to cool.

Preheat the barbecue grill to high. Lightly brush the sausages with some extra olive oil and cook for about 6 minutes, turning every couple of minutes until the meat is no longer pink. These are quite small so basically once they look cooked all over they will be ready. Serve with the jam on the side and sprinkle with za'atar, if desired.

SMOKY **PORK KEBABS**

The pork here is kept quite thick and chunky, larger than you would expect skewered meat to be. But the idea is to slide the tasty and tender medallions of pork off the skewer onto your plate. The paprika gives the pork a great colour and a really smoky aroma.

SERVES 4

750 (1 lb 10 oz) pork fillet, cut into
    2 cm (¾ in) thick slices
1 teaspooon hot smoked paprika
2 teaspoons sweet smoked paprika
3 garlic cloves, finely chopped
125 ml (4 fl oz/½ cup) fino sherry
½ teaspoon dried oregano
soft baguette or Italian bread rolls,
    to serve
salad leaves, to serve

Put the pork in a non-metallic bowl or dish. Combine the paprikas, garlic, sherry and oregano in a small bowl, stirring to dissolve the paprika. Pour over the pork and toss around to combine well. Cover and refrigerate for 6 hours or overnight.

Remove the pork from the fridge 30 minutes before you begin cooking.

Preheat the barbecue grill or hotplate to high. Thread several bits of pork onto metal skewers.

Cook for 8–10 minutes, turning every 2 minutes or so until golden on all sides. Remove from the heat and allow to rest for 5 minutes. Serve with the soft baguette or Italian bread rolls and salad leaves.

VEAL CUTLETS WITH ROSEMARY, ANCHOVIES AND RED WINE

This recipe is a cinch. The flavourings are classic and simple, paying respect to the lovely and very special (yes, I know, they are not the easiest things to find) veal cutlets.

SERVES 4

1 tablespoon rosemary leaves
3 anchovies
3 garlic cloves, chopped
3 tablespoons olive oil
125 ml (4 fl oz/½ cup) red wine
4 x veal cutlets, about 250 g
 (9 oz) each

Put the rosemary, anchovies and garlic in a mortar with a generous pinch of sea salt and some freshly ground black pepper. Pound until the anchovies are mashed. Put mixture into a bowl and stir through the olive oil and red wine.

Put the cutlets in a non-metallic dish and pour over the marinade, tossing the cutlets around to coat in the mixture. Cover and then refrigerate for 3 hours or overnight, turning them often.

Remove the cutlets from the fridge 1 hour before cooking.

Preheat the barbecue hotplate or grill to high. Put the cutlets on the hotplate or grill and cook for 5 minutes with the lid closed. They should look quite dark from the marinade. Turn over and cook for another 5 minutes, again with the lid closed. Turn the barbecue heat off, lightly wrap the meat in cooking foil and sit on the warm lid for 5 minutes. Remove from the lid and rest for another 10 minutes in the foil before serving.

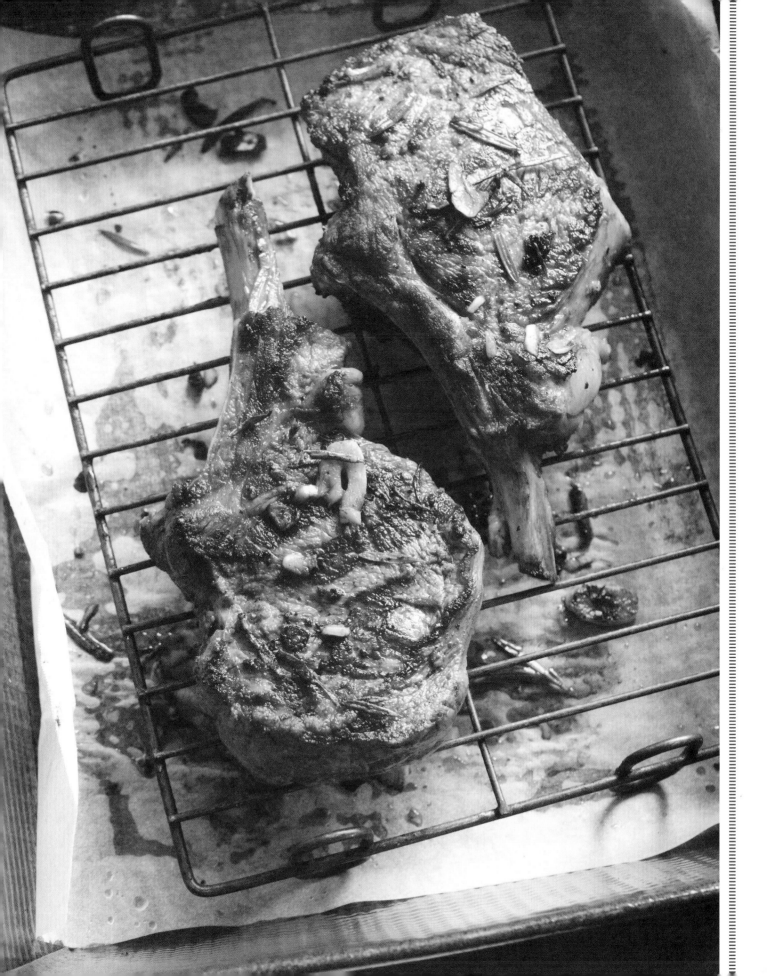

BEEF RIBS WITH BARBECUE SAUCE

Most of the recipes you see for any of these more traditional 'American-style' barbecue ribs will have you pre-cook the ribs in the oven before they make it to the barbecue. I am not sure I see the point of calling something a barbecue if it has spent more time in the kitchen! So be patient with these and you will be rewarded, as this version is cooked entirely on the barbecue. When I bought these ribs the butcher asked what I was planning on doing with them. When I told him my plan he declared that it would easily be a 'three tin number'. By this he meant three cans of beer and he was spot on!

SERVES 4

2 x 800 g (1 lb 12 oz) beef ribs, each with eight rib bones about 5 cm (2 in) long

SPICE RUB
1 teaspoon dried thyme
2 teaspoons smoked paprika
2 teaspoons chilli powder
½ teaspoon freshly ground black pepper

BARBECUE SAUCE
2 tablespoons brown sugar
2 tablespoons cider vinegar
150 g (5½ oz/½ cup) tomato sauce (ketchup)
1 tablespoon chicory
2 teaspoons mustard powder
1 tablespoon Worcestershire sauce

Combine the spices for the spice rub in a small bowl. Put the beef ribs in a snug-fitting non-metallic dish and rub over the ribs. Cover and refrigerate overnight, turning often.

Remove the ribs from the fridge 1 hour before cooking. Wrap each rack in baking paper, then wrap in foil.

Combine the barbecue sauce ingredients in a bowl and set aside.

Preheat the barbecue hotplate to low. Sit the ribs on a rack and sit the rack on the hotplate. Cook for 1½ hours, turning often so the ribs steam in the paper. Unwrap the ribs and put them on the hotplate. Turn the heat to medium and start to baste. Brush the ribs with the sauce and turn over. Continue to baste and turn the ribs for 15–20 minutes, until all the sauce has been used and the ribs are very tender. Remove to a plate, cover with foil and rest for 10 minutes. Cut each rack in half and serve.

TOPSIDE **STEAK SANDWICHES**

How good is a steak sandwich? I've used topside here but scotch fillet, with its snug layer of fat, is a good meat to grill; it stays tender and is very tasty. Ask your butcher to cut the meat to your preferred thickness.

SERVES 4

600 g (1 lb 5 oz) topside steak
3 tablespoons olive oil
6 rosemary sprigs
1 garlic clove
freshly ground black pepper
4 soft bread rolls
butter, to serve
3 tomatoes, thinly sliced
2 large handfuls baby rocket (arugula)

GARLIC CRÈME
10–12 garlic cloves, peeled
1 tablespoon sweet German mustard
2 egg yolks
125 ml (4 fl oz/½ cup) olive oil

BALSAMIC ONIONS
6 red onions
2 tablespoons olive oil
1 tablespoon balsamic vinegar
handful flat-leaf (Italian) parsley,
    roughly chopped

To make the garlic crème, preheat the barbecue hotplate to medium. Tear off a sheet of cooking foil, put the garlic in the centre and loosely wrap. Sit the foil-wrapped garlic on the hotplate and cook for 20 minutes, it should be able to squash a little when squeezed. Put the cooked garlic directly into a food processor. Add the mustard and egg yolks and season well with sea salt and freshly ground black pepper. Process for a few seconds to combine and with the motor running gradually pour in the oil until you have a thick custard-like mixture. Put in a bowl, cover and refrigerate until needed.

Trim any excess fat from the topside, but leave a little on the edge, and cut into eight thin slices. Put a piece of meat between two layers of plastic food wrap and gently pound so it is an even thickness all over, less than 5 mm (¼ in) thick, then cut in half. Put in a non-metallic dish with the olive oil, rosemary, garlic and pepper, then set aside for 30 minutes.

Peel the onions and cut into 5 mm (¼ in) wide rounds. With the hotplate on medium, drizzle a little olive oil over and spread evenly with a flat metal spatula. Put onions on hotplate and leave them to sizzle gently for 8–10 minutes. Don't turn the onions over until they are really dark golden. When they are, turn them over and let them do the same thing on the other side. Put the onions in a heatproof bowl with the remaining oil, vinegar, parsley and a good seasoning of sea salt and freshly ground black pepper. Move to a warm place on the barbecue, away from direct heat and leave for at least 30 minutes for the flavours to really develop.

Preheat the barbecue grill to high. Season the meat well with sea salt. Put the steak on the grill and cook for 2 minutes on each side until evenly browned. Remove to a plate.

Lightly butter the rolls then spread a little of the garlic crème on each side. Put 2–3 pieces of meat on the bottom half, top with a spoonful of balsamic onions, tomatoes and rocket, then serve.

LAMB CHOPS WITH ANCHOVY BUTTER

Anchovies and lamb, I hear you say? It is not unusual to insert slivers of anchovy and garlic into a leg of lamb before roasting. Très French. This gives some status to the humble chop.

SERVES 4

12 lamb chops
2 tablespoons olive oil
4 sprigs rosemary

ANCHOVY BUTTER
1 vine-ripened tomato
125 g (4½ oz) unsalted
   butter, softened
1 clove garlic, crushed
2 anchovies, finely chopped
1 tablespoon finely chopped
   flat-leaf (Italian) parsley

Place the lamb chops, olive oil, rosemary and salt and pepper to taste in a dish. Toss to combine well, then cover and set aside for 1 hour.

For the anchovy butter, remove the stem from the tomato and cut out the core. Cut a small and shallow cross on the opposite end and place in a small heatproof bowl. Pour enough boiling water over the tomato to cover, then stand in the hot water for 1 minute, or until the skin starts to peel. Remove the tomato, refresh in iced water and peel the skin. Cut in half and scoop and discard all the seeds, then cut the flesh into small dice. Place the tomato, butter, garlic, anchovies and parsley in a bowl and stir to combine well.

Lay a sheet of plastic wrap on a work surface and spoon the anchovy butter down the centre. Roll the butter up in the plastic to make a log, twisting the ends to seal. Refrigerate until needed, up to a day in advance.

Preheat a chargrill to high. When smoking hot, cook the lamb chops for 3 minutes on each side. Transfer to a plate, cover loosely with foil and rest for 5 minutes. Slice the anchovy butter into thin coins and serve on the lamb.

FAJITA **RUMP STEAK**
WITH MASHED AVOCADO

There is a story here. Apparently the word 'faja' is Spanish for belt or girdle. Traditionally, a fajita would really use skirt steak, a cut of meat popular in North America. I have tried this both with skirt and rump and I am unconvinced about all the fuss made about this skirt steak – sorry, guys!

SERVES 4

4 x beef rump steaks, about
    200 g (7 oz) each
2 ripe avocados
1 teaspoon sea salt
4 burritos, to serve

FAJITA MARINADE
1 small bunch coriander (cilantro),
    leaves only, finely chopped
2 tablespoons lime juice
1 teaspoon chilli powder
1 tablespoon ground cumin
1 teaspoon Tabasco sauce
2 teaspoons olive oil

Put the marinade ingredients in a non-metallic dish and stir around well so you have the sort of marinade that looks like something you would dip a corn chip into. Add the steaks and toss them around to really coat in the marinade. Cover the bowl and refrigerate for 3–6 hours.

Remove the steaks from the fridge 1 hour before cooking.

Preheat the barbecue hotplate to high and drizzle with a little olive oil to grease. Shake the excess marinade off the steaks, put on the hotplate and cook for 3 minutes on each side. You want the steaks to really sizzle for their short cooking time. Remove the steak on to a plate, lightly cover in foil, and leave to rest for 5 minutes.

Put the flesh of the avocado in a bowl with the salt and mash well. Add a squeeze of lime juice if you like and serve with the fajita steak wrapped in a warm burrito.

HAND-MADE PORK AND FENNEL **SAUSAGES**

These are not really a true sausage as they have no casing. But they take the shape of a sausage and taste as good. The combination of pork, fennel and chilli flakes is very southern Italian where sausages are traditionally cooked on a grill in a large coil or spiral shape.

SERVES 4–6

1 kg (2 lb 4 oz) minced (ground)
    pork neck
1 teaspoon chilli flakes
1 tablespoon rice flour
1 tablespoon fennel seeds
1 teaspoon sea salt
8 garlic cloves, crushed
3 tablespoons finely chopped flat-leaf
    (Italian) parsley, plus extra, to serve
25 g (1 oz/¼ cup) finely grated
    pecorino cheese
chargrilled lemon wedges, to serve

Use your hands to combine all the ingredients, except the olive oil and lemon wedges, in a bowl. Pick the mixture up and firmly throw it back into the bowl or onto a clean work surface to remove any air.

Using wet hands, roll ¼ cup portions of the mixture into little sausages, about 10 cm (4 in) long.

Preheat the barbecue hotplate to high and lightly brush with some olive oil to grease. Cook sausages for 4–5 minutes each side, until well browned and just cooked through. Scatter over the extra parsley and serve with the lemon wedges on the side.

ROAST **BEEF FILLET** WITH PAPRIKA MAYONNAISE

Here is a recipe from my old catering days. These beef fillets could be made in advance, grilled and just left to sit for a short while before being sliced to serve. Ready when you are. The prosciutto wrapped around the beef is cooked crisp, imparting even more flavour on the tender cut of beef.

SERVES 6

1.5 kg (3 lb 5 oz) beef fillet
8 garlic cloves
500 ml (17 fl oz/2 cups)
   Spanish sherry
200 g (7 oz) thinly sliced prosciutto
   (about 10–12 slices)
8 fresh bay leaves
1 tablespoon olive oil

PAPRIKA MAYONNAISE
185 ml (6 fl oz/¾ cup) good
   quality mayonnaise
1 garlic clove, crushed
½ teaspoon Spanish paprika
2 teaspoons lemon juice

Trim the beef of any fat and sinew. Cut the garlic into thin slivers. Make incisions all over the beef and slip in the garlic slivers. Lay the beef fillet in a bowl and pour over the sherry. Set aside at room temperature for 2 hours, or cover and refrigerate for several hours or overnight, turning the beef every now and then.

Remove the beef from the fridge 1–2 hours before cooking.

Lay the slices of prosciutto, side by side, on a work surface.

Remove the beef from the sherry, draining well. Lay the beef fillet on the prosciutto and put the bay leaves on the beef. Wrap the beef and bay leaves up in the prosciutto. Secure with cooking string.

To make the paprika mayonnaise, combine all ingredients in a small bowl and set aside.

Preheat the barbecue hotplate to medium. Lay the beef on the hotplate, close the lid and cook the beef for 20 minutes with the lid on, turning every 5 minutes. Turn the barbecue off and wrap the beef in foil. Sit the beef on the hot barbecue lid for 10 minutes. Remove from the lid, leave wrapped in foil and rest for another 10 minutes. Thickly slice, remove the bay leaves and serve with the paprika mayonnaise.

CHINATOWN **PORK**

You see these unctuous and shiny glazed morsels hanging in Chinatown windows. It's probably a toss-up between the roast duck and the barbecue pork (or char siu) as to which is the most popular. The roast duck is one of those things you would never really want to cook at home. The pork on the other hand is dead easy. All you need are a few Chinatown grocery staples (sauces that will keep for ages in the cupboard) and away you go.

SERVES 4

2 pork fillets, about 400 g (14 oz) each

CHAR SIU GLAZE
1 teaspoon Chinese five-spice powder
2 tablespoons honey
2 tablespoons hoi sin sauce
2 tablespoons light soy sauce

Put all the glaze ingredients in a non-metallic dish and stir around until combined. Add the pork fillets and rub the glaze all over the pork. Cover and refrigerate for 3 hours. Don't marinate it for any longer – the salt content is quite high and, left too long, the meat will become tough and chewy.

Remove the pork from the fridge 30 minutes before you begin cooking.

Preheat the barbecue hotplate to medium. Sit the pork on a cooking rack and sit the rack on a roasting tin half-filled with water. Cook for 20 minutes, turning and basting with the marinade every 2–3 minutes. The fillet will have shrunk a little and should look beautiful reddish-brown and be charred in some places. Remove and allow to cool to room temperature before cutting each fillet in half or finely slicing onto a serving plate.

T-BONE WITH BERCY SAUCE

Bercy sauce is very much a ye-olde-worlde recipe, tangy and piquanty. It's often suggested to serve bercy sauce with seafood but I reckon it's too full-on for that. The tang of the dominant vinegar flavour cuts through and complements red meat. Nice with a juicy big t-bone.

SERVES 4

4 thick t-bones steaks, about 400 g (14 oz) each
2 cloves garlic, peeled and halved
70 g (2½ oz) butter
4 French shallots, thinly sliced
125 ml (4 fl oz/½ cup) white wine
125 ml (4 fl oz/½ cup) veal or beef stock
1 handful flat-leaf (Italian) parsley leaves, finely chopped
2 teaspoons lemon juice

Rub both sides of the steaks, including the bones, with the garlic cloves. Lightly brush the steaks with oil, season with sea salt and freshly ground black pepper and set aside.

Melt 50 g (1¾ oz) butter in a small frying pan over high heat. Add the shallots and cook, stirring regularly for 4–5 minutes or until soft. Add the wine and let it sizzle and reduce by about half. Add the stock, parsley and lemon juice and cook for a couple of minutes, then stir through the remaining 20 g (¾ oz) butter and remove from the heat. Season to taste.

Heat a chargrill on high. When hot, cook the steaks for 4 minutes each side for rare.

Transfer the steaks to a plate, cover loosely with foil and rest for 5 minutes.

Reheat the sauce on low heat for 1 minute, then pour over the steaks and serve.

MINTY SALMORIGLIO
LAMB STEAKS

Salmoriglio is a flavour-packed southern Italian herb concoction, usually made solely with oregano leaves, but here I've added some mint – making this sexy sauce a very suitable partner to some equally sexy little lamb rump steaks. Oh, and this is as quick as they come, in terms of preparation, marinating and cooking times.

SERVES 4

1 handful oregano leaves
1 small bunch mint leaves
2 garlic cloves, chopped
1 teaspoon sea salt
2 tablespoons olive oil
1 tablespoon lemon juice
8 x 100 g (3½ oz) lamb rump steaks
lemon wedges, to serve

Pound the oregano, mint, garlic and sea salt to a paste using a mortar and pestle or whiz in a small food processor. Stir through the oil and lemon juice and set aside for the flavours to develop.

Put the lamb steaks in a non-metallic dish and evenly coat with the sauce. Cover and set aside for 1 hour, or if it's a really hot day just leave it for 30 minutes. You can make this and place in the refrigerator a few hours in advance, but if you do so just add the lemon juice 30 minutes before cooking.

Preheat the barbecue grill to high and brush with a little light olive oil to grease. Put the lamb steaks on the grill and cook for 2 minutes on each side, with the lid on. Put on a plate, cover and rest for about 5 minutes. Serve with lemon wedges on the side.

NEXT TIME Lamb is not always an easy thing to find (outside the Antipodes, where people are spoilt for any cut of lamb) and it may be expensive where you are. But the lamb can be replaced with tuna steaks, or other full-flavoured, oily fish, and cooked accordingly.

BEEF RISSOLES WITH HARISSA

Harissa is a Moroccan chilli-based condiment and takes on many guises. Large dried red chillies can be used, after being soaked and softened in hot water. I make harissa using roasted large fresh red chillies. Harissa would usually include cumin, ground or whole. You could add ground coriander, mint or caraway. Make a big batch of the stuff and stir through mayonnaise, tagines and stews, or just enjoy its unadulterated chilli goodness spread on sandwiches. Or with eggs for breakfast.

SERVES 4

500 g (1 lb 2 oz) minced (ground) beef
1 onion, grated
1 tablespoon ground cumin
3 tablespoons finely chopped
   curly parsley
rocket (arugula), to serve
lemon wedges, to serve

HARISSA
500 g (1 lb 2 oz) large fresh red chillies
2 garlic cloves, chopped
½ teaspoon dried mint
½ teaspoon caraway seeds
250 ml (9 fl oz/1 cup) light olive oil

To make the harissa, preheat the barbecue grill to high. Put the chillies onto the grill and cook for 4–5 minutes, turning often so the chillies are slightly charred and softened.

Set the chillies aside. When cool enough to handle, pull off the stem and put the chillies, including the seeds, into a food processor. Add the garlic, mint and caraway seeds and process, scraping the sides of the bowl, until finely chopped. Add the olive oil to make a chunky paste. Transfer to an airtight container and refrigerate until needed. This will keep for a couple of weeks in the fridge.

To make the rissoles, combine the beef, onion, cumin and parsley in a bowl. Season with sea salt and freshly ground black pepper. Using your hands mix together to make a paste. Refrigerate for 2–3 hours or longer, for flavours to develop.

With wet hands, form the beef mixture into balls that are the size of a golf ball, then flatten to make discs or patties. These can be kept in the fridge for up to a day.

To cook the rissoles, preheat the barbecue hotplate to high. Drizzle some olive oil over the hotplate to grease and cook the rissoles for 3–4 minutes each side.

Serve the rissoles with the rocket, lemon wedges, harissa and chargrilled pitta bread, if desired.

VIETNAMESE GARLIC, BLACK PEPPER AND LIME **STEAKS**

I really do reckon one of the best things about barbecuing is that it can easily incorporate bits and pieces of cooking from all over the world. This recipe uses Vietnamese ingredients, which are characteristically fresh and intense – perfect for marinades, where you really do need strong flavours to penetrate and linger in the cooked meat.

SERVES 4

4 thick beef fillet steaks, about 4 cm
    (1½ in) thick
6 garlic cloves
1 tablespoon fish sauce
1 tablespoon olive oil
1 teaspoon sugar
4 spring onions (scallions), white part
    only, finely chopped
1 teaspoon freshly ground
    black pepper
1 tablespoon rice vinegar
1 tablespoon lime juice
1 tablespoon soy sauce

To make the marinade, peel the garlic and roughly chop. Sprinkle with a pinch of sea salt and begin to chop some more and crush with the side of the knife. The salt will break down the fibres in the garlic and allow it to be effectively crushed without losing half the clove like you do in a crusher. Put the garlic in a bowl with the fish sauce, oil, sugar, spring onions and black pepper.

Put a steak on a chopping board and use a sharp knife to carefully cut each fillet, cutting parallel to the chopping board, to make two pieces about 2 cm (¾ in) thick. Repeat so you have 8 fillets. Put the meat into a non-metallic dish, pour over the marinade and rub all over the steaks. Cover and refrigerate for 3–6 hours, turning occasionally.

Remove the steaks from the fridge 30 minutes before you begin cooking.

Combine the rice vinegar, the lime juice and the soy sauce in small bowl.

Preheat the barbecue hotplate to high with the lid on so it is really hot. Drizzle a little olive oil on the hotplate to grease and then add the steaks. Cook for 2 minutes, without moving or turning, so a golden crust forms. Turn over and cook for a further 2 minutes for medium-rare. Put the steaks in a bowl and pour over the lime sauce mix. Use some tongs to turn the steaks over to coat in the sauce, then serve.

PERSIAN **LAMB CUTLETS**

Both lamb and pork can handle sweet spices. Like a few other recipes in this book, the Middle Eastern influence here is obvious. You could try this spice mixture on pork cutlets.

SERVES 4

16 lamb cutlets

PERSIAN MARINADE
1 red onion, chopped
1 tomato, chopped
4 garlic cloves, chopped
1 teaspoon ground cumin
1 teaspoon allspice
1 teaspoon ground cinnamon
½ teaspoon cayenne pepper
1 small bunch coriander (cilantro),
    leaves only, chopped

MINT YOGHURT
185 g (6½ oz/¾ cup) Greek-style
    natural yoghurt
2 Lebanese (short) cucumbers
2 garlic cloves, crushed
1 handful mint, finely chopped

For the Persian marinade, put all the ingredients in a food processor and whiz until well combined and you have a chunky-looking paste.

Put the lamb in a flat non-metallic dish and smear the paste all over them, cover and refrigerate overnight.

Remove the lamb from the fridge 30 minutes before you begin cooking.

Preheat the hotplate to high and drizzle with a little olive oil to grease. Put the lamb on the hotplate and cook for 2 minutes on each side, so it is still pink in the middle. Cook for an extra 2 minutes each side for well done. You may need to adjust the temperature if cooking longer as the marinade will burn. Remove the lamb to a serving platter, cover and rest for about 5 minutes.

Combine the mint yoghurt ingredients and put in a bowl. (It's best to make this at the last minute because the cucumber will go soggy in the yoghurt if it is left to sit.) Serve the lamb cutlets with the mint yoghurt.

SIRLOIN STEAKS WITH CHIMICHURRI BUTTER

Sirloin is also known as a New York cut. I reckon it is best appreciated when cut quite thick, leaving a nice bit of fat along one side. Sirloin and rump are my two fave cuts of steak. And the butter used in this recipe would go nicely with rump too. Chimichurri is South American in origin, probably Argentinian. It is a highly addictive, herb-filled, vinegar-spiked sauce.

SERVES 4

4 sirloin steaks
olive oil, for cooking

CHIMICHURRI BUTTER
1 handful coriander (cilantro) leaves
1 handful flat-leaf (Italian) parsley
½ teaspoon dried Greek oregano
2 garlic cloves, crushed
2 tablespoons red wine vinegar
125 g (4½ oz) unsalted butter, softened
    to room temperature

To make the chimichurri butter, put all the ingredients in a food processor and process until well combined. Lay a sheet of plastic wrap on a work surface. Put spoonfuls of the butter along the centre of the plastic, then firmly wrap and form into a log. Refrigerate for 2–3 hours, or until firm.

Remove the steaks from the fridge 1–2 hours before cooking. Brush with the olive oil, sprinkle a little sea salt on the top side of each steak and leave for 5–10 minutes.

Preheat the barbecue hotplate or grill to medium–high. Put the seasoned side of the steaks on the hotplate or grill and sprinkle a little sea salt on the top side of the steaks. Cook for 4 minutes. Turn over and cook for another 3 minutes. Remove from the hotplate, cover with foil and rest for 5 minutes.

Slice the butter and serve on the hot steaks. Serve with chargrilled corn, if desired.

MIXED MEAT GRILL

I am not too sure what a mixed grill is exactly. I do remember seeing them on breakfast menus in the '70s in country motel restaurants; lots of bacon, sausages and steak with fried eggs. Actually, this is making me hungry! This is a slightly more posh version, using fillet and T-bone, but if the mention of bacon and sausage leaves you hankering then by all means add these. The eggs, too, if you like.

SERVES 6

2 T-bone steaks, about 150 g
   (5½ oz) each
2 fillet steaks (quite thick, about
   3–4 cm/1¼–1½ in), about 150 g
   (5½ oz) each
8 lamb cutlets
1 garlic bulb, cloves separated,
   left unpeeled
6 sprigs rosemary
1 small bunch thyme
3 tablespoons olive oil
3 tablespoons sherry vinegar
1 teaspoon freshly ground
   black pepper

Put the steaks and the cutlets in a snug-fitting non-metallic dish. Add all the other ingredients and toss everything together so the herbs and garlic are evenly distributed over, under and between the pieces of meat. Cover and refrigerate overnight, tossing a few times.

Remove the plate of meat from the fridge 1 hour before you begin cooking.

Preheat the barbecue hotplate and grill to high. Now you will need a timer or some sort of stopwatch to make things easier here. All the meat is cooked medium-rare.

Put the fillets on the hotplate with some of the garlic and herbs strewn about the meat and cook for 2 minutes, pressing down occasionally with a flat metal spatula but without moving or turning. When the fillet steaks have been cooking for 2 minutes, put the T-bones on the grill, again with some of the garlic and herbs, and cook both for another 4 minutes. Turn both the fillet and T-bone steaks over.

Cook for another 4 minutes, then remove the T-bone steaks to a heatproof plate, covered with foil. Cook the fillet steaks for another 2 minutes then put these too with the T-bones and cover. Cook the cutlets for 3 minutes on the grill then turn over and cook for another 2 minutes and add to the other meat. Turn the barbecue off and set the plate of meat, covered with foil, on the lid of the barbecue to rest for 10 minutes.

Serve the mixed grilled meats with an arrangement of sauces and condiments on the side.

RUMP STEAK WITH GINGER, GARLIC AND SOY

Here is my earliest barbecue memory — eating a steak, marinated in these Asian flavours, pool side at Aunty Betty's in the Sydney summer. You can't go past rump. I still like to throw it out there at barbecues and ask people what their favourite cut of barbecued steak is. Most say rump. If you are lucky enough to get a really big piece of rump you will see how it is divided into several muscle groups, which are separated by lines of fat. The tiny part is the most tender.

SERVES 4

2 x 400 g (14 oz) pieces beef rump steak, about 1.5 cm (⅝ in) thick

GINGER SOY MARINADE
125 ml (4 fl oz/½ cup) light soy sauce, preferably Japanese
1 tablespoon sesame oil
½ teaspoon sugar
2 garlic cloves, roughly chopped
5 cm (2 in) piece ginger, peeled and very finely sliced

Put the ginger soy marinade ingredients in a small bowl and stir to combine. Put the pieces of rump in a large non-metallic dish and pour over the marinade. Cover and set aside for 1 hour, turning the pieces often. You could put the steaks in the fridge for a couple of hours but be aware the salt in the soy can make the meat tough. I find the steak has a better flavour and texture if left to marinate at room temperature for a short time.

Preheat the barbecue grill to high and brush with a little vegetable oil to grease. Put the steaks on the grill and cook for 3 minutes on each side. Remove the steaks to a plate, cover lightly with foil and rest for 5 minutes. The steaks will be quite pink in the centre, medium-rare. If you'd prefer the steaks less pink, cook for 5 minutes each side for medium and 7 minutes each side for well-done. Cut each steak in half to serve 4 or into smaller pieces as part of a barbecue banquet.

BUTTERFLIED LAMB MASALA

Do keep your eye on this one. It is thick in parts so it is not to be rushed, causing it to burn before cooking on the inside. Having said this, lamb is best pink. But if that is not your thing, cook on low heat for an extra 15 or 20 minutes. And let it sit, covered, on the hot barbecue lid for 20 minutes. The green masala marinade is a base curry paste that can be used in curries. Just fry off in a little oil, add some cubed lamb or beef, top with water and cook on a very low heat until the meat is fork tender.

SERVES 6-8

1 small leg lamb, about 1.8 kg (4 lb), butterflied

GREEN MASALA MARINADE
1 tablespoon black mustard seeds
1 tablespoon cumin seeds
1 tablespoon coriander seeds
1 teaspoon turmeric
4 cardamom pods
1 cinnamon stick, broken up
4 spring onions (scallions), white part and a little of the green finely chopped
4 garlic cloves
3 large green chillies
1 small bunch coriander (cilantro), chopped
1 tablespoon finely grated ginger
½ teaspoon ground black pepper
3 tablespoons olive oil
3 tablespoons lemon juice

For the green masala, put the mustard seeds, cumin seeds, coriander seeds, turmeric, cardamom and cinnamon in a small dry frying pan over high heat. Shake the pan over the heat until the mustard seeds pop and the mixture emits an aromatic smoke. Allow to cool then grind in a small spice mill (or mortar and pestle) to a rough powder. Put the spices in a food processor with the other ingredients, except the meat, and whiz to a chunky darkish-green paste. Remove to a bowl. This can be made in advance and kept in a non-metallic dish, covered in the refrigerator.

Cut 5 mm (¼ in) deep incisions on the skin side of the lamb about 5 cm (2 in) apart. This will help the lamb to cook more evenly, and allow the intense flavour of the marinade to penetrate into the meat. Put the lamb into a large, flat non-metallic dish with the masala marinade and rub the marinade all over the lamb, making sure you rub into the incisions. Cover and refrigerate overnight, turning often.

Remove the lamb from the fridge at least 1 hour before you begin cooking.

Preheat the barbecue hotplate and grill burners to high. Sit the lamb on a cooking rack and sit the rack over a roasting tray half-filled with water. Put the tray on the hotplate, cover with the lid and cook for 15 minutes. Turn all the burners to low and cook for a further 25 minutes. Cover with cooking foil and rest for 20 minutes before carving.

NEXT TIME Rub the marinade over 4 chicken leg quarters. Allow to marinate for 3–6 hours and cook on a medium barbecue for 12 minutes on each side.

FILLET STEAK WITH CAFÉ DE PARIS BUTTER

This is amusing as it inspires much who-made-what-and-where debate. The original recipe is guarded as secretly as one Colonel Sanders' 11 secret herbs and spices. Some recipes list as many as 30 ingredients. But let's not get carried away. This is a barbecue after all. This version of Café de Paris butter only has 10 ingredients but it is pretty bloody good. (PS: this will keep for ages in the fridge.)

SERVES 4

4 x 200 g (7 oz) thick-cut beef
    fillet steaks
250 ml (9 fl oz/1 cup) red wine
2 tablespoons olive oil

CAFÉ DE PARIS BUTTER
1 tablespoon mild mustard
2 teaspoons Worcestershire sauce
2 tablespoons tomato sauce (ketchup)
1 garlic clove
1 tablespoon capers, rinsed and
    well drained
6 anchovies
2 tablespoons roughly chopped
    flat-leaf (Italian) parsley
2 teaspoons thyme leaves
1 teaspoon Madras curry powder
250 g (9 oz) butter, softened

To make the Café de Paris butter, put all the ingredients, except the butter, in a food processor and whiz until you have a chunky paste. Remove to a bowl, cover and leave at room temperature for a few hours for the flavours to develop.

Put the butter in a bowl and add the mixture. Stir for a few minutes, making sure the butter is evenly combined. Lay a sheet of plastic wrap on a work surface. Put spoonfuls of the butter along the centre of the plastic, then firmly wrap and form into a log. Refrigerate until needed. Remove the butter from the fridge to come to room temperature before using.

Put the beef fillets in a snug-fitting non-metallic dish. Add the red wine and olive oil, tossing the meat around to coat in the marinade. Cover and refrigerate overnight.

Remove the meat from the fridge 1 hour before cooking.

Preheat the barbecue grill to high and brush with a little olive oil to grease. Put the steak on the grill and cook for 5 minutes on each side. Wrap the meat in some foil and, leaving the heat on, close the lid and sit the meat on top for 5 minutes. Remove and allow to rest for another 10 minutes in the foil before serving with the butter sliced or spooned over the meat.

ROAST **BEEF**

How many recipes for roast beef have you come across? Or maybe you don't follow a recipe? Either way, the tricky thing about a good roast-beef meal is the timing. Many recipes are written forgetting that the home cook simply doesn't have enough space in the oven to cook the beef and the vegies at the same time and, if you are British, probably the Yorkshire puds too! You can cook a pretty close to perfect bit of beef on the barbecue, and why not serve it with barbecue-roasted vegies and some horseradish sour cream?

SERVES 6

4 garlic cloves, chopped
1 tablespoon thyme leaves
2 large handfuls flat-leaf (Italian) parsley, roughly chopped
1 teaspoon sea salt flakes
2 tablespoons olive oil
1–1.25 kg (2 lb 4 oz–2 lb 12 oz) roasting beef fillet, with a nice thin layer of fat

HORSERADISH CREAM
185 g (6½ oz/¾ cup) sour cream
1 tablespoon horseradish

Using a mortar and pestle, pound the garlic, herbs, salt and oil until you have a coarse paste. Rub all over the beef and set aside for 1 hour to come to room temperature.

Preheat all the barbecue burners to high, with the lid on, creating a hot-oven effect. Half-fill a roasting tin with boiling water and sit a rack on top, making sure it is steady and not going to fall off during cooking. Sit the roasting tray on the grill side of the barbecue.

Starting with the fat side down, cook the beef for 1 minute on each of its four sides on the hotplate, so it is just brown all over. Sit the beef on the rack, skin side up, close the lid and cook for 20 minutes, so the beef is just verging on dark brown in some places. Turn the barbecue off, wrap the beef in foil and then sit the beef on top of the hot lid for 15 minutes. Remove and allow to rest for another 20 minutes. While the beef is resting combine the sour cream and horseradish in a bowl. Carve the beef and serve with the horseradish cream.

MARRAKESH **CHOPS**

Truth be known, the inspiration for this recipe comes from a snack I had at a market place in Marrakesh. The snack involved the cheek off a head of lamb and a cumin and salt concoction. The heads were slow cooked, whole, and the cheek meat just fell off the bone. Putting this image to one side, it was very delicious. There is no lamb head here, just some very tasty, and slightly more accessible, lamb loin chops.

SERVES 6

12 thick lamb loin chops
3 tablespoons white wine
3 tablespoons lemon juice
½ teaspoon dried oregano
lemon wedges, to serve

CUMIN SALT
1 teaspoon sea salt
1 teaspoon ground cumin

To make the cumin salt, combine the salt and cumin in a small frying pan. Cook over high heat, shaking the pan, until the mixture starts to smoke and is aromatic. Tip into a bowl and cool. Grind to a fine powder in a spice mill or use a mortar and pestle. Set aside until needed.

Put the lamb in a large dish with the wine, lemon juice and oregano, turning to coat in the marinade. Cover and refrigerate for 3 hours or overnight, turning the chops every now and then.

Remove the lamb from the fridge 1 hour before cooking.

Preheat the barbecue hotplate to high. Drizzle a little olive oil on the hotplate to lightly grease. When smoking hot, cook the lamb for 5 minutes. Turn over and then cook for a further 3 minutes.

Put the cooked chops on a serving plate and quickly sprinkle the cumin salt all over. Cover loosely with foil and rest for 5–10 minutes. Serve with the lemon wedges.

SPANISH **RUMP STEAK**

This is a very broad title. After all, Spain is a big place and Spanish cooking uses many flavours. But I do find myself drawn to smoked paprika and sherry, two of the big boys of flavour in Spanish cooking. They are so intense and unique.

SERVES 4

4 rump steaks, about 200 g (7 oz) each and about 1.5 cm (⅝ in) thick
6 garlic cloves, finely chopped
2 bay leaves
250 ml (9 fl oz/1 cup) Spanish or dry sherry
2 tablespoons olive oil

Put the steaks in a flat dish. Combine the garlic, bay leaves, sherry and olive oil in a bowl and pour over the steaks. Turn the steaks over a couple of times to coat in the marinade. Cover and refrigerate for at least 6 hours or overnight, turning the steaks every now and then.

Remove the steaks from the fridge 1 hour prior to cooking.

Preheat the barbecue hotplate to high. When the hotplate is smoking hot, add the steaks and cook for 4 minutes, turn over and cook for another 3 minutes. Rest the steaks for 5 minutes before serving.

PORK SHOULDER
WITH FENNEL AND GARLIC

This as an autumnal barbecue favourite but need not be saved for the cooler months. One of the great benefits of barbecuing is you can cook these big cuts of meat outdoors in summer – getting out of that hot kitchen.

SERVES 6-8

2 tablespoons fennel seeds
6 garlic cloves, crushed
1 tablespoon sea salt
2 tablespoons white vinegar
1.5 kg (3 lb 5 oz) rolled pork shoulder, skin on
6 bay leaves
1 large fennel bulb, thickly sliced

Pound the fennel seeds in a mortar and pestle until just split – don't pound them too finely. Add the garlic, salt and vinegar, and pound until they combine into a thick paste. Set aside.

Remove the pork from the fridge and use a sharp knife (a Stanley knife is ideal) to cut 5 mm (¼ in) deep incisions across the skin, about 1 to 2 cm (½ to ¾ in) apart. Smear the paste mixture over the meaty ends of the rolled pork and the skin, rubbing it into the cuts. Leave the pork to sit for 1 hour.

Preheat the barbecue hotplate and grill burners to high and close the lid to create a hot-oven effect. Put the bay leaves in a deep-sided baking tin. Pour enough boiling water in to come halfway up the sides. Put two layers of foil on a cooking rack and arrange the fennel slices in the centre. Sit the pork on the fennel, skin side up and cook for 45 minutes with the lid on until the fennel is tender and golden. Remove the fennel to a plate and cover. Turn all the burners down to low. Rotate the baking tin 180 degrees to promote even cooking and cook the pork for another 45 minutes to 1 hour, until the skin is crackling and dark golden. Remove to a serving plate, cover with foil and allow to rest for 20 minutes before carving. Serve with the fennel.

T-BONE FLORENTINE

Despite its fancy-pants name this is the style of cooking that is the essence of a great barbecue – the meat is the star attraction with a couple of support acts on the side. Choose a great bit of meat; I use T-bone because it is one of the few cuts of beef with a bone that can be easily barbecued, except maybe for ribs but these aren't always available or affordable.

SERVES 4

4 T-bone steaks, about 2 cm (¾ in) thick at the bone
2 garlic cloves, cut in half
4 lemons, cut in half
1 tablespoon sea salt
2 tablespoons roughly chopped flat-leaf (Italian) parsley, to serve

Remove your steaks from the fridge 45 minutes to 1 hour before barbecuing. This will allow the meat to come to room temperature. The cooking time is quite quick here and because the meat is on the bone the centres of the steak will be cold if cooked straight from the fridge. Rub the cut garlic halves all over the T-bones, including the bone.

Preheat the barbecue grill to high and brush with a little olive oil to grease.

Rub the cut lemons over the steaks and then cook the lemons on the grill for 5 minutes, until they are scored and starting to caramelise. Remove and set aside.

Rub the meat with about 1 tablespoon of olive oil and sprinkle the salt on both sides of the steaks. Put the steaks on the grill and cook for 4 minutes. Turn over and cook for another 4 minutes for medium-rare. Serve with the parsley sprinkled over and the grilled lemons on the side to squeeze.

LAMB WITH GREEN OLIVE SALSA

Lamb cuts from young animals are perfect for quick cooking – backstrap, fillet, loin chops, cutlets and medallions. But the leg may well be the thing we most associate with lamb. Leaving the skin and fat on allows the meat to cook without burning.

SERVES 6

1 small leg of lamb, about 1.6 kg
    (3 lb 8 oz), butterflied
125 ml (4 fl oz/½ cup) dry white wine
3 tablespoons lemon juice
3 tablespoons olive oil, plus extra,
    for cooking
1 handful rosemary sprigs
10–12 garlic cloves, peeled
    and crushed
Sicilian grilled vegetable salad,
    to serve (see page 301)

GREEN OLIVE SALSA
175 g (6 oz/1 cup) green olives, pitted
6 baby gherkins (cornichons)
2 large handfuls flat-leaf
    (Italian) parsley
2 large handfuls mint
2 garlic cloves, chopped
3 anchovy fillets
3 tablespoons lemon juice
125 ml (4 fl oz/½ cup) olive oil

As the lamb will be thicker at one end, make several deep cuts into the thicker part to allow more even cooking. Put the lamb in a large ceramic dish or bowl with the wine, lemon juice, olive oil, rosemary and garlic. Set aside at room temperature for 2–3 hours or cover and refrigerate for up to a day, turning the lamb often.

To make the salsa, put all the ingredients in a food processor and process to a paste. Set aside.

Remove the lamb from the fridge 1 hour before cooking.

Preheat the barbecue hotplate and grill to high and close the lid to create a hot-oven effect. Drizzle a little olive oil on the hotplate to grease. Remove the lamb from the marinade, reserving the marinade. Cook the lamb skin side down on the hotplate for 8–10 minutes, or until the skin is browned. Turn the lamb over and cook for another 5 minutes. Put the lamb on a 'V'-shaped barbecue rack and spoon over the marinade. Reduce the heat to medium. Sit the rack on the hotplate, close the lid and cook for 20–25 minutes, or until cooked as desired. Remove the lamb to a large serving plate, cover loosely with foil, and rest for 15–20 minutes.

Thickly slice the lamb and arrange on a serving platter with the green olive salsa spooned over. Serve with the Sicilian grilled vegetable salad.

PEPPER **BEEF FILLET**

A special piece of meat is this fillet – larger at one end and tapers down to a tail. Ask your butcher to give you two fillets which are even in size, to keep the cooking time the same. The tip here of shaking away the fine pepper powder is a good one. It ensures you get an intense pepper flavour without the unpalatable heat. But a couple of things to remember when using this prime cut – make use of the hot lid of the barbecue in finishing off the cooking and do remember to let the meat rest.

SERVES 4

2 x 400 g (14 oz) best beef fillets
    (both from the mid cut so they
    are even sizes)
1 tablespoon white peppercorns
1 tablespoon black peppercorns
1 tablespoon olive oil
1 garlic bulb, cloves separated and
    lightly smashed
1 bunch thyme

Trim the meat of any excess fat and put in a non-metallic dish.

Put all the peppercorns in a spice mill and roughly grind. Put the pepper in a sieve and shake away the fine powder. Rub the remaining rough powder all over the beef fillets. Put in the refrigerator and leave uncovered overnight, turning a few times. You can do this up to 2 days in advance.

Remove the beef from the fridge and add the olive oil, garlic and thyme to the dish, turning the beef. Set aside for 1 hour.

Preheat the barbecue hotplate to medium. Put the beef fillets on the hotplate and cook for 8 minutes with the lid on, turning every 2 minutes, so that each surface (including the sides) is cooked for the same length of time. Turn the barbecue off and wrap the meat in two layers of foil. Sit the beef on top of the warm lid of the barbecue for 10 minutes. Remove to a plate and leave to rest, still wrapped in the foil, for 10 minutes.

Cut the beef into thick slices and serve with easy béarnaise sauce (see page 364) if you like.

STOUT **BEEF BURGERS**

The inclusion of stout, a dark and malty brew, will give the prosaic burger something to really talk about.

SERVES 4

40 g (1 ½ oz) butter
1 small onion, finely chopped
1 clove garlic, crushed
2 rashers streaky bacon, rind removed, finely chopped
500 g (1 lb 2 oz) minced (ground) beef
60 ml (2 fl oz/¼ cup) stout beer
1 egg, lightly beaten
toasted burger buns, shredded lettuce, sliced tomato, crispy bacon, sliced beetroot, cheddar cheese and barbecue sauce, to serve

Melt the butter in a small frying pan over medium heat. Add the onion, garlic and bacon and cook for 2–3 minutes, or until soft. Transfer to a bowl, cool slightly, then add the beef and beer and season to taste. Using your hands, combine well, then cover and refrigerate for a few hours, so the beer flavours the beef.

Add the egg to the beef and combine with your hands. Divide the mixture into four equal portions then shape into patties. Place on a plate, cover and refrigerate until needed. The patties can be made up to 1 day in advance.

Remove the patties from the refrigerator 30 minutes before cooking.

Preheat a barbecue flat plate to high and drizzle with a little olive oil. Cook the patties for 5 minutes on each side, or until well cooked on the outside. They may still be slightly pink in the centre. Cook for an extra 2 minutes each side to cook all the way through if desired. Serve with the toasted buns, salad, bacon, beetroot, cheese and sauce.

RUMP STEAK
WITH TABASCO BUTTER

Rump is my most favourite cut of beef to grill. While most meat comes pre-sliced you can ask your butcher for a large piece of rump, 2–3 kg (4 lb 8 oz–6 lb 10 oz), not the whole side. All you need is a sharp knife to cut restaurant thick steaks at home. Try the butter with fries. Wow!

SERVES 4

4 rump steaks, about 200 g (7 oz) each
olive oil, for brushing
lime wedges, to serve

TABASCO BUTTER
125 g (4½ oz) unsalted butter,
    softened to room temperature
¼ teaspoon green Tabasco sauce
1 small clove garlic, crushed
1 tablespoon finely chopped flat-leaf
    (Italian) parsley
1 tablespoon finely chopped
    coriander (cilantro)

For the Tabasco butter, place all the ingredients and a pinch of sea salt in a bowl and combine well. Lay a sheet of plastic wrap on a work surface. Spoon the butter mixture down the centre to make a log about 10 cm (4 in) long. Firmly wrap the butter up in the plastic to make a log. Refrigerate until needed. This can be made up to 2 days in advance.

Lightly brush the steaks with oil and season well with sea salt and freshly ground black pepper.

Preheat a chargrill to high. When smoking hot, cook steaks for 3 minutes on each side for medium-rare. Transfer to a plate, cover loosely with foil and rest for a couple of minutes.

Slice the Tabasco butter into thin coins and serve on the warm steaks, with lime wedges on the side.

NEW YORK **COWBOY**

A New York cut steak is also called porterhouse. It is a thick cut of beef, about 2–3 cm (about an inch), with a healthy layer of fat hugging one side. Like most people, I sometimes use the internet when I'm doing research. While I was looking at recipes I found a spice rub called New York cowboy spice rub. Intrigued? I was, especially when I read it asked for 6 tablespoons of salt in the mixture! Mental note, don't automatically assume the written word on the internet is gospel. If I had followed this I would have ruined some expensive meat. But, I do like the name of the rub, so here is my version.

SERVES 4

4 New York or sirloin steaks, about
   200 g (7 oz) each
2 teaspoons sea salt flakes

NEW YORK COWBOY SPICE RUB
2 teaspoons chilli powder
2 teaspoons Hungarian paprika
2 teaspoons black peppercorns
4 garlic cloves, crushed
80 ml (2½ fl oz/⅓ cup) olive oil

Put the chilli powder, paprika and black peppercorns in a spice mill and whiz together until the peppercorns are crushed and the mixture is powder-like. Put the powder in a non-metallic dish large enough to fit the steaks. Add the garlic and oil and stir around so you have a fiery red paste. Add the steaks and rub the paste all over them.

Cover and refrigerate for 6 hours or overnight. Remember to take them out of the fridge 1 hour before cooking. These are thick cuts of meat so they will need to come to room temperature, otherwise the steaks will still be fridge cold in the centre when you eat them.

Preheat the barbecue grill to medium. Sprinkle the salt on the steaks, put on the grill and cook for 6 minutes with the lid on. Turn over and cook for another 6 minutes. Wrap the meat in foil, turn the barbecue heat off and sit the meat on the warm barbecue lid for 5 minutes. Remove the meat from the lid and leave covered for another 5 minutes to rest before eating.

LAMB SHOULDER WITH ROSEMARY AND GARLIC

Not the prettiest cut of meat, but pretty tasty nonetheless. Leftovers can be made into a toothsome sandwich, smeared with tomato and honey jam.

SERVES 4

1 shoulder of lamb, about 1–1.25 kg
　(2 lb 4 oz–2 lb 12 oz)
1 garlic bulb
1 bunch rosemary
1 bunch thyme
3 tablespoons olive oil
12 baby potatoes (optional)

Using a small, sharp knife, cut about 10–12 incisions in the skin of the lamb, about 1 cm (½ in) wide, but not going into the meat. Peel 2 garlic cloves and finely slice. Slide the garlic slices in under the skin of the lamb. Cut 3–4 cm (1¼–1½ in) lengths off the rosemary tops and use the knife to carefully slide these too under the skin with the garlic. Rub a generous amount of sea salt evenly over the skin of the lamb and leave the lamb to sit at room temperature for 1 hour.

Separate the remaining garlic cloves and put them, unpeeled, in a deep-sided baking tin with the remaining rosemary and thyme.

Preheat the barbecue hotplate and grill to high and close the lid to create a hot-oven effect. Pour enough water to come halfway up the sides of the baking tin and sit a rack on top of the dish, making sure it is steady and even. Sit the lamb on the rack and drizzle the oil over the skin. Put the baking dish on the hotplate of the barbecue and cook for 30 minutes with the lid on. Within about 10 minutes you should hear the skin start to sizzle. After 30 minutes, add the potatoes if using, placing them around the shoulder. Turn the heat to low and cook for another 1½ hours. Check every 30 minutes or so, topping up with boiling water if needed and turning the potatoes. Remove the potatoes and keep warm, loosely cover the lamb with foil and cook for a further 30 minutes.

Remove the lamb to a large serving plate, cover with foil and rest for 20–30 minutes. Serve with the potatoes.

ORANGE AND SPICE
PORK MEDALLIONS

Grated onion not only adds flavour to meat but also tenderises it. The marinade here is very basic yet tasty — a good one to have up your sleeve. It would also work nicely with chicken thigh fillets or rump steak.

SERVES 4

600–700 g (1 lb 5 oz–1 lb 9 oz)
　　pork tenderloin
1 white onion
2 teaspoons sea salt
2 tablespoons orange juice
1 tablespoon ground cumin
2 teaspoons paprika
1 tablespoon olive oil
1 orange, cut into 1 cm (½ in) slices
salad leaves, to serve
coriander (cilantro) sprigs,
　　to serve (optional)

Trim and cut the tenderloin into 1.5 cm (⅝ in) thick slices and put into a non-metallic dish.

Coarsely grate the onion into a bowl and stir through the sea salt. Set aside for 10 minutes. Press the onion into a sieve so the juice drips over the pork. Discard the onion pulp. Add the orange juice, cumin, paprika and olive oil to the pork and stir to combine. Cover and refrigerate for a few hours or overnight, stirring every now and then.

Remove the pork from the fridge 1 hour before cooking.

Preheat the barbecue hotplate to high. Cook the pork for 3 minutes each side. Set aside. Cook the orange slices for 1–2 minutes on each side, or until caramelised. Serve the pork with the orange slices and salad leaves, with the coriander sprigs scattered over, if using.

FILET MIGNON WITH
ROAST GARLIC BUTTER

Fillet steaks can be pricey. If they are, then simply substitute the expensive cut with whatever you like. The garlic butter will be lovely with any grilled red meat or chicken.

SERVES 4

6 cloves garlic, left whole and
    unpeeled
75 g (2½ oz) unsalted butter, softened
4 fillet steaks, about 200 g (7 oz) each
    and about 2 cm (¾ in) thick
4 rashers streaky bacon
1 tablespoon light olive oil

Preheat the oven to 220°C (425°F/Gas 7).

Wrap the garlic cloves in a piece of foil, place on an oven tray and bake for 20 minutes or until the cloves are soft when squeezed. Allow to cool. Once cooled, peel, then mash and combine well in a bowl with the softened butter. Set aside or refrigerate until needed.

Gently pound each steak so they are an even 1.5 cm (⅝ in) thickness all over. Season with sea salt and freshly ground black pepper and wrap a rasher of streaky bacon around the centre of each steak, tucking in the ends to secure. Set aside for 30 minutes.

Heat a chargrill or barbecue flat plate to high. Lightly brush the steaks with oil and cook for 3 minutes on each side for rare. Remove and rest for 5 minutes.

While the steaks are resting, place the garlic butter in a small frying pan over medium heat and cook for 1 minute or until the garlic is sizzling. Transfer the steaks to a serving plate and pour over the hot butter.

SEARED **CALVES' LIVER**

**I loved lambs fry as a child. Then I realised what it was and I stopped loving it.
Then I got over myself and now love it again. Smother it in bacon flavoured
gravy or sear it very quickly and squeeze some lemon over the top.**

SERVES 4

1 kg (2 lb 4 oz) calves' liver
2 tablespoons olive oil
4 cloves garlic, roughly chopped
1 tablespoon lemon juice
handful flat-leaf (Italian) parsley
  leaves, roughly chopped
grilled garlic toasts and lemon
  wedges, to serve

Peel the membrane off the liver and discard. Trim the liver of
any connecting fatty tissue or tubes and discard. Cut the liver
crossways into 2 cm (¾ in) thick steak-like pieces.

Place the liver in a non-metallic dish with the oil and garlic.
Season to taste with sea salt and freshly ground black pepper,
turn to coat and set aside for 30 minutes.

Heat a barbecue hot plate to high. When smoking hot, add
the liver slices and cook for 2–3 minutes. Turn over and cook
for 2 minutes. Pour the lemon juice over the liver, letting it
sizzle on the hot plate, then quickly turn the liver once more
to coat in the juices. Transfer to a plate and sprinkle over the
parsley. Serve with grilled garlic toasts and lemon wedges
on the side.

CHRISTMAS BARBECUED
GLAZED HAM

In my book a garnish is something that should be eaten, except for any ingredients you use on a Christmas ham to make it look pretty. The ham is already cooked, of course, so all you are doing is making it look drop-dead gorgeous – the star of the Christmas table.

SERVES MANY

2 x 450 g (1 lb) tins pineapple rings, liquid reserved
water or orange juice, if needed
45 g (1¾ oz/¼ cup) light brown sugar
2 tablespoons mild mustard
2 tablespoons whole cloves
2 x 100 g (3½ oz) packets glacé cherries
1 whole cooked leg ham, about 8–9 kg (17–19 lb)

Drain the pineapple and measure the liquid. You will need 500 ml (17 fl oz/2 cups) of liquid. If you don't have enough pineapple juice, make up the rest with water or orange juice. Slice each pineapple ring through the centre to give two thinner rings. Put the juice in a frying pan with the sugar and mustard and cook over medium heat, stirring, until the sugar dissolves. Boil for 5 minutes so the liquid thickens a little. Add the rings and toss them to coat in the juice, then cook for 5 minutes so the rings darken just a little. Set aside to cool.

Preheat all the barbecue burners to medium, with the lid on to create a hot-oven effect.

To remove the skin from the ham, cut a line through the thick rind a few centimetres from the shank end with a sharp knife. Run your thumb around the edge and carefully pull back the skin, leaving the fat on the leg. When the skin is removed, lightly score the fat in a diamond pattern (if you score too deeply the fat will fall off during the cooking process).

Start to arrange the pineapple rings on the fat, starting at the shank end. Secure the rings with one or two cloves then secure a glacé cherry in the centre of each ring with a clove. Repeat so the ham is covered all over with the pineapple and cherries.

Half fill a large roasting tray with water. Sit the ham on a cooking rack and sit this on top of the tray. Brush some of the pineapple glaze over the ham and put on the barbecue. Cover with the lid. Now you simply have to cook the ham until it looks good. This will take about 1½ to 2 hours, brushing more glaze over the ham every 20 minutes or so and making sure the water doesn't dry out, until the pineapple rings are almost dark caramel in colour and some of the fat and juices of the ham have dripped down forming toffee stalactites around the sides.

Allow to rest for 30 minutes before carving.

BEEF RIB EYE FILLET
WITH HORSERADISH BUTTER

This is a good example of how meat can benefit from sitting at room temperature before cooking and from resting after cooking. Rib eye does not require much cooking. This means if you cook it directly from the fridge it will still be cold in the centre. It doesn't generally have much fat so if overcooked it will be dry and if not rested it will be tough. Basically, this cut deserves a little respect.

SERVES 4

750–800 g (1 lb 10 oz–1 lb 12 oz)
   rib eye beef fillet
1 teaspoon sea salt
1 teaspoon freshly ground
   black pepper
1 tablespoon olive oil

HORSERADISH BUTTER
125 g (4½ oz) unsalted butter,
   softened to room temperature
1 tablespoon finely grated
   fresh horseradish
2 teaspoons Worcestershire sauce
1 garlic clove, crushed
1 tablespoon finely chopped spring
   onion (scallion)
1 tablespoon small salted capers,
   rinsed and well drained
2 anchovy fillets
2 tablespoons finely chopped
   flat-leaf (Italian) parsley

To make the horseradish butter, put all the ingredients in a food processor and process until well combined. Lay a sheet of plastic wrap on a work surface. Put spoonfuls of the butter along the centre of the plastic, then firmly wrap and form into a log about 2 cm (¾ in) wide. Refrigerate for 2–3 hours, or until firm.

Rub the beef all over with the salt and pepper and set aside at room temperature for 1–2 hours.

Preheat the barbecue hotplate to medium and close the lid to create a hot-oven effect. Drizzle the olive oil over the hotplate to grease. Put the fillet on the hotplate, cover and cook for 5 minutes. Give the beef a quarter turn and cook for another 5 minutes. Repeat twice more so the beef is well browned on all sides. Wrap the beef loosely in foil and sit on the hot barbecue lid for 15 minutes. Remove and allow to rest for 15 minutes, wrapped in the foil. Thickly slice and serve on a platter with slices of the butter on top and oven-baked potato chips on the side, if desired.

CHUNKY **LAMB LEG STEAKS**

Depending on how your butcher bones the leg, or how it is sold in the supermarket, I am hoping you can get four 'steaks' of equal size from the leg. If not, don't stress. If the lamb leg is thin in parts, cut into smaller portions.

SERVES 4

1 small boned leg of lamb,
    about 1 kg (2 lb 4 oz)
2 teaspoons ground cumin
1 teaspoon ground turmeric
2 teaspoons sea salt
70 g (2½ oz/¼ cup) plain yoghurt
2 onions, chopped
1 handful coriander leaves and stems
2 tablespoons finely grated ginger
2 garlic cloves, chopped
1 teaspoon garam masala

Cut the lamb into several steaks, about 2 cm (¾ in) thick and put into a bowl with the cumin, turmeric and sea salt. Toss the lamb around to coat evenly in the spices and set aside.

Put the yoghurt, onion, coriander, ginger and garlic in a food processor and process to a paste. Spoon over the lamb and stir well to combine. Cover and set aside at room temperature for 2–3 hours, or refrigerate for at least 6 hours or overnight.

Remove steaks from the fridge 1 hour before cooking.

Preheat the barbecue grill to medium. Cook the steaks for 5 minutes each side. Sprinkle over the garam masala and quickly turn the steaks on the grill for a few seconds each side so the spices cook and are aromatic.

FILLET STEAK WITH GREEN PEPPERCORN SAUCE

The sauce here will need to be made in a small saucepan. It can be made just before the meat is cooked or made in advance and kept warm in a thermo flask, conveniently ready to pour over the steaks.

SERVES 4

4 fillet steaks, about 180 g
   (6½ oz) each
50 g (1¾ oz) unsalted butter
1 tablespoon olive oil
1 clove garlic, finely chopped
1 tablespoon plain (all-purpose) flour
125 ml (4 fl oz/½ cup) white wine
125 ml (4 fl oz/½ cup) beef stock
2 tablespoons green peppercorns
   in brine, drained
60 g (2¼ oz) thick
   (double/heavy) cream

Pound the steaks lightly until they are an even 1 cm (½ in) thickness all over. Season both sides with salt and pepper and set aside.

Heat the butter and oil in a small saucepan on medium heat. Add the garlic and cook for just a few seconds, until aromatic but not burnt. Remove the pan from the heat. Add the flour and stir until smooth.

Return the pan to the heat. Add the wine and stir for 1 minute, until thickened. Add the stock and peppercorns and bring to the boil, stirring regularly. Reduce the heat to low then add the cream. Stir well to combine and season to taste. Set aside while cooking the steaks.

Heat a barbecue hotplate or grill to high heat and brush the surface of the grill lightly with cooking oil. Cook the steaks for 2 minutes each side then put on serving plates. Serve with the warm sauce.

CURRIED **LEG OF LAMB**

The ingredient list here is about as lengthy as you will find in this book, or with my recipes in general for that matter. Sometimes with Indian flavours this is unavoidable for an authentic result. A curry really is just a blend or combination of spices. If you have any shop-bought curry powder or paste have a look at the ingredient list and you'll see what I mean. Making your own, though, is one sure way to ensure a more flavoursome, pungent and aromatic curry.

SERVES 6–8

1 leg of lamb, about 1.5 kg (3 lb 5 oz),
    boned and butterflied
3 tablespoons lemon juice
2 tablespoons olive oil
½ teaspoon chilli powder
2 tablespoons sea salt
pomegranate seeds,
    to serve (optional)

SPICE PASTE
1 teaspoon saffron threads
1 onion, chopped
2 garlic cloves, chopped
1 tablespoon finely grated ginger
2 teaspoons black mustard seeds
2 whole cloves
4 cardamom pods
1 teaspoon coriander seeds
1 teaspoon cumin seeds
1 teaspoon fennel seeds
130 g (4½ oz/½ cup) plain yoghurt
2 tablespoons pomegranate molasses

Put the lamb in a large flat dish. Combine the lemon juice, olive oil, chilli powder and sea salt in a small bowl and pour over the lamb. Cover and set aside for about 1 hour, but do not refrigerate.

To make the spice paste, put the saffron in a bowl with 60 ml (2 fl oz/¼ cup) boiling water. Leave for 10 minutes, until the water is a vibrant saffron colour. Put all the remaining ingredients in a food processor, including the saffron water. Process for several seconds then scrape down the side of the processor with a spatula. Repeat several more times. Pour the paste over the lamb. Toss the lamb around so it is completely covered with the spice paste. Cover and leave at room temperature for 2–3 hours, or refrigerate overnight.

Remove the lamb from the fridge 1 hour before cooking.

Preheat the barbecue hotplate and grill to high and close the lid to create a hot-oven effect.

Sit the lamb on a 'V'-shaped barbecue rack. Sit the rack on the hotplate, close the lid and cook for 20 minutes. Reduce the heat to medium and cook for another 20 minutes.

Remove the lamb to a large serving plate, cover loosely with foil and allow to rest for 20 minutes before carving. Serve with the pomegranate seeds, if desired.

SIRLOIN STEAK WITH BÉARNAISE

**All sounds a bit posh, doesn't it? Check out the ingredient list. It's not very long.
And the method? It's pretty straightforward.**

SERVES 4

4 sirloin steaks, about 200 g
   (7 oz) each
1 tablespoon light olive oil

BÉARNAISE
3 egg yolks
1 tablespoon tarragon vinegar
60 ml (2 fl oz/¼ cup) light olive oil
200 g (7 oz) butter

For the béarnaise, place the egg yolks and vinegar in a small food processor. With the motor running, gradually add the oil in a very slow, steady stream until all the oil has been added and the mixture is thick and emulsified. Place the butter in a small saucepan and cook over high heat until melted and sizzling. With the motor running again, pour the hot butter into the mayonnaise in a thin steady stream and process until thick and smooth. This can be made several hours in advance, then transferred to a warmed thermos where it will keep warm for 2 hours. Makes about 310 ml (10¾ fl oz/1¼ cups).

Brush the steaks with the oil and put on a plate. Season the tops with sea salt and freshly ground black pepper to taste. Stand at room temperature for 30 minutes.

Heat a chargrill or barbecue flat plate to high. When smoking hot, add the steaks, seasoned side down, and cook for 4 minutes. Season the other side to taste, then turn and cook for another 4 minutes for medium-rare. This will vary according to the thickness of the steaks. Remove, cover loosely with foil and rest for 5 minutes.

Spoon over the béarnaise to serve.

PORK SHOULDER WITH VINEGAR, GARLIC AND SPICE

You know, we often think that we need to eat meat as soon as it comes off the barbecue. And most things, like a good steak, may well taste better when eaten straight after cooking. But then there are some things which you just have to rest, like whole chickens and big, beefy cuts of meat. And then there is a recipe like this, which is just as tasty cold as it is hot.

SERVES 6–8

1.5 kg (3 lb 5 oz) pork shoulder, skin on
375 ml (13 fl oz/1½ cups) red wine vinegar
6 garlic cloves, lightly crushed
2 bay leaves
2 teaspoons allspice
1 teaspoon sea salt
1 teaspoon smoked paprika
1 teaspoon cayenne pepper

Sit the pork, skin side up, in a non-metallic dish. Combine the remaining ingredients in a bowl and pour them over the pork. Cover and refrigerate for 24 hours, turning the pork every 6 hours or so.

Remove the pork from the marinade 1 hour before you begin cooking.

Preheat the barbecue hotplate and grill to high and close the lid to create a hot-oven effect. Sit the pork, skin side up, on a cooking rack set over a deep-sided baking tray half-filled with water. Put the tray on the hotplate, close the lid and cook for 30 minutes. Turn heat down to low and cook for another 1¼ hours, topping up the tray with water as it evaporates.

Remove the pork to a serving plate, cover loosely with foil and allow to rest for 15–20 minutes before carving.

CHAR SIU **LAMB** WRAPS

You may not associate cumin with Chinese flavours. In the north and west of China, lamb and wheat is abundant and dominates the cooking there. So you find lots of barbecued lamb flavoured with chilli and cumin and served with steamed buns and breads. Very nice.

SERVES 4

2 large lamb backstrap fillets, about 400 g (14 oz) each
2 teaspoons sesame oil
2 garlic cloves, finely chopped
2 teaspoons chilli flakes
2 teaspoons ground cumin
3 tablespoons Chinese barbecue sauce (char siu), plus extra, for serving
4 soft tortillas or burritos
4 spring onions (scallions), thinly sliced on the angle
2 Lebanese (short) cucumbers, halved lengthways and sliced

Put the lamb in a bowl with the sesame oil, garlic, chilli and cumin. Toss the lamb around to coat all over with the marinade. Cover and set aside at room temperature for a couple of hours or cover and refrigerate for 3–6 hours, removing from the fridge 1 hour before cooking.

Preheat the barbecue hotplate to high.

Put the lamb on the hotplate and cook for 2 minutes. Turn over and cook for another 2 minutes. Brush the lamb with the barbecue sauce and turn. Continue to baste and turn the lamb, using all the remaining sauce for 4–5 minutes. Remove the lamb to a chopping board and cover loosely with foil for 5 minutes.

Slice the lamb. Spread a little of the extra char siu sauce down the centre of each tortilla. Top with sliced lamb, spring onions and cucumbers. Roll up each tortilla and serve.

VEAL CUTLETS WITH HERBS AND PROSCIUTTO

The inspiration for this is the classic veal saltimbocca (jump in the mouth!). It's that quick-cook veal schnitzel cooked with one sage leaf, and a few extra bits. I always like the idea of this but it often leaves me a bit unsatisfied asking 'Why only one sage leaf?' True, sage is a strong herb, but it does seem all a bit twee to have but one. Here is a robust barbecue veal saltimbocca.

SERVES 4

4 veal cutlets, about 250 g (9 oz) each
1 bunch sage
1 small bunch rosemary
1 small bunch thyme
8 thin slices prosciutto

Gently pound the veal cutlets to tenderise them. Grab a couple of sage leaves, with stems intact, a sprig of rosemary and a small sprig or two of thyme and place these on one side of the cutlet to form a little herbaceous clump. Grind some freshly ground black pepper over the top. Now take a piece of prosciutto and wrap around the veal. One piece may not be long enough to go entirely around the veal so use another piece to wrap around from where the two ends of the first piece don't meet up.

Preheat the barbecue hotplate to high and drizzle with a little olive oil to grease. Put the veal on the hotplate, herby-clump side down, and cook for 5 minutes, until the prosciutto looks crispy and the herbs cook and release oils to flavour the veal. Turn over and cook for another 5 minutes. Turn the barbecue off, wrap the veal in foil and sit on the hot barbecue lid for 10 minutes. Remove and allow to rest for another 5 minutes before serving.

ROAST SIRLOIN WITH ROOT VEGIES AND GARLIC CRÈME

This is a great cool weather option. In summer, try serving the beef cold, cooked rare, thinly sliced and served with heirloom tomatoes, baby rocket and some olives.

SERVES 4–6

1 teaspoon sea salt

2 teaspoons dried Greek oregano

2 teaspoons ras-el-hanout (Moroccan spice blend)

3 tablespoons olive oil

1 sirloin roast, about 1.25 kg (2 lb 12 oz)

1 medium sweet potato, cut into sticks 10 x 1 cm (4 x ½ in)

2 red onions, skin on, halved

2 parsnips, peeled and halved

freshly ground black pepper, to serve

GARLIC CRÈME

1 garlic bulb

1 tablespoon dijon mustard

½ teaspoon sea salt

¼ teaspoon ground white pepper

3 egg yolks

250 ml (9 fl oz/1 cup) rice bran oil

Combine the salt, oregano, half the ras-el-hanout and half the olive oil in a non-metallic bowl and rub over the meat. Set aside at room temperature for 2–3 hours, or cover and refrigerate overnight.

Remove the meat from the fridge 2 hours before cooking. Preheat the barbecue hotplate to medium. To make the garlic crème, loosely wrap the garlic in foil. Sit the garlic on the hotplate, close the lid and cook for 15–20 minutes, until softened and aromatic. Remove and cool, then cut the whole bulb in half crossways and squeeze the flesh out. Put the flesh into a food processor with the mustard, salt, pepper and egg yolks. Process to combine, then very slowly start to add the oil. With the food processor running, pour the rice bran oil in a steady stream until the mixture resembles thick custard. Put into a bowl and set aside.

Increase the barbecue hotplate to high and grill to medium. Put the fat side of the sirloin on the hotplate and cook for 10 minutes. Cook the sirloin for 3 minutes on all sides, until well browned. Reduce the heat to medium. Sit the meat in a 'V'-shaped barbecue rack and sit the rack on the hotplate.

Put the vegetables in a bowl with the remaining olive oil, ras-el-hanout and extra sea salt. Toss to evenly coat in the spice and salt mixture. Strew the vegies over the grill. Close the lid and cook for 15–20 minutes, turning once, until they are golden and tender.

Remove the meat, cover loosely with foil and allow to rest for 15–20 minutes. Carve and serve with the vegetables and spoon over the garlic crème.

FRUITS OF THE SEA

LAKSA **PRAWN SKEWERS**

HOTPLATE **FISH CAKES**

SWORDFISH KEBABS

TOM YUM LIME LEAF AND CORIANDER **PRAWNS**

SEAFOOD LEMONGRASS SKEWERS

GRILLED **WHITING**

PRAWN AND CHORIZO SKEWERS

GRILLED FISH CUTLETS WITH REMOULADE

SEARED RARE TUNA WITH BAY LEAF AND LEMON

PRAWNS WITH GARLIC AND VINEGAR

LOBSTER TAILS WITH CHILLI AND GARLIC BUTTER

EXOTIC SPICED **CUTTLEFISH**

CHERMOULA **FISH CUTLETS**

PARCHMENT **BAKED WHITING** WITH LEMON SALSA BUTTER

GRILLED TUNA WITH CAPER MAYONNAISE

PIRI PIRI **PRAWNS**

WHOLE BABY TROUT WITH LEMON AND DILL

BARBECUED SNAPPER WITH A RYE ROMESCO SAUCE

TROUT WITH PERSIAN RICE

SICILIAN FLAVOURED **FISH**

FIVE-SPICE **FISH PARCELS**

LING FILLET WITH CHAMPAGNE, LEEKS AND DILL BUTTER

SWORDFISH WITH PAPRIKA, LEMON AND HERBS

MUSSELS IN LIME PICKLE BUTTER

WHOLE SNAPPER WITH GINGER AND SPRING ONIONS

NEWSPAPER-WRAPPED **SALMON** WITH FRESH HERBS, LEMON AND CHILLI

SHICHIMI TUNA WITH WASABI CRÈME

WHOLE FLOUNDER WITH BURNT BUTTER AND SAGE SAUCE

BLUE EYE WITH CURRY BUTTER

BARBECUED SNAPPER WITH MEXICAN SALSA

THAI PEPPER GARLIC **PRAWNS**

RAS-EL-HANOUT SPICED **SWORDFISH**

WHOLE SNAPPER WITH LEMON

ADOBO **COD**

WHOLE FISH WITH JALAPEÑO CHILLIES, LEMON AND HERBS

OCEAN TROUT FILLET WITH GINGER AND SHALLOTS

LAKSA **PRAWN SKEWERS**

You will pretty much always find a jar of authentic laksa paste in my cupboard. Some say the word means 'ten thousand', which refers to the number of ingredients needed to make an authentic paste. So I do avoid making it myself. Good-quality pre-made pastes are available and they are used in coconut milk based soups, with thin rice noodles, chicken, fried tofu and bean sprouts and some fresh lime on the side to cut through the richness. The paste, made creamy with a little coconut milk and balanced with sugar and salty fish sauce is an easy marinade for big prawns and could all too easily be used to marinate chicken in. Then barbecued, of course.

SERVES 4

125 ml (4 fl oz/½ cup) coconut cream
2 tablespoons good-quality
  laksa paste
1 tablespoon fish sauce
1 tablespoon brown sugar
125 ml (4 fl oz/½ cup) coconut milk
6 limes, cut into quarters
24 large raw prawns (shrimp),
  deveined

Put the coconut cream in a small saucepan and bring to the boil for about 5 minutes, until little volcanic-like pools form, bubbling as the oils separate from the liquids. Stir the mixture as the coconut cream darkens around the edge and boil for another 2 minutes until it looks curdled. Add the laksa paste and stir to combine. Add the fish sauce and the sugar and then cook for 1 minute. The mixture will look dark at this stage. Stir through the coconut milk and bring to the boil for a minute. Remove and allow to cool completely.

Put the prawns in a non-metallic dish, pour over the laksa marinade and toss around to coat the prawns evenly. Cover and refrigerate for 3 hours. Soak 12 bamboo skewers in cold water for 30 minutes.

Remove the prawns, reserving the marinade and thread two prawns onto each of the skewers with a lime wedge on the end.

Preheat the barbecue hotplate to high and drizzle with a little vegetable oil to grease. Put the skewers on the barbecue and cook for 2 minutes. Turn over and cook for another minute so they are pink all over. Start brushing the prawns with the reserved marinade, turn over and cook for 1 minute. Repeat once more so the prawns are looking really golden as the paste is cooked onto the shell. Serve with a bowl for shells, finger bowls and napkins.

HOTPLATE **FISH CAKES**

Perfect for many occasions – on a Good Friday barbecue, for a non-meat, fish-eating barbecue guest ('a pescatarian') or something to serve up for kids that they will love. And they look good.

SERVES 4

2 potatoes, about 500 g (1 lb 2 oz), peeled and quartered
1 salmon cutlet, about 250 g (9 oz)
3 spring onions (scallions), white and a small amount of the green part, finely chopped
1 large handful flat-leaf (Italian) parsley, finely chopped
½ bunch dill, finely chopped
1 teaspoon sea salt
1 egg, beaten
40 g (1½ oz/½ cup) stale breadcrumbs
mayonnaise, to serve

Bring a large saucepan of lightly salted water to the boil and add the potatoes. Cook for 12 minutes then add the salmon cutlet. Put the lid on and cook for another 3 minutes, so the salmon is now a soft pink colour. Drain both and allow to cool. When cool enough to handle, remove the skin and bones from the fish and roughly flake into a large bowl.

Roughly mash the potatoes and add to the salmon with all the other ingredients. Use a large spoon to stir the mixture so the salmon is broken up and spread evenly throughout the mix. Wet your hands with water and divide the mixture into eight equal portions. Roll into balls. Put onto a tray lined with baking paper and gently press down to make a slightly flattened pattie. Repeat to make eight patties. Cover and refrigerate for a few hours or leave overnight.

Remove your patty from the fridge 30 minutes before you begin cooking.

Preheat the barbecue hotplate to medium and drizzle with a little vegetable oil to grease. Cook the patties for about 5–6 minutes, gently pressing down once or twice with a flat metal spatula, until they develop an even golden-coloured crust. Turn over and cook for another 5–6 minutes.

SWORDFISH KEBABS

Swordfish to me is about the texture of the meat. And this is a meaty fish. Like tuna, it lends itself to being cooked as you would a steak and when cubed and skewered it doesn't fall apart like soft-textured fish.

SERVES 4

750 g (1 lb 10 oz) swordfish steaks, skin removed and cut into 3–4 cm (1¼–1½ in) pieces
3 tablespoons olive oil
4 garlic cloves, finely chopped
3 tablespoons finely chopped flat-leaf (Italian) parsley
3 tablespoons lemon juice
4 roma (plum) tomatoes, quartered
2 red onions, peeled and each cut into 8 wedges
1 green capsicum (pepper), cut into 2–3 cm (¾–1¼ in) pieces
chargrilled lemon cheeks, to serve

Put the swordfish in a bowl along with the olive oil, garlic, parsley and lemon juice. Set aside at room temperature for 30 minutes.

Preheat the barbecue hotplate to high. Thread pieces of fish, tomato, onion wedges and green capsicum onto eight long metal skewers. Reserve the marinade.

Cook the skewers for about 8 minutes, basting with the reserved marinade, turning every 2 minutes, until the fish is cooked through. Serve with the chargrilled lemon cheeks.

TOM YUM LIME LEAF AND CORIANDER **PRAWNS**

Cheating at its finest, I am a huge fan of authentic Thai tom yum paste, which means it must be made in Thailand! Please do avoid those brands which are trying to jump on the Thai bandwagon as we have finally embraced the fresh flavours of Thailand. So besides always having a big jar of tom yum paste in the fridge, ready to add the usual suspects for a quick and spicy soup supper, I now have one sitting near the barbie ready to use as a ready-made marinade and baste. This is really good, not to mention easy.

SERVES 4

24 raw large prawns (shrimp),
   peeled and deveined, leaving
   the tails intact
1 tablespoon tom yum paste
1 tablespoon lime juice
4 small makrut (kaffir lime) leaves,
   very finely shredded, plus 4 extra
   whole leaves
1 tablespoon olive oil
handful coriander (cilantro), chopped
4 extra makrut (kaffir lime) leaves
1 lime, cut in half

Combine the prawns in a non-metallic dish with the tom yum paste, lime juice, makrut leaves, olive oil and the coriander, tossing the prawns around so they are evenly coated in the marinade. Cover and set aside for 30 minutes.

Preheat the barbecue hotplate to high and drizzle with a little vegetable oil to grease. Put the prawns and whole makrut leaves on the barbecue and then cook for 2 minutes, drizzling or brushing with any of the left-over marinade. Turn over and cook for another 2 minutes, making sure the prawns are sizzling the whole cooking time and are turning pink all over. Squeeze the lime over the prawns and quickly turn the prawns over on the hotplate to coat in the juices and spices, cooking for another minute on each side. Serve with finger bowls and lots of napkins.

SEAFOOD LEMONGRASS SKEWERS

This recipe has Vietnam written all over it. Simple, fresh flavours, with lemongrass of course. I have an indelible memory of lemongrass, which I use here as a skewer. Tinned sugarcane, split or cut into thinner pieces, is also an effective and exotic skewer.

SERVES 6

5 large red chillies, chopped
4 garlic cloves, chopped
4 spring onions (scallions), chopped
¼ teaspoon ground turmeric
½ teaspoon ground coriander
1 teaspoon shrimp paste
2 tablespoons tamarind purée
2 makrut (kaffir lime) leaves, finely shredded
1 tablespoon finely chopped lemongrass, white part only
2 tablespoons rice bran oil
3 tablespoons coconut cream
2 tablespoons brown sugar
400 g raw prawn (shrimp) meat
400 g white fish fillet
6 lemongrass stalks, cut in 15 cm (6 in) lengths, to make 12 skewers
coriander (cilantro) sprigs, to serve

Put the chilli, garlic, spring onions, turmeric, ground coriander, shrimp paste, tamarind purée, lime leaves, lemongrass, rice bran oil, coconut cream and brown sugar in a food processor. Process until finely chopped and then scrape the mixture into a bowl.

Put the prawn meat and fish in the food processor and process to a mince. Scrape into the bowl with the spice mix and stir well to combine.

Using wet hands, take a generous 3 tablespoons of the mixture and form into a log around a length of lemongrass. Repeat with the remaining mixture.

Preheat the barbecue hotplate to high. Cook the skewers for 5 minutes. Carefully turn over and then cook for another 5 minutes. Serve with the coriander sprigs.

GRILLED **WHITING**

Whether we cook for a living, cook for a family or we only cook on the weekend it is easy to forget the simple things. And this always strikes me as a little odd when it is the simple things that are the most important. Cooking doesn't get much simpler (or more impressive) than this, and it's the type of dish that fond food memories are made of.

SERVES 4

2 whole whiting, about 450–500 g
    (1 lb–1 lb 2 oz) each, cleaned
    and gutted
2 tablespoons olive oil
2 teaspoons sea salt
lemon, to serve

Make a couple of slashes in each side of the fish. Put the fish in a baking tin lined with baking paper and lightly brush each side of the fish with about half of the olive oil, then sprinkle the salt evenly over the skin. Cover and set aside.

Preheat the barbecue hotplate to high. If you have grills, put them on too to get the heat really cranked up. Drizzle the remaining olive oil over the hotplate to grease. Put the fish on the hotplate and cook for 5 minutes with the lid on, without moving the fish so it develops an even, golden crust. Use a large metal spatula to quickly turn the fish over and cook for another 5 minutes without moving. The skin should be slightly crispy and the flesh firm yet succulent. One fish can be shared between two.

PRAWN AND CHORIZO SKEWERS

Chonza is the nickname I have for the chorizo we use, actually called 'cheeky chorizo' because of the extra chilli used in it. Raw chorizo is used here so it has to be cooked before eating. Chorizo should be a deep, rich colour and jam-packed with garlic and paprika. Please don't use the chorizo that looks like cabanossi.

SERVES 4

3 raw chorizo, about 350 g (12 oz)
16 raw large prawns (shrimp),
    peeled and deveined, leaving
    the tails intact
2 tablespoons olive oil
2 tablespoons lemon juice
½ teaspoon good quality dried mint
lemon cheeks, to serve
barbecued truss cherry tomatoes,
    to serve (optional)

Cut the chorizo into 16 chunks similar in thickness to the prawns. Put the chorizo in a bowl with the prawns, olive oil, lemon juice and mint. Toss the ingredients around to combine. Set aside at room temperature for 30 minutes or cover and refrigerate for 3–6 hours.

Remove from the fridge 30 minutes before cooking. Preheat the barbecue grill or hotplate to high.

Put 2 pieces of chorizo and 2 prawns on each of eight metal skewers. Cook the skewers for 3–4 minutes on each side, or until cooked through. Serve with the lemon cheeks and cherry tomatoes, if desired.

GRILLED FISH CUTLETS
WITH REMOULADE

Remoulade is like a flavoured mayonnaise to go with meats, fish or chicken. This version has the inclusion of grated celeriac. Not the prettiest of vegies, celeriac makes up for it in flavour.

SERVES 4

1 tablespoon light olive oil
4 salmon cutlets, about 200 g
   (7 oz) each
2 teaspoons sea salt
lemon cheeks, to serve

CELERIAC REMOULADE
1 tablespoon lemon juice
½ small head celeriac,
   about 300 g (10½ oz) peeled
60 g (2¼ oz/¼ cup)
   good-quality mayonnaise
2 teaspoons capers, rinsed, drained
   and finely chopped
2 teaspoons dijon mustard
2 tablespoons thick
   (double/heavy) cream
2 tablespoons torn flat-leaf
   (Italian) parsley

For the remoulade, pour the lemon juice into a bowl. Using the coarse holes on a cheese grater, grate the celeriac directly into the bowl with the lemon juice. Use your hands to toss the grated celeriac with the lemon juice, separating the strands as you go. Set aside for 30 minutes so the celeriac softens. Add the mayonnaise, capers, mustard, cream and parsley, season to taste and combine well. Set aside while cooking the fish.

Using your hands, rub the oil over the fish and sprinkle one side of each of the cutlets with half the salt.

Preheat a chargrill to high. When cooking fish, it is best that the cooking surface is hot and not to turn the fish too early or it will stick and tear the flesh.

Add the fish, salted side down. Sprinkle the remaining salt on the fish and cook for 2 minutes. Turn over and cook for another 2 minutes, or until cooked to your liking. Serve with the remoulade and lemon cheeks on the side.

SEARED RARE TUNA
WITH BAY LEAF AND LEMON

This is an extravagance, no doubt about it. But if you are a fan of good quality tuna then you know where I am coming from. You don't need to mess around with this fantastic fish too much, but the biggest mistake is overcooking. Just sear it, keeping its flesh rare. I like to use a whole piece, but you could also use smaller fillets.

SERVES 4

2 x 400 g (14 oz) pieces
    sashimi-quality tuna
3 tablespoons olive oil
1 tablespoon light soy sauce
    (preferably Japanese)
1 tablespoon lemon juice
4 bay leaves
1 lemon, thinly sliced
Japanese soy sauce (extra)
    and wasabi, to serve

Put the tuna in a non-metallic dish and add the other ingredients. Cover and refrigerate for 3 hours, making sure you turn the tuna every so often.

Remove the tuna from the fridge 30 minutes before you begin cooking.

Preheat the barbecue hotplate to high.

Remove the tuna from the oil and put on the hotplate with the bay leaves and the lemon. These will cook and impart their flavour to the fish. Cook the tuna for 2 minutes each side so it sizzles quickly and cooks to a golden brown. Cut each piece in half or use a sharp knife to cut into fine slices, sashimi style. Serve with soy sauce and wasabi.

PRAWNS WITH GARLIC AND VINEGAR

Pouring hot oil on garlic (or on any combination of garlic, ginger and spring onion, for that matter) is very Cantonese. It is also, as I recently discovered, a technique used in Iberian cooking. The hot oil softens the garlic, making it more palatable, at the same time as infusing the oil with the flavour of the garlic.

SERVES 4

8 garlic cloves, finely chopped
3 tablespoons light olive oil
3 tablespoons white wine vinegar
1 tablespoon Spanish sweet paprika
1 teaspoon sea salt
24 raw large prawns (shrimp),
    peeled and deveined, leaving
    the tails intact
baby rocket (arugula) leaves, to serve

Put the garlic in a small heatproof bowl. Put the olive oil in a small saucepan and heat over high heat until hot. Pour the oil over the garlic, allowing it to sizzle for just a few seconds then quickly add the vinegar, paprika and sea salt. Stir to combine and set aside until cool.

Put the prawns in a large bowl. Pour over the garlic mixture, stirring well so the prawns are coated in the sauce. Set aside at room temperature for about 30 minutes, or cover and then refrigerate for 3–6 hours.

Remove the prawns from the fridge 30 minutes before you begin cooking.

Preheat the barbecue hotplate to high.

Spread the prawns over the hotplate so they don't overlap. You may have to cook them in a couple of batches. Cook for 3 minutes, turn over and cook for another 2 minutes, until pink, curled up and cooked through. Scatter over the rocket and then serve.

LOBSTER TAILS WITH CHILLI AND GARLIC BUTTER

Lobsters are odd creatures. But then again, so are prawns, which I personally prefer. There is something about the expense of lobster that puts pressure on the cook to do something really fancy with it. This is where mistakes are made. Keep it simple. No béchamel or white sauce, no cheese and no flambé. Cook the lobster simply and quickly, basted with some lovely, fresh flavours. That's all you need to do.

SERVES 4

75 g (2½ oz) unsalted butter, softened
    to room temperature
½ teaspoon chilli flakes
2 garlic cloves, crushed
1 tablespoon finely chopped flat-leaf
    (Italian) parsley
2 lobster tails, about 320 g
    (11¼ oz) each
lemon cheeks, to serve

Combine the butter, chilli flakes, garlic and parsley in a small bowl. Season with a little sea salt and set aside.

Cut the lobster tails in half lengthways and spread the butter mixture over the cut sides.

Preheat the barbecue hotplate to medium. Lay the lobster, shell side down, on the hotplate, close the lid and cook for 10 minutes, or until the lobster meat is white and cooked through. Serve with the lemon cheeks.

EXOTIC SPICED **CUTTLEFISH**

Fresh cuttlefish is a gem to cook with. Many fresh seafood outlets may even clean it for you. I find it more tender than squid and its rather unattractive looks scare people off, which means it costs less.

SERVES 4

1 teaspoon sea salt
½ teaspoon ground coriander
½ teaspoon ground cumin
½ teaspoon smoked paprika
½ teaspoon ras-el-hanout
     (Moroccan spice blend)
750 g (1 lb 10 oz) cuttlefish
     hoods, cleaned
1 tablespoon olive oil
lemon wedges, to serve (optional)

Put the salt and spices in a small frying pan and cook over high heat, shaking the pan, until the spices begin to smoke. Remove from the heat, tip into a bowl and set aside.

Use a sharp knife to scrape any bits of dark skin off the cuttlefish. Cut open the hood of the cuttlefish and use a small knife to scrape it clean. Slice the cuttlefish into strips, no wider than 1 cm (½ in). Put into a bowl with the olive oil, tossing to coat the cuttlefish.

Preheat the barbecue hotplate to high.

Put the cuttlefish on the hotplate, using tongs to spread out. Cook for just a minute or two, until white and curled up. Turn over and then cook for another minute. Put cuttlefish in a bowl and sprinkle over the spice mixture, shaking the bowl to coat. Tumble onto a plate to serve.

CHERMOULA **FISH CUTLETS**

I think I have harped on in a few recipes about how good north African flavours are for use in barbecuing – they are made for it. The essentials of this traditional rub are garlic, cumin, some sort of chillies and some sort of fresh herbage. Often, the seafood is rubbed and marinated in a chermoula then added to a simple, fresh tomato sauce for a seafood tagine. I have used big blue eye cutlets here, but any white fish will do. The cutlets are a horse-shoe or oval cut, which is the cross-section of the fish, with that big bone down the centre.

SERVES 4

1 large red chilli, chopped
1 large green chilli, chopped
2 garlic cloves, chopped
½ teaspoon sea salt
3 tablespoons olive oil
½ teaspoon ground cumin
½ teaspoon ground coriander
1 large handful coriander (cilantro)
    leaves, roughly chopped
1 large handful flat-leaf (Italian)
    parsley leaves, roughly chopped
1 large handful mint leaves,
    roughly chopped
2 x blue eye cutlets (or cod),
    about 350 g (12 oz) each

Put the chillies, garlic and salt in a mortar and pound until you have a chunky paste. Add the olive oil, cumin, ground coriander and fresh herbs and keep pounding until you have an aromatic, green thick paste.

Put the fish in a non-metallic dish and rub the chermoula all over. Cover and refrigerate for 3 hours.

Remove from the fridge 30 minutes before cooking.

Preheat the barbecue hotplate to medium. Tear off two sheets of baking paper about the same size as the hotplate. Put the baking paper on the hotplate and drizzle with a little olive oil to grease. Cook the fish for 5 minutes on each side until golden.

PARCHMENT **BAKED WHITING** WITH LEMON SALSA BUTTER

It seems very '70s to wrap something in paper, usually white fish fillets, and cook in the oven. A delicate method for this rather delicate fish that translates well to the barbecue and made more contemporary with some green chilli and coriander thrown in. I use whiting here, but any firm white fish will do.

SERVES 4

2 x whiting fillets, about 350–400 g
(12–14 oz) each

LEMON SALSA BUTTER
125 g (4½ oz/½ cup) butter
1 large handful coriander (cilantro)
    leaves and stems, finely chopped
3 spring onions (scallions), finely
    chopped
1 tablespoon finely snipped chives
1 large green chilli, seeded and
    finely chopped
2 tablespoons lemon juice

Put the butter in a small saucepan and cook over a low heat until just melted, but don't let the butter boil. Add the other lemon salsa ingredients, with a pinch of sea salt and some freshly ground black pepper, stirring for a minute or so to combine, then set aside to cool to room temperature. Put the butter in a bowl, cover and refrigerate until needed.

Tear off two large pieces of baking paper, large enough with room to spare to wrap a whiting fillet in. Sit a fillet in the centre of the paper and spoon over half of the salsa butter. Bring the two long sides of the paper together and firmly fold over a few times then twist the ends to seal. Tie each twisted end with kitchen string. Now sit each parcel in a large piece of cooking foil. Fold the edges of the foil to firmly seal and form a parcel.

Preheat the barbecue hotplate to high. Put the fish parcels on the hotplate and cook for 10 minutes, with the lid on. The fish will be white and flaky and can be eaten directly from the parcels. Serve a parcel between two people to share.

GRILLED TUNA
WITH CAPER MAYONNAISE

I've converted more than one person to bay. The woody, sweet aroma of a bay leaf needs either a long slow cooking time to be released or a quick blast of heat so aromatic oils to flavour the food it is cooked with. It's the latter that makes it a good herb to grill. Bay are tough leaves, so can withstand the heat of a hot grill.

SERVES 4

4 tuna steaks, about 150–180 g
   (5½ –6½ oz) each
60 ml (2 fl oz/¼ cup) olive oil
4 bay leaves
1 lemon, thinly sliced

CAPER MAYONNAISE
2 egg yolks, at room temperature
1 teaspoon dijon mustard
2 teaspoons lemon juice
125 ml (4 fl oz/½ cup) light olive oil
1 tablespoon small capers in salt,
   well rinsed, drained and
   roughly chopped
1 tablespoon finely chopped chervil,
   plus extra chervil sprigs, to serve

Place the tuna in a non-metallic dish with the olive oil, bay leaves and lemon. Cover and set aside for 30 minutes.

For the caper mayonnaise, place the egg yolks, mustard, lemon juice and a pinch of sea salt in a small bowl. Wet a dish cloth and fold up into a square on a work surface. Sit the bowl on top. This will allow you to use both hands to whisk and add oil at the same time without the bowl moving too much. Or have someone hold the bowl for you. Start to whisk the egg yolk mixture and as you do, add a thin steady stream of the oil. Keep whisking and adding the oil until all the oil has been added and the mixture is thick and emulsified. Stir through the capers and chervil and check the seasoning. Transfer to a serving bowl, cover closely with plastic wrap and refrigerate until needed. This can be made several hours ahead.

To cook the tuna, preheat a chargrill to high. Shake off excess oil from the tuna, reserving the bay leaves and lemon. When smoking hot, cook the tuna for 2 minutes on each side. Transfer to a serving plate. Add the bay leaves and lemon slices to the grill and cook for 1 minute, or until charred.

Serve the tuna garnished with the grilled bay leaf, lemon and the extra chervil sprigs with the caper mayonnaise on the side.

PIRI PIRI **PRAWNS**

There has been a huge number of Portuguese-style fast-food chicken outlets opening in recent times. My dirty secret is I kind of like them, especially the day after the night before. Although, the origins of the chilli condiment is African, from Mozambique actually, which was a former colony of Portugal. I have made up my own here for these prawns, but the flavours would also work well with fish and chicken.

SERVES 4

24 raw large prawns (shrimp), peeled and deveined, leaving the tails intact

PIRI PIRI SAUCE
1 large red capsicum (pepper)
1 tablespoon white wine vinegar
1 tablespoon olive oil
2 large red chillies, seeded
2 garlic cloves

For the piri piri sauce, put the capsicum in a hot oven and cook until the skin is blackened and puffed all over, or put the capsicum on a hot barbecue grill, turning often with tongs and cook until blackened all over, then put in a clean plastic bag until cool enough to handle. Peel and seed the capsicum, without being too fussy as the odd blackened bit will add flavour. (And don't rinse under water or you'll lose the flavour.) Put the capsicum in a food processor with the other piri piri ingredients. Whiz until you have a fiery red paste. Put in a bowl, cover and set aside until needed. This will keep in the refrigerator for a few days.

Put the prawns in a bowl and add the sauce, tossing them around to coat evenly. Set aside for 30 minutes.

Preheat the barbecue hotplate to high and drizzle with a little olive oil to grease. Cook the prawns for 2 minutes on each side, so they turn bright pink all over. Generously brush the prawns with any left-over sauce and quickly turn them on the hotplate so the sauce cooks just a little.

Quickly remove the prawns from the heat and serve with lots of finger bowls and napkins.

WHOLE BABY TROUT
WITH LEMON AND DILL

The combination of ingredients here is not reinventing the wheel. But it is a much-loved favourite. The trick here is to cook the fish (as I do with much barbecued seafood) on a couple of sheets of greaseproof paper directly placed on the hotplate. The paper conducts all the heat off the hotplate without the delicate skin of the fish tearing or sticking.

SERVES 4

2 x 500 g (1 lb 2 oz) trout, cleaned
    and gutted
1 lemon, very finely sliced
1 red onion, very finely sliced
1 bunch dill

Lay the trout on a clean work surface. Inside the cavity of each trout put 3–4 slices of lemon, a few slices of red onion, 3–4 sprigs of dill, another layer of onions and lemon, and season the outside of the fish well with sea salt and freshly ground black pepper.

Preheat the barbecue hotplate to high. Tear off two sheets of baking paper about the same size as the hotplate and put onto the hotplate. Lightly brush the paper with olive oil. Put the fish on the paper and cook for 8 minutes, with the lid on. Turn over and cook for another 5 minutes. Both sides of the fish should be dark golden and the skin crispy. One fish can be shared between two.

BARBECUED SNAPPER
WITH A RYE ROMESCO SAUCE

A bit like pesto, this sauce comes in many shapes and sizes. From the fish-loving Catalonian region of Spain it is a rich emulsion of olive oil, tomatoes, chillies and spices. I use rye bread as I like eating it toasted for breakfast and always have some left over. It lasts for ages and gives an extra nutty edge to go with the almonds.

SERVES 4

4 x small snapper (about
    300 g/10½ oz each), cleaned
    and gutted
1 bunch thyme
3 tablespoons olive oil
3 tablespoons lemon juice
lemon wedges, to serve

RYE ROMESCO SAUCE
4 ripe tomatoes, cut in half
1 large red chilli, seeded and
    thickly sliced
4 garlic cloves, sliced
50 g (1¾ oz/⅓ cup) blanched almonds
2 x 1 cm (½ in) thick slices rye bread,
    toasted and roughly torn
1 teaspoon smoky paprika
2 tablespoons red wine vinegar
1 handful chopped coriander (cilantro)
3 tablespoons extra virgin olive oil

For the romesco sauce, preheat the barbecue hotplate to high and drizzle with a little olive oil to grease. Put the tomatoes on the hotplate, cut side down. Scatter over the chilli and garlic and cook for 3–4 minutes, using tongs to turn the chilli and garlic but leaving the tomatoes. Remove the chillies and garlic from the hotplate. Turn the tomatoes over and cook for another 5 minutes until they are really soft and slightly charred.

Put the almonds in a food processor and whiz until they are finely chopped. Add tomatoes, garlic, chilli, bread, paprika, vinegar and coriander to the food processor and whiz so they are all combined and chunky looking. With the processor on, add the oil in a steady stream until it is all incorporated and you have a thick red sauce. Put into a container, cover and refrigerate until needed. Just remember to allow the sauce to come to room temperature before serving.

Cut several diagonal, deep incisions across each side of the snapper and put into a large, flat non-metallic dish with the thyme, olive oil and lemon juice. Brush the marinade over the fish and into the incisions then leave to stand for 30 minutes.

Preheat the barbecue hotplate to medium. Tear off two sheets of baking paper about the same size as the hotplate and put onto the hotplate. Lightly brush the paper with olive oil, put the fish on the paper and cook for 8–10 minutes, with the barbecue lid on, until the flesh is golden brown. Use a flat metal spatula to quickly and carefully turn the fish over and cook for another 5 minutes, again with the lid on. Serve the fish with romesco sauce.

CUTTLEFISH WITH CHORIZO AND POTATOES

'Surf and turf' with Spanish flavours. You may want to just cook the chorizo part of this recipe. Chorizo is packed full of hidden spices and garlic, quite rich actually, so the red wine vinegar really does temper it a tad.

SERVES 4

500 g (1 lb 2 oz) large cuttlefish hoods
3 tablespoons olive oil
2 tablespoons lemon juice
½ teaspoon smoky paprika
1 quantity hotplate wedges
   (see page 324)
2 chorizo sausages, sliced
2 tablespoons beer
2 tablespoons red wine vinegar
1 handful small mint leaves

Put the cuttlefish hoods in a non-metallic dish with the olive oil, lemon juice and paprika, tossing the cuttlefish around to coat. Cover and refrigerate for 3 hours.

Make a quantity of hotplate wedges (see page 324) and put them in a heatproof bowl. Sit them on a warm part of the barbecue away from direct heat.

Preheat the barbecue hotplate to high and drizzle with a little olive oil to grease. Cook the chorizo for 1 minute on each side, until lightly crisp and golden. Pour the beer and vinegar over the chorizo so the liquids sizzle as they hit the hotplate. Push the chorizo around on the hotplate to coat in the sauce and cook for 1 minute, until the liquids evaporate, then put in a large bowl.

Cook the cuttlefish on the hotplate for 1 minute on each side, drizzling over a little of the tasty marinade. Remove the cuttlefish and slice into 1 cm (½ in) wide strips. Add to the bowl with the chorizo, then add the potatoes and mint leaves, tossing around to combine. Put on a serving plate.

TROUT WITH PERSIAN RICE

It is very typical of north African and Middle Eastern cookery to have sweet and aromatic spices used with meat, fish and chicken. There is that amazing Moroccan dish 'bastilla', a pie made of chicken or pigeon meat, cooked in filo and sprinkled with cinnamon and icing sugar. The flavours sound incongruous but it actually works like a treat. Like using cinnamon with fish; who would have thought?

SERVES 4

4 small rainbow trout, cleaned,
    gutted and scaled
olive oil, for cooking

PERSIAN RICE
2 tablespoons butter
1 small red onion, thinly sliced
2 teaspoons finely grated ginger
2 teaspoons ground cinnamon
2 tablespoons slivered almonds,
    roughly chopped
110 g (3¾ oz/½ cup) short-grain rice
2 tablespoons finely chopped
    coriander (cilantro) leaves
2 tablespoons finely chopped mint
2 tablespoons finely chopped
    flat-leaf (Italian) parsley

For the Persian rice, heat the butter in a small saucepan over medium heat. When the butter is sizzling, add the onion and cook for 2–3 minutes, or until softened. Stir in the ginger and cinnamon and cook for 1 minute or until aromatic. Stir in the almonds and rice. Add enough water to the pan so it just covers the rice and bring to the boil. Reduce the heat and simmer for about 10 minutes, or until most of the liquid has been absorbed by the rice. Quickly fluff with a fork then cover and set aside for 20 minutes. Stir through the herbs and season to taste.

Spoon the rice mixture into the trout cavity.

Preheat the barbecue hotplate to medium. Lay a sheet of baking paper on the hotplate and brush the paper with the olive oil. Lay the trout on the paper, close the lid and cook for 10 minutes. Carefully turn the trout over and cook for another 8–10 minutes, or until just cooked through.

SICILIAN FLAVOURED **FISH**

Wonderful flavours and cooking method here, something I stumbled across by accident. I bought a rather large 'V'-shaped barbecue rack, which did not fit on my barbecue, unless it was inverted to be an upside down 'V'. Perfect for a whole fish to sit on and cook to perfection. I am a big fan of the fennel seed and chilli flake combo, but if you find these too spicy or intense don't let that stop you from experiencing cooking fish this way.

SERVES 6

1 big snapper, about 2 kg (4 lb 8 oz),
    cleaned, gutted and scaled
1 teaspoon chilli flakes
1 teaspoon fennel seeds
2 garlic cloves, chopped
1 teaspoon sea salt
3 tablespoons olive oil
2 tablespoons finely chopped flat-leaf
    (Italian) parsley (optional), to serve
lemon cheeks, to serve

Give the fish a good wash and dry with paper towel. Make several, deep diagonal cuts across each side of the fish. Scrunch up some baking paper and run under cold water. Shake out any excess water and put the scrunched paper inside the cavity of the fish.

Combine chilli flakes, fennel seeds, garlic, sea salt and olive oil in a small bowl. Brush all over the fish and into the cuts.

Preheat the barbecue hotplate and grill to high and close the lid to create a hot-oven effect. Turn a 'V'-shaped barbecue rack upside down. Sit the fish on the inverted V of the rack so it is upright.

Sit the rack on the hotplate, close the lid and cook for 20–25 minutes, until the flesh of the fish is white and easily pulls away from the bones.

Transfer to a serving plate. Sprinkle with the parsley, if using, and serve with the lemon cheeks.

FIVE-SPICE **FISH PARCELS**

Okay, so there are only four spices here. Sichuan pepper would also be included in any traditional five-spice mixture, which is endemic to Chinese cookery. Although, there is a Bengali five-spice combination called panch phora – but that's another thing altogether.

SERVES 4

4 x 200 g (7 oz) blue eye, or a firm
   white-fleshed fish, fillets

FIVE-SPICE SAUCE
8 star anise
4 whole cloves
½ teaspoon fennel seeds
4 small cinnamon sticks
3 tablespoons light soy sauce
1 tablespoon shaved palm sugar
   (jaggery) or dark brown sugar
1 tablespoon finely grated ginger

Combine all the sauce ingredients in a small saucepan. Bring to the boil over high heat, stirring to dissolve the sugar. Reduce the heat and simmer for 2–3 minutes. Pour into a bowl and set aside to cool.

Add the fish to the sauce mixture, tossing to coat all over. Cover and refrigerate for up to 3 hours.

Remove the fish from the fridge 30 minutes before you begin cooking.

Tear off four sheets of baking paper large enough to wrap a piece of the fish entirely. Wet the paper, then shake off any excess water.

Sit a piece of fish in the centre of each piece of paper. Spoon over the sauce ensuring you have 2 star anise, 1 whole clove and 1 cinnamon stick on each. Wrap the fish in the paper to firmly enclose.

Preheat the barbecue grill to high. Sit the parcels on the grill, close the lid and cook for 8–10 minutes. Serve with Asian greens, if desired.

LING FILLET WITH CHAMPAGNE, LEEKS AND DILL BUTTER

I didn't mean for this to sound as posh as it does but I do use the term Champagne loosely, although to some this is a sin.

SERVES 4

1 leek
125 g (4½ oz/½ cup) butter
2 garlic cloves
1 small bunch dill, finely chopped
1 handful flat-leaf (Italian) parsley, roughly chopped
250 ml (9 fl oz/1 cup) Champagne or a dry sparkling wine
800 g (1 lb 12 oz) ling fillet

Finely chop the white part of the leek and slice off 5 mm (¼ in) thick rings from the green and set aside.

Put about 1 tablespoon of the butter in a small saucepan over high heat. When the butter has melted and sizzling add the leek and cook for 2–3 minutes, stirring often so the leek softens. Add the garlic, dill and parsley and cook for 1 minute then add the champagne. Bring to the boil, then reduce the heat to a simmer until the liquid has reduced by half. Add the remaining butter to the pan and stir until the butter has melted. Put in a bowl and refrigerate until needed.

For the fish, tear off a large piece of baking paper and fold over to give double thickness. Place the leek rings down the centre of the paper and sit the fish on top. Spoon the Champagne butter down the length of the fish. Firmly fold the baking paper over to form a parcel and tuck the ends underneath to enclose the fish.

Preheat the barbecue hotplate to high.

Put the fish on the hotplate and cook with the lid on for 15 minutes. Remove to a platter and allow the fish to rest for 5 minutes before unwrapping and serving directly from the paper with the melted butter spooned over. The fish will be so tender you should be able to use a spoon to cut and serve it.

SWORDFISH WITH PAPRIKA, LEMON AND HERBS

Here's some oddball trivia to share as you fire up the barbecue. The swordfish is a fast creature. It is a fish, which means it is cold blooded, of course. That is, except for its eyes! This cunning predator has evolved to have warm eyes that move faster and therefore better to see their prey with. And continuing on a whimsical note, there are records of stabbings with the 'nose' of a swordfish – which is a sinister twist as we usually enjoy them skewered, which you could do here.

SERVES 4

4 swordfish steaks, each about
    2.5 cm (1 in) thick
3 tablespoons olive oil
1 teaspoon paprika
2 tablespoons lemon juice
4 bay leaves
1 small bunch thyme

Put the fish in a snug-fitting non-metallic dish. Combine the olive oil, paprika and lemon juice in a small bowl then pour over the fish. Add the bay leaves and thyme, and rub the marinade all over the fish, evenly distributing the herbs. Cover and refrigerate for 3–6 hours. Remove the fish from the fridge 30 minutes before cooking.

Preheat the barbecue hotplate to medium and drizzle with a little olive oil to grease. Remove the fish from the marinade, shaking off the excess, and put onto the hotplate with the bay leaves and thyme. (Cooking the herbs will bring out their flavours.) Cook the fish for 8–10 minutes. Use some cooking tongs to move the herbs around on the hotplate so they sizzle in the oil and cooking juices of the fish. Turn the fish over and cook for another 5 minutes. Unlike tuna, it's best for swordfish to be cooked all the way through.

MUSSELS IN LIME PICKLE BUTTER

Mussels are big, mussels are bold and mussels are made to share. This is a toothsome number for four, with a very tasty and tangy lime pickle butter, which I have only recently discovered vary greatly in flavour. Some lime pickles leave me feeling like I have just sucked on a lemon, yet others I want to eat with cheese and crackers. Odd, I know. This butter can be used on just about any fish, white fish especially.

SERVES 4

2 kg (4 lb 8 oz) mussels, beards
   removed and scrubbed
125 ml (4 fl oz/½ cup) white wine
1 bunch coriander (cilantro) leaves
   and 2–3 cm (¾–1¼ in) stems,
   finely chopped

LIME PICKLE BUTTER
100 g (3½ oz) butter, softened
2 spring onions (scallions), chopped
1 tablespoon good quality lime
   pickle, chopped
½ teaspoon turmeric
1 teaspoon finely grated ginger
2 garlic cloves, crushed
1 tablespoon lime juice
½ teaspoon freshly ground
   black pepper
1 handful coriander (cilantro) leaves,
   finely chopped
1 handful mint leaves, finely chopped

For the lime pickle butter, put 1 tablespoon of the butter in a small saucepan with the spring onions, pickle, turmeric, ginger, garlic, lime juice and pepper and cook over a medium heat until the ingredients have softened and become aromatic. Put into a bowl and stir through the herbs and remaining butter until well combined. Cover and refrigerate until needed.

Remove the lime pickle butter from the fridge to soften.

To cook the mussels, preheat the barbecue hotplate to high. Put the mussels onto the hotplate, pour over some of the wine and cook for 2 minutes on each side with the lid on, until the mussels open. Discard any that do not. Put the mussels in a large bowl and spoon over the softened butter. Add the coriander. Use a large pair of tongs to toss the mussels around and serve.

WHOLE SNAPPER WITH GINGER AND SPRING ONIONS

This is a classic Chinese dish usually all done in a restaurant kitchen. But it is all smoke and mirrors, as all you are doing is assembling. The celestial duo of scallions and ginger has heavenly status in Chinese cooking, so honour them and only use the freshest. Again, a few simple barbecuing tricks here are the only prerequisites for a perfectly steamed fish.

SERVES 4-5

1 large, whole snapper, about 2 kg
    (4 lb 8 oz), cleaned and gutted
3 tablespoons Chinese rice wine
10 cm (4 in) piece ginger
1 bunch spring onions (scallions)
1 bunch coriander (cilantro), chopped
3 tablespoons light soy sauce
3 tablespoons chicken stock
1 teaspoon white sugar
3 tablespoons light peanut oil
1 tablespoon sesame oil
½ teaspoon white pepper

Cut several diagonal incisions across the skin and flesh of the fish. Put the fish in a large non-metallic dish and pour over the rice wine. Cut the piece of ginger in half and cut one half into thin discs. Cut half of the bunch of spring onions into 10 cm (4 in) lengths. Put the ginger discs, spring onion pieces and half of the coriander in the cavity of the fish. Cover and set aside for 20 minutes.

Peel and cut the remaining ginger into thin match-sticks. Cut the remaining spring onions on the angle into similar-sized pieces as the ginger. Set both aside. Combine the soy, chicken stock and sugar in a small bowl, stir to dissolve the sugar and set aside.

Preheat the barbecue hotplate to medium–high. Tear off two large sheets of baking paper and put these on top of two sheets of cooking foil. Sit the fish in the centre of the baking paper. Fold the sides of the foil to form a parcel, firmly enclosing the fish. Sit the fish on a cooking rack. Put the rack on the barbecue hotplate and cook for 20 minutes, so the fish cooks and steams in the parcel.

Remove the fish to a serving platter and leave the barbecue heat on. Pour the sauce over the fish then scatter over the ginger and spring onions. Put the light peanut oil and sesame oil in a small frying pan and sit it on the hotplate. When the oil is smoking hot pour over the fish then quickly scatter over the remaining coriander and white pepper to serve. This is a real event and can be done at the table creating a bit of drama and anticipation.

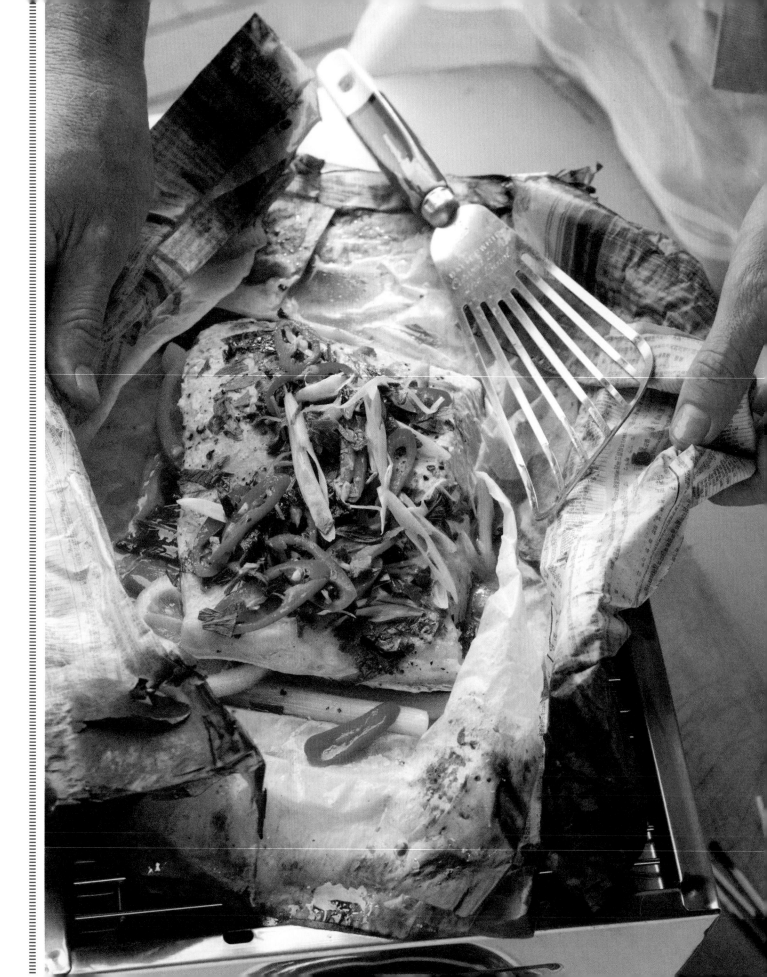

NEWSPAPER-WRAPPED **SALMON** WITH FRESH HERBS, LEMON AND CHILLI

Wetting the newspaper prevents it from burning on the hotplate (although it will a little anyway, which is fine) and creates a steamy environment for the fish to cook in. This makes cooking for a crowd too easy. Only limited by the size of your hotplate, you could easily cook six or eight of these and feed an army with little effort.

SERVES 4

2 x salmon fillets, mid cut,
    about 400 g (14 oz) each
1 bunch spring onions (scallions)
1 large handful flat-leaf (Italian)
    parsley leaves, roughly chopped
1 large handful coriander (cilantro)
    leaves, roughly chopped
1 handful mint leaves,
    roughly chopped
1 large red chilli, finely sliced
    (seeded if it's a hot one)
1 lemon, sliced
3 tablespoons olive oil
3 tablespoons lemon juice
1 teaspoon sea salt

Preheat the barbecue hotplate to high.

Lay out two large sheets of newspaper on top of each other and liberally brush the newspaper all over with water to dampen. Tear off a piece of baking paper, slightly larger than a fish fillet and sit it in the middle of the newspaper. Repeat for the other fillet.

Finely slice 3 spring onions and put in a bowl with the other herbs and the chilli. Cut the remaining spring onions in half, lengthways, and lay these on top of the baking paper. Now lay the lemon slices on the spring onions. Sit the fish on the lemons and season well with sea salt and freshly ground black pepper. Scatter the herb mix evenly all over the top of the fillets. Combine the olive oil and lemon juice in a small bowl and pour over the fish. Fold up the newspaper to form a parcel by bringing the two long sides together, and folding down. Tuck the two shorter ends in underneath and sit the parcel, with the tucked sides on the hotplate. Cover with the lid and cook for 20 minutes. Remove and then allow to rest for 5 minutes before carefully moving the fish to a plate. Drizzle over the cooking juices and serve.

SHICHIMI TUNA
WITH WASABI CRÈME

Shichimi is a Japanese chilli spice mix and its name means seven flavours. The spice mix will vary, depending on where you are in Japan. Here is my version, not completely traditional, but it should be a hit with tuna lovers. The aonori is a tricky ingredient to find – sold in glass jars and individual little bags, it can be found in good Asian specialty food supermarkets.

SERVES 4

4 tuna steaks, about 200 g (7 oz) each

SHICHIMI SPICE RUB
1 teaspoon chilli powder
1 teaspoon chilli flakes
2 teaspoons freshly ground
   black pepper
1 teaspoon mustard powder
3 tablespoons white sesame seeds
2 teaspoons poppy seeds
2 tablespoons aonori (fine,
   dried seaweed flakes)

WASABI CRÈME
2 egg yolks
2 tablespoons light sour cream
200 ml (7 fl oz) light olive oil
2 teaspoons wasabi paste

Combine the spices in a bowl and set aside.

Put the tuna steaks on a tray lined with baking paper. Evenly sprinkle the spice mix and a little sea salt over both sides of the tuna and set aside.

Put the yolks and sour cream in a bowl and whisk to combine. Very slowly add the oil, whisking constantly, to make a smooth creamy sauce. Stir through the wasabi until combined.

Preheat the barbecue hotplate to medium and drizzle with a little vegetable oil to grease. Put the tuna on the hotplate and cook for 2 minutes on each side until the spice mix is cooked, crusted and golden on the tuna. Serve with the wasabi crème.

WHOLE FLOUNDER WITH
BURNT BUTTER AND SAGE SAUCE

Seems strange to cook a whole fish on the barbecue without fear of ruining the whole thing. But here's the trick – tear off a large sheet of baking paper to lay over the grill or hotplate. Flounder is a good fish to cook this way as, unlike most fish we cook, its two sides are not the same. Rather, it has a top side and a bottom side. Odd thing, it is.

SERVES 4

4 flounder, about 600 g (1 lb 5 oz) each
2 tablespoons olive oil
100 g (3½ oz) butter
24 small sage leaves

Rinse the flounder and pat dry well with paper towel. Rub the top side of the flounder with the oil and season well with sea salt and freshly ground black pepper.

Preheat the oven to 180°C (350°F/Gas 4) and a barbecue flat plate to high.

Tear off a large sheet of baking paper and place on the flatplate. Place the fish on the baking paper, top side down, and cook for 5 minutes. Turn the fish over and cook for another 5 minutes, then place, top side up, on an oven tray and bake for 5 minutes. Remove from the oven and transfer to warm serving plates and cover loosely with foil.

Melt the butter in a frying pan over medium heat, swirling the pan around so it melts evenly. Add the sage leaves and cook until the sage leaves crispen and the butter starts to froth and become nutty and aromatic. Remove from the heat before the sediment in the bottom of the pan starts to burn. Spoon the hot butter over the fish.

BLUE EYE WITH CURRY BUTTER

These flavoured butter ideas are always a good thing. They can be made some time in advance and they can be frozen. Lots of lovely spices here. And remember, spices do lose their punch as they often sit in the back of the cupboard for several months or even years. If this is the case, throw them away, please, and buy some fresh ones.

SERVES 4

2 teaspoons sea salt
4 blue eye cod fillets, about 180 g
    (6½ oz) each, skin on
1 tablespoon light olive oil
lime cheeks, to serve
coriander (cilantro) sprigs, to serve

CURRY BUTTER
125 g (4½ oz) unsalted butter,
    room temperature
1 teaspoon finely grated ginger
1 garlic clove, crushed
2 tablespoons finely chopped
    spring onion
½ teaspoon ground cumin seeds
¼ teaspoon ground coriander seeds
¼ teaspoon ground fennel seeds
¼ teaspoon ground turmeric
¼ teaspoon sea salt

For the curry butter, heat 40 g (1½ oz) butter in a frying pan over high heat. When sizzling but not burnt, add the ginger, garlic and spring onions and stir for 2–3 minutes, or until the spring onions have softened. Stir in the spices and cook for another minute, or until the mixture is aromatic. Add the salt then remove from the heat and cool to room temperature. Place the mixture in a bowl with the remaining butter and stir until well combined. Place a piece of plastic wrap on a work surface and spoon the butter down the centre, then roll up to make a log. Twist the ends to seal and refrigerate until needed. This can be made a day in advance.

Sprinkle the sea salt on the skin of the fish fillets.

Preheat a barbecue flat plate to high. When smoking hot, add the oil and use a metal spatula to spread the oil evenly over the surface of the flat plate. Cook the fish, skin side down, for 3–4 minutes, without moving or turning the fish for a crisp skin. When the skin is crisp and golden the fish can be easily flipped over without tearing the skin. Turn the fish over and cook for another 2 minutes.

Place the fish, skin side up on serving plates, top with slices of the curry butter and serve with the lime cheeks and coriander sprigs on the side.

BARBECUED SNAPPER
WITH MEXICAN SALSA

The same smoky flavour you get when cooking eggplant for baba ghanoush can be achieved with any other soft vegies, such as tomatoes, garlic and shallots. If you decide to go down the Thai flavour path, these vegies would be peeled and processed with some fish sauce and sugar. Or you could take a completely different turn and add some Mexican flavours, like fiery chipotle and coriander. This is a very flavoursome base for a sauce to use with barbecued fish or chicken.

SERVES 6

1 large snapper, about 2 kg (4 lb 8 oz),
  cleaned, gutted and scaled
2 tablespoons olive oil, plus extra,
  for cooking
2 teaspoons sea salt
coriander (cilantro), roughly chopped,
  to serve
lime wedges, to serve

MEXICAN SALSA

2 tomatoes
4 garlic cloves, unpeeled
1 onion, skin left on and halved
3 tablespoons orange juice
2 tablespoons red wine vinegar
1 tablespoon chipotle chilli powder
2 tablespoons brown sugar
3 tablespoons chopped coriander
  (cilantro) leaves

Preheat the barbecue grill to high.

To make the Mexican salsa, put the tomatoes, the garlic and the onion on the grill, turning constantly and removing from the grill when the skin of each is charred and blistered. Allow to cool.

Peel the vegetables, roughly chop and put them into a food processor along with the the orange juice, vinegar, chipotle chilli powder, brown sugar and coriander. Process to a smooth paste.

Make several deep, diagonal cuts across each side of the fish. Combine the olive oil and sea salt in a bowl and rub all over the fish.

Preheat the barbecue hotplate to medium and close the lid to create a hot-oven effect.

Brush a large sheet of baking paper with a little olive oil. Lay the fish on the baking paper and spread 1 tablespoon of the salsa onto each side of the fish and put onto the hotplate. Close the lid and cook for 15 minutes. Carefully turn the fish over and cook, covered, for 10 minutes.

Slide the fish onto a serving platter. Spoon over the remaining salsa, sprinkle with the coriander and serve with the lime wedges.

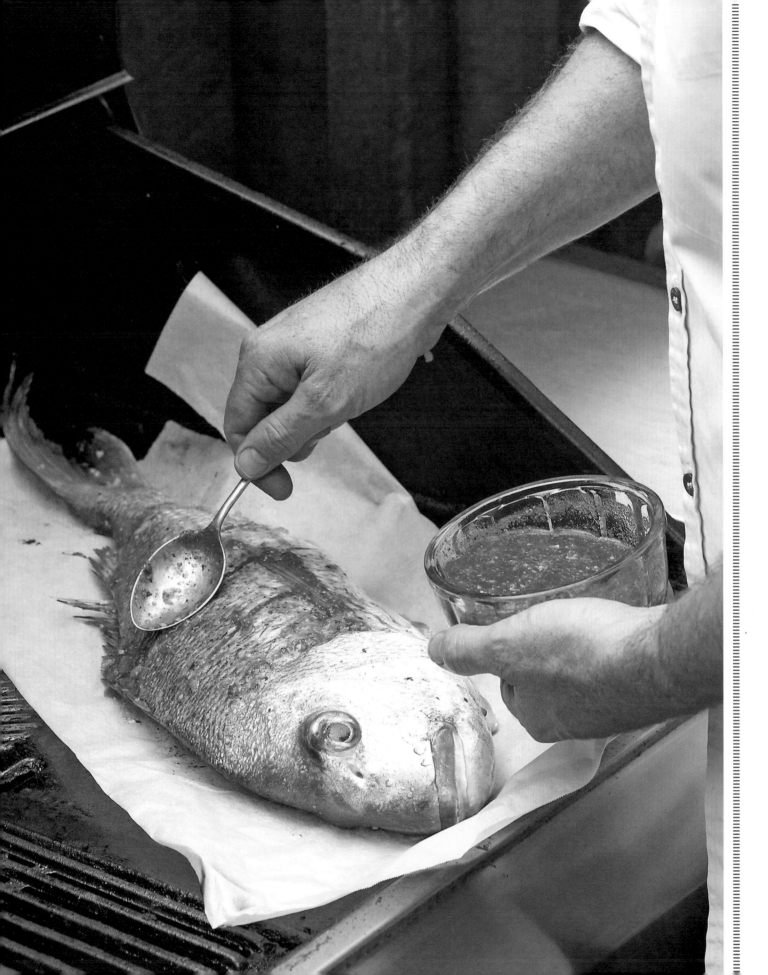

THAI PEPPER GARLIC **PRAWNS**

The trick to a well-cooked prawn is not to overcook it. As soon as the prawn has changed colour and is curled up, it is ready. The flavour combo of coriander, garlic and fish sauce is very Thai – using all the coriander, from roots to crown. This could be used with whole fish or chicken drumsticks. Cutting deep slashes into the thicker parts of the fish or chicken drumstick will ensure more even cooking.

SERVES 4

1 bunch coriander (cilantro)
4 garlic cloves, chopped
1 tablespoon white peppercorns
2 tablespoons brown sugar
2 tablespoons fish sauce
16 raw large prawns (shrimp),
    peeled and deveined, leaving
    the tails intact
lime wedges, to serve

Cut about 3–4 cm (1¼–1½ in) from the root end of the coriander. Rinse the roots, then finely chop and put into a mortar. Roughly chop the coriander leaves and set aside.

Add the garlic and peppercorns to the coriander roots and, using a pestle, pound to a paste. Tip the paste into a bowl. Stir in the brown sugar and fish sauce. Add the prawns and toss to coat with the paste. Set aside at room temperature for 30 minutes or cover and refrigerate for 3–6 hours.

Remove the prawns from the fridge 30 minutes before you begin cooking. Heat the barbecue hotplate to high. Drizzle the vegetable oil over the hotplate to grease. Add the prawns and cook for 2 minutes each side, until pink, curled up and aromatic. Serve with the reserved chopped coriander leaves sprinkled over and the lime wedges on the side.

RAS-EL-HANOUT
SPICED **SWORDFISH**

In the Derb, or market laneways in Marrakesh, each spice shop will have its own
ras-el-hanout, or 'top shelf' spice blend. A bit like the Indian spice blend garam
masala, each version will be different from the next.

SERVES 4

750 g (1 lb 10 oz) swordfish,
    cleaned, gutted and scaled,
    cut into large chunks
2 tablespoons olive oil
lemon wedges, to serve

SPICE MIX
1 teaspoon sea salt
1 teaspoon smoked paprika
1 teaspoon ras-el-hanout
    (Moroccan spice blend)

To make the spice mix, put the spices in a small frying pan.
Cook on high heat, shaking the pan, until the spices just start to
smoke but do not burn. Tip spices into a bowl and set aside.

Put the swordfish into a bowl with olive oil and toss to coat.
Preheat the barbecue hotplate to high.

Tumble the fish pieces over the hotplate and cook for
6–8 minutes, turning every couple of minutes until the fish is
golden and cooked through. Put the fish in a bowl. Add the
spice mix to the fish, shaking the bowl so the fish is coated
in the spices.

WHOLE SNAPPER WITH LEMON

What you really need here are very fresh fish. There are not many other ingredients so the fish have to be really good. And do take note of the cooking method. Whole fish, with skin on, are wonderful to barbecue. But let the skin crisp up. It will be easier to flip over and less likely the skin will tear.

SERVES 4

4 baby snapper, about 300 g
    (10½ oz) each
1 tablespoon sea salt flakes
3 lemons, halved
1 tablespoon light olive oil

Make several diagonal slashes on both sides of the fish. Rub the sea salt all over the fish and into the cuts. Stand the fish on a wire rack for 15 minutes. Squeeze one of the lemons all over the fish.

Preheat a barbecue hotplate to high. Wait for the plate to be hot before adding the oil.

Place the lemons, cut side down, in one corner of the hotplate. Put the fish on the hotplate and cook for 5 minutes, without turning or moving or the fish or the skin will tear. Use a large metal spatula to slide under the fish in one quick movement and turn over. Cook for another 4–5 minutes, or until just done. Put the fish on a serving plate. By this time, the lemons should be golden and soft on the cut side.

Serve the fish with the barbecued lemon.

ADOBO **COD**

I think we all know what cod is, but what is adobo? It is a Spanish word used to describe a dish, some say to be a national dish of the Philippines – usually using meat, but the flavours are also good with a meaty white fish. I have since tried this with monkfish (a great fish fillet to use in Moroccan tagines, by the way) and it works a treat.

SERVES 4

800 g (1 lb 12 oz) thick cod fillets, cut into large 3–4 cm (1¼–1½ in) chunks

ADOBO MARINADE
1 small red onion, chopped
1 large red chilli
2 garlic cloves, chopped
1 teaspoon finely chopped thyme
1 handful flat-leaf (Italian) parsley, leaves only, roughly chopped
2 bay leaves
3 tablespoons olive oil
3 tablespoons white wine vinegar

For the marinade, put the onion, chilli, garlic, thyme, parsley and bay leaves in a food processor and whiz to a paste. Heat the olive oil in a small saucepan over high heat and then cook the paste for 3–4 minutes, stirring often, until the onion has softened and the mixture is aromatic. Remove from the heat, stir through the vinegar, and allow to cool.

Put the fish chunks in a non-metallic dish, pour over the marinade and toss the fish to coat. Cover and refrigerate for 3 hours, turning often.

Remove the fish from the fridge 30 minutes before you begin cooking.

Preheat the barbecue hotplate to medium and drizzle with a little olive oil to grease. Cook the fish pieces for 3 minutes on each of the larger sides. (The fish pieces will have irregular shapes.) Remove the smaller pieces from the hotplate and cook the larger, thicker, more triangular-shaped pieces cut from the centre of the fillet for an extra minute on each of the smaller sides. The marinade will have cooked to a slightly charred red paste coating the fish.

WHOLE FISH WITH JALAPEÑO CHILLIES, LEMON AND HERBS

Cooking fish in foil or baking paper is not a new idea. One of the most simple yet tasty recipes is to wrap fish fillets in baking paper with nothing more than lemon slices, dill and butter. This recipe has more of a punch with the inclusion of jalapeños.

SERVES 4

4 small whole white-fleshed fish, such as snapper, about 400 g (14 oz) each, cleaned, gutted and scaled
1 lemon, thinly sliced
100 g (3½ oz) unsalted butter, diced
2 tablespoons roughly chopped dill
1 tablespoon finely chopped flat-leaf (Italian) parsley
2 tablespoons finely chopped jalapeño chillies, in brine, drained
3 tablespoons lemon juice

Preheat the barbecue grill or hotplate to high.

Rinse the fish with cold water and pat dry with a paper towel. Tear off four large pieces of foil and place four slightly smaller pieces of baking paper on top and put a fish on each.

Put some lemon slices inside the cavity of each fish. Put about 1 tablespoon of butter on top of each fish, top with the herbs and chilli and pour over the lemon juice. Season well with sea salt and freshly ground black pepper. Loosely wrap the fish in the foil and sit on the barbecue. Close the lid and cook for 8–10 minutes. Allow to sit in the foil for 10 minutes before opening the parcels to serve.

OCEAN TROUT FILLET
WITH GINGER AND SHALLOTS

Ocean trout is a terrifically coloured fish. Beautiful to look at and beautiful to eat. Please avoid overcooking this one. Ideally, you want the fish to be a dusty pink on the outside while retaining a glossy orange centre. Despite its robust colour this is a delicately flavoured fish which is complemented by light Asian flavours.

SERVES 4

1 ocean trout fillet, about 1 kg (2 lb 4 oz), skin on
1 tablespoon Chinese rice wine
pinch of ground white pepper, plus extra, to serve
3 tablespoons chicken stock
1 tablespoon light soy sauce
1 teaspoon caster (superfine) sugar
5 cm (2 in) piece of ginger, shredded as finely as possible
6 spring onions (scallions), white and green parts thinly sliced on an angle, and kept separate
4 lime cheeks, to serve
3 tablespoons rice bran oil
1 handful chopped coriander (cilantro) leaves and stems, to serve

Put the fish on a large plate or baking tray. Rub the Chinese rice wine all over the fish and season with sea salt and ground white pepper. Set aside for 30 minutes.

Tear off a large sheet of foil and lay on a work surface. Tear off a similar-sized sheet of baking paper and lay on top of the foil. Sit the fish in the centre, skin side down.

Combine the stock, soy sauce and sugar in a small bowl to dissolve the sugar, then pour the mixture over the fish.

Scatter the ginger and the white part of the spring onions over the fish. Loosely wrap the fish in the foil.

Preheat the barbecue hotplate to high and close the lid to create a hot-oven effect.

Lay the fish on the hotplate, close the lid and cook for 10 minutes. Leave the fish wrapped and then transfer to a serving platter.

Barbecue the lime cheeks for 1–2 minutes, or until caramelised.

Put the oil in a small saucepan and sit the saucepan on the hotplate. When the surface of the oil is shimmering and smoking hot, unwrap the fish and carefully pour the hot oil over the fish.

Scatter the green parts of the spring onion and the coriander on top and sprinkle over some white pepper. Serve with the lime cheeks.

ENCHANTED VEGIES

ZUCCHINI, EGGPLANT AND **HALOUMI SKEWERS**

BIG MUSHROOMS WITH MARINATED FETA

NAKED **SAMOSAS**

SMOKED TOFU, CHILLI AND **VEGETABLE CABBAGE ROLLS**

TOFU, TOMATO AND SHIITAKE SKEWERS WITH GINGER AND SPRING ONION DRESSING

LIME AND TURMERIC TOFU STEAKS WITH FRESH SAMBAL

CHICKPEA AND SQUASH **PAKORAS**

KAFFIR LIME LEAF AND LEMONGRASS **TOFU**

BLACKENED **PANEER SKEWERS**

SILVERBEET AND FETA **GÖZLEME**

CHAKCHOUKA

MUSHROOM **BULGOGI**

PANEER AND TOMATO **SKEWERS**

FRAGRANT FIVE-SPICE **VEGETABLE PARCELS**

HALOUMI WITH PICKLED CHILLI AND CAULIFLOWER SALSA

ZUCCHINI, EGGPLANT AND
HALOUMI SKEWERS

Haloumi is one of those ingredients that seemed to appear from out of nowhere to become one of my favourite things to cook. Here, it is cubed and skewered with eggplant and zucchini. You could also slice the haloumi into 'steaks' about 1 cm (½ in) thick, marinate them in a mixture of chilli flakes, dried oregano, olive oil and lemon juice, then cook on the grill until a golden crust forms. Serve with couscous, if desired.

SERVES 4

500 g (1 lb 2 oz) haloumi cheese
2 Japanese eggplant (aubergines)
2 zucchini (courgettes)
2 tablespoons olive oil, plus extra
    for brushing
2 tablespoons apple cider vinegar
2 teaspoons cumin seeds
1 teaspoon chilli flakes
baby rocket (arugula) leaves, to serve

Soak eight bamboo skewers in cold water for 30 minutes.

Cut the haloumi, eggplant and zucchini into 2 cm (¾ in) chunks. Onto each skewer, alternately thread two bits of haloumi with some eggplant and zucchini. Lay the skewers on a flat dish.

Mix the olive oil, vinegar, cumin and chilli in a small bowl, then pour the mixture over the skewers. Cover and set aside at room temperature for a couple of hours to allow the flavours to infuse.

Preheat the barbecue hotplate to high. Brush with a little olive oil to lightly grease.

Put the skewers on the hotplate, reserving the marinade in the dish, and cook for 2–3 minutes, or until a dark-golden crust has formed on the haloumi.

Use a metal spatula to turn the skewers over, then cook for another 2 minutes.

Scatter rocket on a serving plate and pile the skewers alongside. Drizzle with the reserved marinade and serve.

BIG MUSHROOMS
WITH MARINATED FETA

I would say the top two vegies to cook on the barbecue are eggplant (aubergine) and mushrooms. They lend themselves to all sorts of cooking styles and pair well with many different flavours. I have made my own herb-infused oil here, but if you can get your hands on soft feta marinated in oil with garlic and herbs, then by all means use that. All you'll then have to do is spoon the ready-marinated cheese into the mushroom caps and cook them on your barbecue. Very nice.

SERVES 4

2 thyme sprigs
2 garlic cloves, sliced
2 spring onions (scallions), finely
    sliced on an angle
125 ml (4 fl oz/½ cup) light olive oil
½ teaspoon sea salt
2 tablespoons sherry vinegar
200 g (7 oz) semi-soft goat's
    feta cheese
8 large field mushrooms, or pine
    mushrooms if available
1 teaspoon sumac (see Note)
finely chopped flat-leaf (Italian)
    parsley (optional), to garnish

Put the thyme, garlic and spring onions in a heatproof bowl.

Heat the olive oil in a small frying pan over medium heat. When the oil is smoking hot, pour in the spring onion mixture, allowing it to sizzle in the oil and release the flavours. Stir in the salt, vinegar and some freshly ground black pepper to taste.

Cut the feta into small bite-sized cubes and arrange in a flat non-metallic dish. Spoon the spring onion mixture over the feta. Cover and marinate in the refrigerator for up to 3 days.

Preheat the barbecue grill to high.

Remove the stems from the mushrooms and spoon some pieces of feta and the marinade into the caps. Sit the mushrooms on the grill, then close the barbecue lid, or cover the mushrooms with a baking tray. Cook for 15 minutes, or until the mushrooms are tender. Serve warm, sprinkled with the sumac, and parsley if desired.

NOTE Sumac is a spice ground from a purple berry, widely used in Middle Eastern cuisine. It has a pleasantly astringent lemony flavour and is available from specialty shops.

NAKED **SAMOSAS**

So called because they have no pastry. This is more like a vegetable patty or burger with all the tasty flavours of Indian cooking. You could serve this up as a take on a vegie burger – put the samosa on a piece of warm, grilled naan bread and top with the chutney, yoghurt and coriander.

SERVES 4

4 medium russet (idaho) or king
    edward potatoes
2 tablespoons light olive oil, plus
    extra, for cooking
½ teaspoon black mustard seeds
1 onion, thinly sliced
1 garlic clove, finely chopped
2 teaspoons finely grated ginger
½ teaspoon cumin seeds
1 teaspoon fennel seeds
75 g (2½ oz/½ cup) frozen
    peas, defrosted
¼ teaspoon ground turmeric
2 teaspoons sea salt
¼ teaspoon chilli powder
½ teaspoon garam masala
1 small bunch coriander (cilantro),
    finely chopped
mango chutney, to serve
plain yoghurt, to serve
coriander (cilantro) sprigs, to serve

Peel and wash the potatoes. Cut each into eight pieces and put into a medium saucepan. Cover with cold water and bring to the boil, cooking for 15 minutes, or until just cooked. Drain well then tip the potatoes out onto a clean chopping board to cool and dry.

Put the potatoes into a large bowl and roughly mash.

Heat the olive oil in a frying pan over high heat. Add the mustard seeds and cook until the seeds start to pop. Add the onion and cook, stirring, for about 4–5 minutes, until golden. Add the garlic, ginger, cumin seeds and fennel seeds and stir-fry for 1 minute, until aromatic. Add the peas and mix through. Pour the onion mixture over the potatoes. Add the turmeric, sea salt, chilli powder, garam masala and coriander. Use a large spoon to stir, making sure the ingredients are really well combined. Set aside at room temperature for 1–2 hours for flavours to develop, or refrigerate until needed.

Using slightly wet hands, roughly divide the mixture into eight equal portions and form into balls. Gently pat down to make a disc or patty.

Preheat the barbecue hotplate to high and drizzle over a little olive oil to grease.

Cook the patties for 10 minutes each side, so they have a golden crust.

Serve with the mango chutney, yoghurt and coriander sprigs.

SMOKED TOFU, CHILLI AND
VEGETABLE CABBAGE ROLLS

**Cabbage leaves are used in so many cuisines, especially throughout Asia.
And anything rolled in them is good – it means you can make them in advance,
refrigerate them, then cook them up at a minute's notice.**

SERVES 4

8 large Chinese cabbage
(wong bok) leaves

TOFU AND CHILLI FILLING
100 g (3½ oz) smoked tofu,
roughly grated
115 g (4 oz/1 cup) bean sprouts
155 g (5½ oz/1 cup) grated carrot
1 teaspoon finely grated fresh ginger
1 small red chilli, finely sliced
½ cup finely chopped coriander
(cilantro) leaves and stalks
2 tablespoons tamari (Japanese
soy sauce)
1 teaspoon sesame oil
1 tablespoon rice vinegar
½ teaspoon sugar
1 teaspoon cornflour (cornstarch)

Bring a large saucepan of water to the boil. Add the cabbage
leaves, turn the heat off and set aside for 2 minutes – the
leaves will be tender but bright green.

Drain well and rinse under cold water until completely cool.
Drain, then trim any thick ends off the cabbage leaves. Lay the
leaves on a clean cloth on a work surface and leave to dry.

To make the filling, combine the tofu, sprouts, carrot,
ginger, chilli and coriander in a bowl. Combine the tamari,
sesame oil, vinegar, sugar and cornflour in another bowl, then
pour the mixture over the vegetables. Season to taste with
freshly ground black pepper and stir to combine.

To assemble, place about ½ cup of the filling on the broad
end of one cabbage leaf. Fold the end over the filling, then
fold the sides in, rolling to enclose the filling, and finishing at
the stem of the leaf. Don't wrap too tightly, and don't worry
if some of the filling sticks out the sides. Repeat with the
remaining filling and leaves to make 8 rolls.

Tear off eight pieces of foil, large enough to fully wrap up
the cabbage rolls, and lay them on a flat surface. Brush the
top of each piece of foil with grapeseed oil. Roll each of the
cabbage rolls up in a sheet of foil, twisting the ends to seal.

Preheat a barbecue hotplate to medium. Sit the cabbage
rolls on the hotplate and cook for 10 minutes, turning every
few minutes. Serve the rolls on a platter, to be unwrapped
at the table.

TOFU, TOMATO AND SHIITAKE SKEWERS WITH GINGER AND SPRING ONION DRESSING

You could try using silky, soft tofu here, but it does tend to stick to the hotplate and break up easily. One way to avoid this is to put some baking paper on the hotplate. I generally prefer soft tofu, but am using the firm variety in this recipe, simply because it looks better when it makes it to the table.

SERVES 4

300 g (10½ oz) firm tofu
24 truss cherry tomatoes
24 small shiitake mushrooms
1 tablespoon rice bran oil
2 teaspoons light soy sauce
coriander (cilantro) sprigs, to garnish

GINGER AND SPRING ONION DRESSING

2 tablespoons julienned fresh ginger
125 g (4½ oz/1 cup) thinly sliced
    spring onions (scallions)
60 ml (2 fl oz/¼ cup) rice bran oil
2 tablespoons light soy sauce
1 teaspoon sesame oil

Soak eight bamboo skewers in cold water for 30 minutes.

To make the dressing, put the ginger and spring onions in a small heatproof bowl. Heat the oil in a small saucepan over high heat until smoking hot. Pour the hot oil over the ginger and spring onions so they sizzle and soften, then stir in the soy sauce and sesame oil. Set aside while preparing the skewers.

Cut the tofu into pieces about the same size as the tomatoes.

Randomly thread some tofu, 3 tomatoes and 3 mushrooms on each skewer. Put the skewers in a flat dish or on a plate. Combine the oil and soy sauce and brush the mixture over the vegies and tofu.

Preheat a barbecue hotplate to high. Cook the skewers for 8 minutes, turning every couple of minutes, until they are golden and tender.

Spoon the dressing over the skewers. Serve scattered with coriander sprigs.

NOTE The ginger and spring onion dressing can be made a day in advance. Store it in an airtight container in the fridge until needed and bring back to room temperature before using.

LIME AND TURMERIC TOFU STEAKS WITH FRESH SAMBAL

The real flavour in this recipe comes from the sambal, and as far as flavours go, you won't be left wanting. Sambal is a chilli-based condiment used throughout South-East Asia. It is generally cooked, but this is a very raw, very fresh and very tasty version.

SERVES 4

600 g (1 lb 5 oz) firm tofu
60 ml (2 fl oz/¼ cup) lime juice
60 ml (2 fl oz/¼ cup) grapeseed oil
¼ teaspoon ground turmeric
lime cheeks, to serve

SAMBAL

1 teaspoon vegetable stock (bouillon)
    powder
2 kaffir lime leaves, thinly sliced
2 lemongrass stems, pale part only,
    finely chopped
2 bird's eye chillies, finely chopped
3 tablespoons finely chopped red
    Asian shallots
2 garlic cloves, finely chopped
1 tablespoon vegetable oil
1 tablespoon lime juice

For the sambal, combine the sambal ingredients in a bowl and stir until the stock powder has dissolved. Cover and set aside for 30 minutes, or refrigerate overnight.

Cut the tofu into four equal portions. Place in a flat dish in a single layer.

Combine the lime juice, grapeseed oil and turmeric in a bowl and stir until the turmeric has dissolved and the oil is vibrantly coloured. Pour the marinade over the tofu and turn to coat all over. Set aside for 30 minutes.

Preheat the barbecue grill to high.

Cook the tofu for 2–3 minutes on each side, or until heated through and slightly crusty. Serve warm, with the sambal spooned over and lime cheeks on the side.

CHICKPEA AND SQUASH **PAKORAS**

Best put, a pakora is a fried snack – although we are barbecuing them, not frying them here. These fritters are delicious, made even more so by their simplicity.

SERVES 4–6

300 g (10½ oz) tinned chickpeas, drained

500 g (1 lb 2 oz) piece of jap pumpkin (winter squash), peeled, seeded and roughly chopped, to yield about 300 g (10½ oz) flesh

140 g (5 oz/1 cup) frozen peas

1 large green chilli, thinly sliced on an angle

2 spring onions (scallions), thinly sliced on an angle

60 g (2¼ oz/½ cup) chickpea flour (besan), plus extra for dusting

1 teaspoon cumin seeds

1 teaspoon ground coriander

3 tablespoons finely chopped coriander (cilantro) leaves and stalks, plus extra leaves to garnish

1 tablespoon lemon juice

½ teaspoon sea salt

rice bran oil, for brushing

iceberg lettuce leaves, to serve

lemon wedges, to serve

plain yoghurt, to serve

Bring a large saucepan of water to the boil. Add the chickpeas and pumpkin and cook for 15 minutes, or until the pumpkin is tender. Drain well, then tip chickpeas and pumpkin into a bowl.

Use a potato masher to mash the chickpeas and pumpkin into a lumpy mixture. Stir in the peas, chilli, spring onions, chickpea flour, cumin, ground coriander, fresh coriander, lemon juice and salt. Cover and refrigerate until chilled.

Divide the mixture into eight even portions. Using wet hands, form the portions into discs or patties. Place on a tray lined with baking paper and refrigerate until ready to cook.

Preheat the barbecue hotplate to medium–high and brush with oil. Lightly dust the the fritters with extra chickpea flour and place them on the hotplate. Cook for 3–4 minutes on each side, or until golden.

Serve warm, garnished with coriander leaves, with lettuce, lemon wedges and yoghurt on the side.

NOTE These fritters can be made a day in advance. Cover with plastic wrap and refrigerate until you're ready to cook them.

KAFFIR LIME LEAF AND LEMONGRASS **TOFU**

I can totally understand if you do not enjoy tofu as it is often cooked really badly.
I mean, if you cooked a fillet steak for 20 minutes each side you probably wouldn't
like it either. Tofu is about the texture. It is a chameleon of sorts and takes on the
flavours it is cooked with. So when cooked well (and by this I generally mean simply
and quickly), and used with other flavours, you will understand why tofu is no longer
only enjoyed by vegetarians. If you can't get your hands on kecap manis, soy sauce
with a little brown sugar will do the job nicely.

SERVES 4

2 lemongrass stalks, white part
   only, chopped
2 garlic cloves, chopped
2 makrut (kaffir lime) leaves,
   thinly sliced
1 tablespoon finely grated ginger
2 tablespoons fish sauce
2 tablespoons vegetable oil
1 teaspoon caster (superfine) sugar
300 g (10½ oz) block firm tofu
kecap manis, to serve
coriander (cilantro) sprigs, to serve

Put the lemongrass, garlic, lime leaves, ginger, fish sauce,
vegetable oil and sugar in a food processor and blend to
make a chunky sauce. Transfer to a bowl with the tofu.
Gently turn the tofu so it is evenly covered in the mixture.
Set aside at room temperature for a couple of hours.

Preheat the barbecue hotplate to medium. Put the block
of tofu on the hotplate, scraping any of the sauce over the
tofu. Close the lid and cook for 5 minutes. Using a large
spatula, turn over the tofu. The lemongrass mixture will have
cooked golden and charred in some places. Cook, covered,
for another 5 minutes.

Cut into large cubes, transfer to a serving plate, drizzle
with the kecap manis and scatter over the coriander.

BLACKENED **PANEER SKEWERS**

Paneer is an Indian 'cheese', though not what Westerners would call cheese. It is a fresh cheese and does not use a setting agent. Have you ever left fresh ricotta in the fridge for several days? It becomes very firm, just like paneer — which, by the way, is so good in curries too.

SERVES 4

400 g (14 oz) block paneer (Indian cottage cheese)
lemon wedges, to serve

BLACKENED SEASONING
60 ml (2 fl oz/¼ cup) rice bran oil
2 teaspoons dried thyme
2 teaspoons dried oregano
2 teaspoons hot smoked
    Spanish paprika
1 teaspoon cayenne pepper
1 teaspoon sea salt

FRESH TOMATO RELISH
2 roma (plum) tomatoes, finely diced
1 small red onion, finely diced
2 teaspoons soft brown sugar
2 tablespoons lime juice
½ teaspoon celery seeds
¼ teaspoon nigella seeds (see Note)

Combine the blackened seasoning ingredients in a bowl, then pour the mixture onto a flat plate.

Cut the paneer into 8 rectangles, about 1.5 cm (⅝ in) wide and 6 cm (2½ in) long — like fat chips. Roll each piece in the blackened seasoning mixture to coat all over. Cover and marinate in the refrigerator for several hours.

Soak eight bamboo skewers in cold water for 30 minutes.

Combine all the tomato relish ingredients in a bowl and set aside for the flavours to develop.

Preheat the barbecue grill to high. Thread a bamboo skewer through each piece of paneer. Cook the skewers, turning every couple of minutes, for 8–10 minutes, or until dark and aromatic. Serve immediately, with the tomato relish and lemon wedges.

NOTE Nigella seeds look like little black sesame seeds, but have a peppery, smoky flavour. They are widely used throughout India, Egypt and the Middle East. You'll find them in spice shops and gourmet food stores.

SILVERBEET AND FETA **GÖZLEME**

Hot dog and donut stalls have been replaced by gözleme (Turkish pizza) stalls at markets. And this is not a bad thing. I love these 'pizzas'. It would be very tricky to try your hand at making the dough yourself but you don't have to, not with so many exotic pre-made breads out there, including some good gluten-free ones, too.

SERVES 4

1 tablespoon olive oil, plus extra,
    for cooking
1 red onion, finely chopped
2 garlic cloves, crushed
180 g (6 oz) finely shredded silverbeet
    (Swiss chard)
200 g (7 oz/2 cups) feta cheese,
    crumbled
50 g (1¾ oz/½ cup) coarsely grated
    cheddar cheese
¼ teaspoon sweet paprika
4 x 26 cm (10½ in) Greek pitta breads
lemon wedges, to serve

Combine the olive oil, onion, garlic, silverbeet, cheeses and paprika in a bowl, mixing well to combine.

Spread half of the mixture over 1 pitta bread and top with another. Repeat with the remaining pitta breads and filling to make a second gözleme.

Preheat the barbecue hotplate to medium–high. Brush both sides of the gözleme with oil. Cook the gözleme one at a time for 3–4 minutes each side, using a spatula to compress it, until crisp and golden. Cut into wedges and serve with lots of fresh lemon juice squeezed over. Cook the second gözleme while your guests eat the first.

CHAKCHOUKA

Translating Arabic to English can be tricky. That is why, in the world of food, you often see the names of Middle Eastern dishes spelt in different ways, as with this fabulously flavoursome dish from North Africa. This must be the vegetarian equivalent to bacon and eggs as hangover food. The name alone makes you want to sit up and take notice.

SERVES 4

60 ml (2 fl oz/¼ cup) rice bran oil
6 ripe tomatoes, cut in half
1 small yellow capsicum (pepper),
    cut into strips
1 small green capsicum (pepper),
    cut into strips
1 small red capsicum (pepper),
    cut into strips
1 red onion, cut into rings
1 large red chilli, finely chopped
1 teaspoon ground cumin
1 teaspoon sweet paprika
1 teaspoon sea salt
8 eggs
3 tablespoons finely chopped
    flat-leaf (Italian) parsley
chargrilled bread, to serve

Preheat the barbecue grill to high.

Put the oil in a large bowl. Add the tomatoes, capsicums and onion and toss the vegies around to coat them in the oil.

Working in batches, tumble some of the vegies over the grill and spread them around so they don't overlap. Cook the vegetables for 8–10 minutes, turning them often using metal tongs until they are tender and scored with grill marks, then transfer to a bowl. Cook remaining vegetables in the same way.

Sprinkle the cooked vegetables with the chilli, cumin, paprika and salt and toss together. Lightly mash using a potato masher, so the tomatoes especially are well crushed. Spoon the mixture onto a heavy-based baking tray. Put the tray on the barbecue grill and allow to heat up and sizzle.

Form eight evenly spaced little wells in the mixture, then crack an egg into each one.

Close the barbecue lid, if your barbecue has one, or place another baking tray over the top. Cook for 8–10 minutes, just until the egg whites are firm. Sprinkle with the parsley and serve hot with the chargrilled bread.

MUSHROOM **BULGOGI**

Okay, so bulgolgi is a popular Korean steak recipe, which translates to something like 'fired meat'. With this recipe, the flavour comes from the marinade. I love a good steak myself, but why should meat get all the fun?

SERVES 4

200 g (7 oz) fresh shiitake mushrooms
200 g (7 oz) oyster mushrooms
200 g (7 oz) medium-sized
    field mushrooms
4 pine mushrooms, or 2 large king
    oyster mushrooms, thickly sliced
1 teaspoon toasted sesame seeds

**SOY, SESAME AND
GINGER MARINADE**
60 ml (2 fl oz/¼ cup) Korean or
    Japanese soy sauce
1 tablespoon sesame oil
1 teaspoon toasted sesame seeds
2 spring onions (scallions), thinly
    sliced on an angle
2 garlic cloves, finely chopped
1 tablespoon finely grated fresh ginger

Combine the marinade ingredients in a bowl and set aside.

Cut off and discard any large stems from the mushrooms. Lay the mushrooms in a large, flat dish, pour the marinade over and turn to coat. Cover and refrigerate for 3 hours, or overnight, turning the mushrooms every now and then.

Remove the mushrooms from the fridge 30 minutes before cooking to bring them to room temperature.

Preheat the barbecue grill to medium.

Use tongs to shake the excess marinade off mushrooms, then arrange them on the grill. Cook the mushrooms, turning them often, for 10–15 minutes, or until dark, tender and aromatic. Serve warm, sprinkled with the sesame seeds.

PANEER AND TOMATO **SKEWERS**

Paneer is an Indian fresh 'cheese', though not really a cheese in the same sense many of us would think as it doesn't have a setting agent like rennet. Like haloumi, it grills well. It can be cubed or cut into steaks and cooked until golden.

SERVES 6

1 large red chilli, thinly sliced
    on an angle
3 tablespoons light olive oil,
    plus extra, for cooking
1 teaspoon sea salt
1 handful roughly chopped
    coriander (cilantro) leaves
1 handful roughly chopped mint
2 tablespoons lemon juice
400 g (14 oz) paneer (Indian
    cottage cheese), cut into
    2–3 cm (¾–1¼ in) cubes
24 cherry tomatoes
1 teaspoon cumin seeds
1 teaspoon fennel seeds
lemon wedges, to serve

Combine the chilli, olive oil, sea salt, coriander, mint and lemon juice in a bowl and set aside. Soak 12 bamboo skewers in cold water for 30 minutes.

Preheat the barbecue hotplate to high and lightly brush with olive oil to grease.

Thread 2 pieces of paneer and 2 tomatoes alternately onto each bamboo skewer. Sprinkle with the cumin and the fennel seeds.

Cook the skewers for 8–10 minutes, turning often until the paneer is golden and the tomatoes softened.

Arrange on a serving platter and pour over the dressing. Serve with the lemon wedges.

FRAGRANT FIVE-SPICE
VEGETABLE PARCELS

Fresh shiitake mushrooms have such a wonderful savoury aroma. Dried shiitakes are even more intense and also work well for this recipe. They store well, are inexpensive and easy to use. Just pour over boiling water to cover and leave to soften for about 30 minutes, then discard the stems and either use the caps whole or chop them up. This dish is great served with steamed brown rice.

SERVES 4

12 medium-sized shiitake mushrooms, stems removed

1 small sweet potato, cut into rounds 1 cm (½ in) thick

200 g (7 oz) peeled daikon, cut into 3 cm (1¼ in) cubes

200 g (7 oz) firm tofu, cut into 2 cm (¾ in) pieces

2 tablespoons thinly sliced shiso leaves (see Note)

60 ml (2 fl oz/¼ cup) good-quality soy sauce

1 tablespoon mirin

½ teaspoon sugar

½ teaspoon Chinese five-spice

1 teaspoon sesame oil

Preheat the barbecue hotplate to high.

Combine all the ingredients in a large bowl. Tear off a sheet of foil about 30 cm (12 in) square and place a similar-sized piece of baking paper over the foil.

Spoon a quarter of the vegie mixture in the middle of the baking paper. Bring the sides of the foil up to enclose the vegetables, and then seal the edges together. Repeat to make four parcels.

Sit the parcels on the hotplate and cook for 12–15 minutes, or until the vegetables are tender and aromatic. Serve hot.

NOTE Also known as perilla, and related to mint, shiso is a herb with round, serrated green or purplish leaves. If you can't get any, use flat-leaf (Italian) parsley instead.

HALOUMI WITH PICKLED CHILLI AND CAULIFLOWER SALSA

I am thinking I like the word salsa, which really means sauce: it evokes such a sense of freshness and simplicity of flavour. And here the star player is cauliflower, which is often overlooked, yet lends itself to all styles of cooking – baking, frying, boiling. Just serve it with something cheesy and it shines.

SERVES 4

400 g (14 oz) haloumi, cut into slices
　　5 mm (¼ in) thick
1 tablespoon rice bran oil

**PICKLED CHILLI AND
CAULIFLOWER SALSA**
1 tablespoon light olive oil
250 g (9 oz/2 cups) small
　　cauliflower florets
1 garlic clove, finely chopped
1 red onion, chopped
2 tablespoons sherry vinegar
60 g (2¼ oz/½ cup) finely sliced
　　pickled red chillies
3 tablespoons finely shredded
　　mint leaves
3 tablespoons finely chopped
　　flat-leaf (Italian) parsley

To make the salsa, heat the olive oil in a large frying pan over high heat. Add the cauliflower and stir-fry for 4–5 minutes, or until golden and tender.

Stir the garlic and onion through and cook for just a minute, then remove from the heat and allow to cool.

Stir in the vinegar, chillies and herbs. Set aside while cooking the haloumi, to allow the flavours to develop.

Preheat the barbecue grill to high.

Brush the haloumi with the rice bran oil. Spread the slices on the grill and cook for 2–3 minutes on each side, or until golden grill marks appear.

Layer the haloumi and salsa on a serving plate. Serve warm.

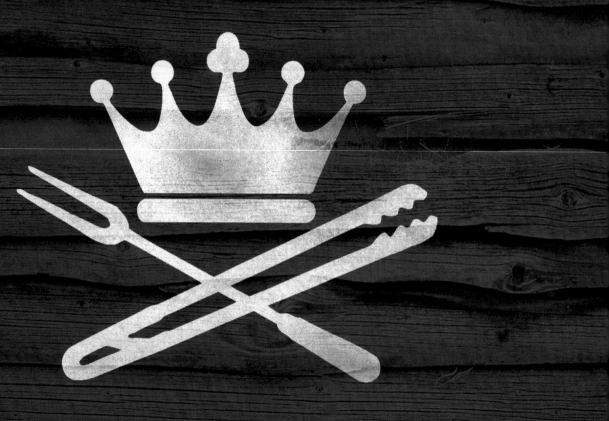

RABBIT FOOD

TANGY SWEET POTATO SALAD

There are some ingredients that, when used with a light hand, give warmth to a dish. Caraway is one of them. Use it sparingly, like fennel seeds, and you will be left wondering what the flavour is exactly. But it doesn't matter, it just tastes very good.

SERVES 6

1 medium-sized sweet potato, sliced into rounds 5 mm (¼ in) thick
2 tablespoons rice bran oil
1 teaspoon caraway seeds
2 dill pickles, finely chopped
3 tablespoons roughly chopped mint leaves
1 large red chilli, finely chopped
2 tablespoons apple cider vinegar
60 ml (2 fl oz/¼ cup) extra virgin olive oil
1 teaspoon caster (superfine) sugar

Preheat the barbecue grill to medium.

Put the sweet potato, rice bran oil and caraway seeds in a bowl and toss to coat the sweet potato well.

Tumble the sweet potato over the grill, then use tongs to spread them out so they don't overlap. Cook for 8–10 minutes on each side, or until caramelised and tender.

Place the hot sweet potato in a bowl. Add the dill pickles, mint and chilli. In a small bowl, combine the vinegar, olive oil and sugar, then drizzle the mixture over the sweet potatoes, gently stirring to combine. Set aside for 30 minutes for the flavours to infuse.

Season to taste with sea salt and freshly ground black pepper and serve.

CLASSIC **WALDORF SALAD**

This one could not be easier so please don't get too worked up about it and make it in advance or even worse, the day before. The freshness of each ingredient here is paramount to making this classic, which I think of as an autumn salad. This is the season when apples are at their best.

SERVES 4

4 young celery stalks, including leaves, thinly sliced on the angle

2 French shallots, thinly sliced

3 red delicious apples, cored and cut into thin wedges

¼ cup flat-leaf (Italian) parsley, torn

60 g (2¼ oz/½ cup) walnuts, lightly toasted and coarsely chopped

185 g (6½ oz/¾ cup) good-quality mayonnaise

2 tablespoons lemon juice

Combine the celery, shallots, apple, parsley and walnuts in a bowl.

Combine the mayonnaise and lemon juice in another bowl, then stir through the apple salad and season with salt and freshly ground black pepper to taste just before serving.

SALAD WITH **RED WINE VINAIGRETTE**

The most basic of salad dressings, second only to olive oil and lemon juice, is a vinaigrette. French in origin, if there were any doubts.

SERVES 4

80 ml (2½ fl oz/⅓ cup) olive oil
2 teaspoons dijon mustard
2 teaspoons red wine vinegar
½ teaspoon crushed garlic
360 g (4¼ oz/8 cups)
   good-quality salad mix

Place the oil, mustard, vinegar, garlic and salt and freshly ground black pepper to taste in a small jar with a tight-fitting lid. Shake well to combine and refrigerate for up to 2 days. Remove from the refrigerator 30 minutes before using.

Place the salad leaves in a large bowl. Shake the dressing, pour over the salad and toss gently to combine.

RED CABBAGE AND BACON SALAD

Warm salads will be really enjoyed by your barbecue guests. Spinach leaves and witlof (chicory) can substitute for the cabbage, served up with pork chops, chicken or lamb.

SERVES 4–6

1 small red cabbage
6 bacon slices, rind removed

**GARLIC AND RED WINE
VINEGAR DRESSING**
2 garlic cloves, crushed
3 tablespoons olive oil
2 tablespoons red wine vinegar
2 tablespoons chopped tarragon
2 tablespoons roughly chopped
   flat-leaf (Italian) parsley

Combine all the dressing ingredients in a bowl and set aside.

Preheat the barbecue grill and hotplate to high.

Pull away any tough leaves from the cabbage. Trim most of the stem off, leaving just enough to help the cabbage hold together when cooked. Cut 1 cm (½ in) wide strips from top to stem of the cabbage.

Drizzle the hotplate with olive oil. Lay the cabbage on the hotplate and sprinkle with sea salt. Lay the bacon on the grill.

Cook the cabbage and bacon for 4–5 minutes each side, until the cabbage is golden and the bacon is starting to crisp up. Turn both cabbage and bacon over and then cook for another 2–3 minutes.

Put the cabbage in a large bowl and while still hot add the dressing. Roughly chop the bacon and then add to the salad. Toss to combine and serve warm.

MEDITERRANEAN SALAD

This salad is one of my all-time favourites. It can be used as a dip, a dressing for grilled vegetables or an accompanying sauce for lamb. Spoon over a classic mix of Mediterranean salad ingredients and you are all set for a memorable side for just about any barbecued meat.

SERVES 4

4 tomatoes, roughly chopped
2 Lebanese (short) cucumbers,
    cut into bite-sized chunks
black olives, to taste
1 iceberg lettuce, torn into
    large pieces
1 handful mint leaves

CREAMY FETA DRESSING
120 g (4¼ oz/1 cup) crumbled
    feta cheese
1 garlic clove, crushed
1 teaspoon dried dill
1 tablespoon white wine vinegar
125 ml (4 fl oz/½ cup) light olive oil
125 ml (4 fl oz/½ cup) milk

Put the feta, garlic, dill, vinegar and olive oil in a food processor and whiz for a few seconds to combine. Add the milk in a steady stream with the motor running so you have a smooth and creamy sauce.

Put the salad ingredients in a large bowl and pour over the dressing to serve.

THE MUST-HAVE
GRILLED VEGIE SALAD

This is a very simple, very tasty recipe to have in your repertoire. Start with a few basics: chopped garlic, chilli, parsley, some sort of oil and something with a tang factor (like vinegar or lemon juice), then just add whatever barbecued vegies you like. In summer, I am partial to vine vegies – eggplant, tomatoes and beans.

SERVES 8

1 kg (2 lb 4 oz) roma (plum)
    tomatoes, halved lengthways
2 large eggplant (aubergines),
    cut into large chunks
500 g (1 lb 2 oz) green beans
2 red onions, cut into thin rings

GRILLED VEGIE SALAD DRESSING
4 garlic cloves, finely chopped
2 large red chillies, finely
    chopped
1 cup roughly chopped flat-leaf
    (Italian) parsley
125 ml (4 fl oz/½ cup) olive oil
60 ml (2 fl oz/¼ cup) sherry
    vinegar
1 teaspoon sea salt

Combine the dressing ingredients in a bowl and then set aside to infuse.

Preheat the barbecue hotplate and grill to high.

Tumble the tomatoes over the hotplate – avoid cooking them on the grill as they will stick.

Spread the eggplant around the grill. Depending on the size of your barbecue, you may need to cook the vegies in batches. Don't overcrowd the barbecue, and make sure the vegies don't overlap. Keep turning the vegies until they are tender and golden.

Put the cooked vegies in a large bowl. While they're still warm, spoon some of the dressing over them, but don't stir the vegies or they'll break up.

Cook the beans and onions on the barbecue in the same manner. When all the vegies are cooked and in the bowl, pour the remaining dressing over.

Tip the salad onto a serving platter and then serve at room temperature.

ISRAELI EGGPLANT SALAD

If you're ever looking for a decent reference book on cooking vegies, try to get your hands on a copy of Mollie Katzen's *The Enchanted Broccoli Forest*. In the 1980s, it was in the kitchen of just about every other student. It is a well-worn book on my shelf and was the inspiration for this delicious recipe.

SERVES 4

2 eggplant (aubergines)
4 truss tomatoes
1 handful coriander (cilantro) leaves
1 cup chopped flat-leaf (Italian)
    parsley, plus extra leaves, to garnish

SPICY LEMON DRESSING
60 ml (2 fl oz/¼ cup) olive oil
60 ml (2 fl oz/¼ cup) lemon juice
2 teaspoons ground cumin
2 teaspoons hot paprika
½ teaspoon cayenne pepper

Preheat the barbecue grill to high.

Sit the eggplant and tomatoes on the grill. When they start to smoke, give them a turn. Continue until the vegies look charred all over, then remove from the grill.

When cool enough to handle, peel the eggplant skins and discard – there's no need to be too fussy about removing all the burnt bits as these add flavour. Tear the flesh of the eggplant into long lengths and place in a bowl.

Peel and discard the skins of the tomatoes. Chop the flesh and add it to the eggplant, along with any seeds and juice. Don't mix them together at this stage.

Put the dressing ingredients in a bowl and stir to combine. Pour the dressing over the vegetables and use a large spoon to gently coat all the vegies – you don't want to break them up too much. Stir the herbs through and season well. Serve warm, or at room temperature, garnished with extra parsley.

TOMATO, ONION AND BREAD SALAD

I remember eating this with leftover roast lamb so it would be good with any of the barbecued lamb recipes, hot or cold. Regarding oregano — try and get Greek oregano (oregani), available at most delis and good providores.

SERVES 4

2 white onions, thinly sliced
½ teaspoon dried oregano
1 teaspoon caster (superfine) sugar
2 tablespoons white wine vinegar
1 teaspoon sea salt
4 thick slices sourdough bread
6 ripe tomatoes
60 ml (2 fl oz/¼ cup) extra
    virgin olive oil

Place the onion, oregano, sugar, vinegar and sea salt in a bowl and toss to combine, separating the onion rings. Cover and refrigerate for at least 3 hours.

Grill the bread until golden on both sides and then allow to cool. Roughly tear into small pieces.

Slice the tomatoes and place in a bowl with the torn bread, onion mixture and olive oil. Toss to combine, the season to taste with freshly ground black pepper and serve.

HERB-MARINATED **POTATO SALAD**

Always on the lookout for a potato salad, I am often drawn to those that are quick and easy. In my book, they are either creamy (mayonnaise-based) or, like this one, tossed with a vinaigrette and lots of fresh herbs. I like to let this one sit in its juices for a short while, so the potatoes are almost marinated and the herby flavour really permeates. Which makes it good to transport without refrigeration and, therefore, equally as good for a barbecue on the beach or in a park as it is in your own backyard.

SERVES 4

16 small waxy potatoes, cut in half
3 tablespoons olive oil
2 tablespoons red wine vinegar
2 teaspoons mild mustard
4 spring onions (scallions),
     finely sliced
1 handful flat-leaf (Italian) parsley,
     finely chopped
1 small handful dill, finely chopped

Put the potatoes in a saucepan and cover with cold water. Cook on a high heat and as soon as the water boils, turn the heat off and cover the pan with a tight-fitting lid. Set aside for 20 minutes so the potatoes are cooked through but still firm.

Drain the potatoes, cut into large bite-sized pieces and put into a large bowl. While they are still warm, quickly whisk the olive oil, red wine vinegar and mustard in a small bowl until well combined. Add this and all the other ingredients to the bowl along with the potatos as well as some sea salt and freshly ground black pepper. Use your hands to toss the potatoes around so each one is well coated in the herby sauce. Cover and set aside for an hour or so, stirring often, for the flavours to develop.

CHARGRILLED PANEER AND SPINACH SALAD

What you're after here is the salad all ready to go in a bowl. To this you are going to toss through warm, golden, just-cooked cubes of paneer and a simple dressing. The warm paneer will soften the spinach and entice the flavours from the dressing.

SERVES 4

200 g (7 oz) baby English
    spinach leaves
200 g (7 oz) small teardrop
    tomatoes, halved
2 spring onions (scallions), thinly
    sliced on an angle
½ cup roughly chopped coriander
    (cilantro) leaves
200 g (7 oz) block paneer
    (Indian cottage cheese)
2 tablespoons olive oil, plus
    extra for drizzling
1 teaspoon ground cumin
2 tablespoons lemon juice

Preheat the barbecue grill or hotplate to high.

Combine the spinach, tomatoes, spring onions and coriander in a large bowl and set aside.

Pat the paneer dry with paper towels and cut into 2 cm (¾ in) cubes. Place in a bowl, drizzle with a little olive oil and toss to coat. Put the paneer cubes on the grill or hotplate and cook for about 8 minutes, turning often so that each side is golden.

Add the warm cheese to the spinach mixture, along with the cumin, olive oil and lemon juice. Season to taste with sea salt and freshly ground black pepper and toss to combine

Serve the salad while the cheese is still warm.

SUGAR PUMPKIN WITH LENTILS
AND TANGY DRESSING

This will not be the first, or the last, time I have used the following technique to make a dressing or a sauce. Gently heating aromatics in some oil teases out the flavours and infuses these through the oil. And don't be afraid of lentils — they are tender, tasty and good for you.

SERVES 4

55 g (2 oz/¼ cup) puy lentils
    or tiny blue-green lentils
1 sugar or butternut pumpkin (squash),
    about 2 kg (4 lb 8 oz)
1 tablespoon rice bran oil
1 red onion, finely sliced
1 cup small mint leaves
1 cup flat-leaf (Italian) parsley leaves

TANGY DRESSING
60 ml (2 fl oz/¼ cup) light olive oil
1 large red chilli, finely sliced
4 garlic cloves, finely sliced
60 ml (2 fl oz/¼ cup) white
    wine vinegar
2 tablespoons sugar
½ teaspoon sea salt

To make the dressing, put the olive oil, chilli and garlic in a small saucepan over medium heat. When the chilli and garlic start to sizzle, cook for just 1–2 minutes longer, then remove from the heat. Stir in the vinegar, sugar and salt and mix until dissolved. Pour into a jar or bowl and set aside to infuse.

Put the lentils in a small saucepan and pour in enough water to cover. Bring to the boil, then reduce the heat and simmer until the lentils are tender but not mushy – this may take as little as 5 minutes, or up to 20 minutes, depending on the age of your lentils, so check them regularly. Drain well and set aside.

Preheat the barbecue grill to medium.

Cut the pumpkin in half, then scoop out and discard the seeds. Leaving the skin on, cut the pumpkin into wedges no thicker than 2 cm (¾ in). Brush the flesh with the rice bran oil and cook on the grill for 10 minutes on each side, or until golden and cooked through, checking regularly to ensure it doesn't burn too much.

Put the hot pumpkin in a large bowl with the onion, herbs and lentils. Stir the dressing, then pour it over the pumpkin.

Toss gently to combine. Serve warm.

MIGAS AND TOMATO SALAD

I'll interpret this in a very broad sense: migas is a dish using leftover bread in Spanish, Portuguese and Mexican cooking. The bread can be soaked in a mixture of milk and water and it is then deep-fried. The traditional way is a tasty technique but impossible to replicate when cooking outside on a barbecue. Here, cooking the soaked bread on a hotplate is a convenient alternative, if not a bit healthier.

SERVES 4

60 ml (2 fl oz/¼ cup) milk
4 slices ciabatta bread
olive oil, for drizzling
3 tomatoes, roughly chopped
2 tablespoons red wine vinegar
1 small garlic clove, crushed
½ cup roughly chopped flat-leaf
  (Italian) parsley

Preheat the barbecue hotplate to high.

Combine the milk and 60 ml (2 fl oz/¼ cup) water in a bowl. Soak each slice of bread in this mixture for 1 minute.

Remove the bread from the milk mixture and gently squeeze out as much liquid as possible.

Drizzle the hotplate generously with olive oil and cook the bread for a couple of minutes on each side, until golden and crispy around the edges.

Remove the bread from the hotplate and allow to cool. When cool enough to handle, roughly tear the bread and place in a bowl with the tomatoes, vinegar, garlic and parsley. Season well with salt and freshly ground black pepper and gently toss to combine. Serve warm.

CLASSIC **COLESLAW**

This is a popular recipe (but a bit like apple pie in that everyone knows someone who makes the best version). For a good coleslaw, you want it to be both creamy and crunchy without too much of an overbearing flavour so it can be eaten with just about all barbecued meats.

SERVES 4

½ head red cabbage, finely shredded
½ head green cabbage,
    finely shredded
2 teaspoons fine sea salt
1 carrot, grated
1 small red onion, very finely sliced
250 g (9 oz/1 cup) whole-egg
    mayonnaise
1 teaspoon mustard powder
125 g (4½ oz/½ cup) thick
    (double/heavy) cream
1 tablespoon prepared horseradish

Put the cabbage in a colander and toss with the sea salt. Set aside for 30 minutes then rinse with cold water. Strain the cabbage thoroughly then use your hands to squeeze out as much liquid as possible and you will hear the cabbage crushing as you do. This will help to soften the texture of the cabbage. Put the cabbage in a bowl with the carrot and onion and toss to combine.

Combine the mayonnaise, mustard, cream and horseradish in a bowl and pour over the cabbage mixture. Use tongs or your hands to combine the ingredients well.

Serve as soon as possible.

SICILIAN GRILLED VEGETABLE SALAD

I'm using eggplant and cauliflower here, but you could also use zucchini (courgette), broccolini and capsicum (pepper). Any vegie will do, really, so long as you add the dressing to the just-cooked vegetables, letting them soak up all the tasty bits – kind of like a reverse marinade.

SERVES 4–6

2 medium-sized eggplant
    (aubergines)
1 small cauliflower
1 tablespoon light olive oil

SICILIAN DRESSING
125 ml (4 fl oz/½ cup) olive oil
2 tablespoons red wine vinegar
2 garlic cloves, crushed
1 cup roughly chopped mint
1 cup roughly chopped flat-leaf
    (Italian) parsley leaves
1 cup basil leaves, torn
2 tablespoons small salted capers,
    rinsed and drained
¼ teaspoon sugar
45 g (1 oz/¼ cup) raisins

For the Sicilian dressing, combine all the dressing ingredients in a large bowl and set aside.

Preheat the barbecue grill to medium.

Slice the eggplant into 1 cm (½ in) rounds, and cut the cauliflower into bite-sized florets. Put them in a bowl with the olive oil, season well with sea salt and freshly ground black pepper and toss to coat.

Tumble the eggplant and cauliflower over the grill and spread them out so they don't overlap. Cook for 8–10 minutes, then turn them over and cook for another 5 minutes, or until just tender.

Put the hot vegetables in a large bowl, pour the dressing over and toss to combine. Cover with plastic wrap and set aside at room temperature for at least 30 minutes or up to 1 hour, allowing all the flavours to infuse.

Toss together, season to taste and serve.

ON THE SIDE

POTATOES IN FOIL WITH
HERBED LABNEH

GRILLED CORN WITH JALAPEÑO,
LIME AND PARMESAN BUTTER

INDIAN SPICED **EGGPLANT**

GRILLED SUMMER **VEGETABLES**

SWEET POTATOES IN JACKETS
WITH CREAMY FETA

SWEET AND SOUR **PUMPKIN**

BOLD **POTATOES**

GRILLED EGGPLANT
WITH CHIPOTLE LABNEH

BRUSSELS SPROUTS WITH BACON

CRUNCHY ROASTED POTATOES
WITH ROSEMARY

CHARGRILLED FENNEL
WITH CHILLI AND HERBS

MISO BROWN RICE
IN LOTUS LEAVES

HOTPLATE **WEDGES**

CUBAN **BARBECUED CORN**

SPICED **PARSNIPS**

LETTUCE WEDGES WITH
BLUE CHEESE DRESSING

RUM AND MAPLE MASHED
SWEET POTATO

SOY AND GINGER **GRILLED
MUSHROOMS**

GRILLED MOZZARELLA WITH TOMATO,
HONEY AND CINNAMON JAM

BARBECUED CORN WITH HOT SALSA

POTATOES IN THEIR JACKETS WITH
SOUR CREAM AND CHIVES

GARLICKY **MASH**

BALINESE GRILLED EGGPLANT
WITH TOMATO SAMBAL

BAKED BEETROOT WITH
HORSERADISH CRÈME

POTATOES IN FOIL
WITH HERBED LABNEH

**Go and get some labneh and try it, please. And use it in all kinds of dishes, as
a substitute for all sorts of other things. Try it in dips instead of sour cream.
Use it as you would hummus – or yoghurt, which is what it is anyway. You can
even use labneh to replace ricotta or cream cheese in sweets such as cheesecake.**

SERVES 4

4 large potatoes, skin on, washed

HERBED LABNEH
125 g (4½ oz/½ cup) labneh (strained
    yoghurt cheese)
1 tablespoon finely snipped chives
1 tablespoon finely chopped flat-leaf
    (Italian) parsley
1 tablespoon finely chopped mint

For the herbed labneh, combine the ingredients in a bowl and
mix together well. Cover and set aside at room temperature,
or refrigerate until needed.

Preheat the barbecue hotplate to medium.

Wrap each potato in foil. Sit them on the hotplate, then
close the barbecue lid, or cover the potatoes with a large
stainless steel bowl or baking tray. Cook for 1 hour, turning
often, until the potatoes are tender. You can check if the
potatoes are cooked without unwrapping them by pressing
on them with tongs or a spatula – when cooked, the potatoes
will feel soft.

Remove the potatoes from the hotplate and leave them in
their foil wrapping for 10–15 minutes. (You can leave them on
the barbecue lid to keep warm.)

Unwrap the potatoes, then press down on them with a
spatula to flatten and split the skin.

Spoon the herbed labneh over the hot potatoes and serve.

GRILLED CORN WITH JALAPEÑO, LIME AND PARMESAN BUTTER

It might sound odd, but the parmesan really does work a treat with the bite and tang of the other ingredients. It actually complements them. Because there are so few ingredients here, quality is the key: good butter, good cheese.

SERVES 4

4 corn cobs, each cut into
    3 smaller rounds
coriander (cilantro) sprigs, to garnish
lime cheeks, to serve

JALAPEÑO, LIME AND
PARMESAN BUTTER

125 g (4½ oz) unsalted butter,
    softened to room temperature
2 tablespoons pickled jalapeño
    chillies, well drained and chopped
1 tablespoon lime juice
25 g (1 oz/¼ cup) finely grated
    parmesan cheese

For the jalapeño butter, put all the ingredients in a food processor and whiz until smooth. Scrape into a bowl, then cover and refrigerate until needed.

Preheat the barbecue grill to high. Cut the jalapeño, lime and parmesan butter into small pieces and leave at room temperature.

Cook the corn on the hotplate for 10–12 minutes, turning often, until the kernels are dark and caramelised.

Using metal tongs, place the hot corn cobs in a bowl, add the butter and toss the corn around so it melts the butter.

Tumble the corn cobs onto a serving plate and pour over any melted butter remaining in the bowl. Garnish with coriander and serve with lime cheeks.

NOTE You can make the jalapeño, lime and parmesan butter up to a week ahead, or wrap it thoroughly and freeze for up to 1 month.

INDIAN SPICED **EGGPLANT**

Take note of this method of adding seasoning and flavour to just-cooked eggplant. The heat of the eggplant releases the fragrant oil in the spices. Eggplant is a highly absorbent vegie – you'll notice how much oil it sucks up when being fried.

SERVES 4–6

2 medium-sized eggplant (aubergines)
2 tablespoons rice bran oil
3 teaspoons sea salt
2 tablespoons olive oil
1 garlic clove, crushed
1 teaspoon ground cumin
½ teaspoon chilli powder
1 cup mint leaves, roughly torn
125 g (4½ oz/½ cup) labneh (strained yoghurt cheese)

Preheat the barbecue grill to medium.

Cut the eggplant lengthways into large wedges. Place in a bowl with the rice bran oil and salt and toss to coat. Tumble the eggplant onto the grill and then cook for 12–15 minutes, using tongs to spread the wedges out and to turn them often, until golden and just tender. Transfer to a bowl.

Combine the olive oil, garlic, cumin and chilli powder in a small bowl. Pour the dressing over the eggplant while it is still hot, then gently toss to coat in the spice mixture. Pile the eggplant onto a serving platter. Serve warm, scattered with the mint, with the labneh on the side.

GRILLED SUMMER **VEGETABLES**

This can be served warm, straight off the hotplate, or it can be one of those things for the super organised that can be made an hour or two before the barbecue has officially started. And it seems to benefit from this anyway, letting all the flavours come together. Add some fresh mint and crumble feta for a point of difference.

SERVES 4

2 red capsicums (peppers)
2 fennel bulbs, thinly
    sliced lengthways
2 tablespoons olive oil
1 eggplant (aubergine), cut into
    thin rounds
1 large zucchini (courgette),
    thinly sliced lengthways
3 tablespoons light olive oil
1 handful flat-leaf (Italian)
    parsley, chopped
1 handful mint, chopped

Preheat the barbecue grill to high. Put the capsicums directly on the grill and cook until the skin is puffed up and starting to blacken. Put into a clean plastic bag and allow to cool.

Meanwhile, brush the fennel with a little olive oil. Put the fennel on the grill and cook for 4–5 minutes on each side, until softened and striped with grill marks. Put into a large bowl. Brush the eggplant rounds with a little oil and cook for 3–4 minutes on each side. Place in the bowl with the fennel. Finally, brush the zucchini with oil and cook for 2–3 minutes on each side and add to the bowl with the other ingredients.

Peel and discard the skin of the capsicums. Pull out and discard the seeds. Roughly tear the flesh into strips and toss with the other vegetables. Season to taste with sea salt and freshly ground black pepper.

SWEET POTATOES IN JACKETS WITH CREAMY FETA

Sweet potato, like potato, cooks up really well on the barbecue, wrapped in foil and cooked until fluffy and soft on the inside, with the skin a little chewy and sweet.

SERVES 4

1 large sweet potato, peeled
80 ml (2½ fl oz/⅓ cup) olive oil
1 teaspoon sea salt

FETA AND DILL CREAM
100 g (3½ oz/1½ cups) soft feta
    cheese, crumbled
1 garlic clove, crushed
3 tablespoons chopped dill
2 tablespoons olive oil
2 tablespoons milk

For the feta and dill cream, put the feta, garlic, dill and olive oil in a food processor and whiz to a thick paste. With the motor running, slowly add the milk, blending until thick and creamy. Set aside.

Cut the pointy ends off the sweet potato, then cut it into four portions about the same size.

Preheat the barbecue hotplate to medium.

Tear off four sheets of foil, large enough to completely wrap each piece of sweet potato. Sit a piece of sweet potato in the centre of each piece of foil. Pour 1 tablespoon of the olive oil over each and sprinkle with the salt. Loosely wrap each portion in the foil and place them on the hotplate.

Close the barbecue lid, or cover the parcels with a baking tray. Cook for 45 minutes, turning often, until the sweet potato is very tender.

Unwrap the sweet potato parcels and spoon the feta and dill cream over while still hot.

SWEET AND SOUR **PUMPKIN**

Sweet and sour is not a flavour combination unique only to Chinese cooking. The Sicilians are masters too, albeit in a much more subtle way. The combination of sugar and vinegar is common in southern Italian cooking.

SERVES 6

1 small jap or kent pumpkin
   (winter squash)
2 tablespoons rice bran oil

DRESSING
80 ml (2½ fl oz/⅓ cup) red wine
   vinegar
60 ml (2 fl oz/¼ cup) olive oil
2 garlic cloves, finely chopped
¼ teaspoon chilli flakes
2 teaspoons soft brown sugar
1 cup mint leaves, roughly chopped
40 g (1½ oz/¼ cup) currants

Cut the pumpkin in half using a large knife. Scoop out the seeds with a large metal spoon and discard. Lay the cut side of the pumpkin flat on a chopping board. Cut the pumpkin into thick wedges, following the natural indentations.

Place the pumpkin in a bowl with the rice bran oil, season well with sea salt and freshly ground black pepper to taste and then toss to coat.

Combine the dressing ingredients in a bowl, mix well to dissolve the sugar, then set aside.

Preheat the barbecue hotplate to medium.

Lay the pumpkin wedges on the hotplate, cut side down, and cook for 10 minutes. Turn the pumpkin over and cook for another 5–10 minutes, until just tender – you want the pumpkin pieces to retain some firmness so they don't break up too much.

Place the hot pumpkin in a large bowl. Pour the dressing over, toss to combine, then season to taste.

Serve warm, or at room temperature.

BOLD **POTATOES**

Those who know even a little Spanish will probably recognise this as patatas bravas, a much bastardised dish. Potatoes are not supposed to be eaten cold and wrinkled. Cold is fine, but not wrinkled too, which is how this dish is done by the lazy chef — even though it is actually less effort to make these splendid potatoes live up to their name. These are very good enjoyed with a glass of rosé or some Spanish beer.

SERVES 4

4 large boiling potatoes,
    such as desiree, scrubbed
    but not peeled
60 ml (2 fl oz/¼ cup) olive oil
1 teaspoon sea salt
1 cup roughly chopped flat-leaf
    (Italian) parsley

SAUCE

250 ml (9 fl oz/1 cup) tomato
    passata (puréed tomatoes)
85 g (3 oz/⅓ cup) good-quality
    mayonnaise
2 garlic cloves, crushed
2 tablespoons white wine vinegar
1 teaspoon smoked paprika
1 teaspoon ground cumin
1 teaspoon chilli flakes

Combine the sauce ingredients in a bowl. Season to taste with sea salt and freshly ground black pepper. Cover and set aside for the flavours to develop while cooking the potatoes.

Preheat the barbecue hotplate to medium.

Cut the potatoes into slices no thicker than 5 mm (¼ in). Place in a bowl, add 1 tablespoon of the olive oil and the salt, then toss around to evenly coat the slices in the oil.

Tumble the potatoes over the hotplate and use tongs to spread the slices out so they don't overlap. Close the lid, if your barbecue has one, and cook for 10 minutes, or until golden. (If your barbecue doesn't have a lid, just cook the potatoes a little longer at a slightly lower temperature.)

Turn the potato slices over, close the lid and cook for another 5–6 minutes, or until golden and tender.

Spread the sauce down the middle of a long serving plate. Tumble the potatoes over, scatter with the parsley and drizzle with the remaining olive oil. Serve hot.

GRILLED EGGPLANT
WITH CHIPOTLE LABNEH

Labneh is a slightly tangy soft cheese made from salted and strained yoghurt, widely enjoyed for breakfast in the Middle East. As it has increased in popularity it is much easier to get your hands on these days. Try it once and you will appreciate its deliciousness! If you can't find labneh, don't despair: it is very easy to make yourself. For every cup of natural yoghurt, stir through 1 teaspoon salt. Spoon it into some clean cloth, such as muslin (cheesecloth), and firmly tie to enclose the yoghurt in the cloth. Suspend it over a bowl so the water drips out, then refrigerate overnight. The next day, have a look in the cloth and you will see labneh.

SERVES 4–6

2 small eggplant (aubergines),
    no more than 15 cm (6 in) long
2 tablespoons rice bran oil
1 garlic clove, crushed
2 tablespoons lemon juice
3 tablespoons roughly chopped
    mint leaves
3 tablespoons roughly chopped
    flat-leaf (Italian) parsley
extra virgin olive oil, for drizzling

CHIPOTLE LABNEH
2 whole smoked chipotle chillies in
    adobo sauce, plus 1 tablespoon
    of the sauce (see Note)
300 g (10½ oz) labneh (strained
    yoghurt cheese)

For the chipotle labneh, put the ingredients in a food processor and whiz until just combined, leaving some flecks of chilli and then set aside.

Preheat the barbecue grill to high.

Cut the eggplant lengthways down the middle, then cut each piece crossways in half. Place in a bowl, drizzle with the rice bran oil and toss to coat the eggplant.

Tumble the eggplant over the grill, using tongs to spread the pieces out so they don't overlap. Cook, turning often, for 10–15 minutes, or until golden all over.

Place the eggplant in a bowl. Add the garlic, lemon juice and herbs and toss together while the eggplant is still hot.

Tumble the eggplant onto a serving plate. Drizzle with olive oil and serve with thick dollops of the chipotle labneh.

NOTE Chipotle chillies are often packed in adobo – a spicy red chilli sauce. You'll find them packed in tins and jars in spice shops and good food stores.

BRUSSELS SPROUTS WITH BACON

I'm loving brussels sprouts – a super tasty and healthy side dish with barbecued meat, chicken or fish. Cook them old-school style (boiled) and combine with a garlicky bacon oil. Yum.

SERVES 4

12 brussels sprouts, halved
1 tablespoon olive oil
60 g (2¼ oz) butter
2 rashers bacon, thinly sliced
2 cloves garlic, crushed

Bring a saucepan of lightly salted water to the boil. Add the sprouts and cook for 5 minutes. Drain well.

Heat the oil and butter in a large frying pan over high heat. When the butter is sizzling, add the bacon and then cook for 4–5 minutes, or until crisp. Stir in the garlic and cook for a further 1 minute, or until aromatic. Add the sprouts and stir for a further 2–3 minutes, or until heated through and evenly coated in the garlicky oil and bacon. Season with sea salt and freshly ground black pepper.

CRUNCHY ROASTED POTATOES
WITH ROSEMARY

Simple trick here. Get your oven nice and hot before putting the potatoes in. You can't go wrong. We all love potatoes at a barbecue – think potato salad and potatoes wrapped in foil. These crispy potatoes are a winner.

SERVES 4

6 medium desiree potatoes, peeled
60 ml (2 fl oz/¼ cup) extra
   virgin olive oil
2 sprigs rosemary
½ teaspoon sea salt

Preheat the oven to 220°C (425°F/Gas 7) and place the oven shelf in the middle.

Cut the potatoes in half and place in a large bowl with the oil, rosemary and sea salt. Toss to combine.

Place the potatoes, flat side down, in a single layer in a roasting pan, cover with foil and then bake for 20 minutes. Remove the foil and cook for another 15–20 minutes.

Using a metal spatula, turn the potatoes over. Roast for another 15 minutes or until potatoes are very golden and crisp.

CHARGRILLED FENNEL WITH CHILLI AND HERBS

Fennel in all its forms is delicious. The feathery tops add flavour to dressings and mayonnaise. The beefy bulbs can be cooked in all sorts of ways — in pasta sauces, risotto, minestrone, and roasted with pork or chicken. Fennel seeds are a staple in my cupboard, ready to be used in Indian- and Italian-inspired recipes.

SERVES 4

4 medium-sized fennel bulbs, preferably with fronds
2 garlic cloves, chopped
3 tablespoons olive oil
2 tablespoons red wine vinegar
2 teaspoons dijon mustard
½ teaspoon sea salt
chilli flakes, to taste
1 cup flat-leaf (Italian) parsley leaves, finely chopped
1 cup mint leaves, finely chopped

If the fennel has feathery fronds, cut these off and roughly chop up enough to give a small handful. Set aside.

Slice the fennel lengthways into slices 5 mm (¼ in) thick. Place in a bowl along with the garlic and 1 tablespoon of the olive oil.

Set aside at room temperature for 30 minutes to infuse.

In a large bowl, combine the remaining olive oil with the remaining ingredients to make a herb dressing.

Preheat the barbecue grill to high.

Tumble half the fennel over the grill and spread the slices out so they don't overlap. Cook for 4–5 minutes on each side, until the fennel is golden and charred and the garlic is golden and aromatic. Add the hot fennel to the herb dressing and toss to coat.

Cook the remaining fennel in the same manner and toss it through the dressing. Serve warm or at room temperature, sprinkled with any reserved fennel fronds.

MISO BROWN RICE
IN LOTUS LEAVES

What started as a small plate option turned very quickly into a big one: it was so tasty I couldn't stop eating it! I then realised how full I was afterwards – another good sign, given all the good-for-you things in this dish.

SERVES 4

2 large dried lotus leaves (available from Asian grocers)
1 tablespoon white miso paste
2 tablespoons light soy sauce
1 teaspoon sesame oil
½ teaspoon sea salt
½ teaspoon sugar
2 tablespoons rice bran oil
2 garlic cloves, finely chopped
1 tablespoon finely grated fresh ginger
2 spring onions (scallions), finely chopped
75 g (2½ oz/1 cup) finely shredded Chinese cabbage
75 g (2½ oz/1 cup) finely shredded bok choy (pak choy) or choy sum
200 g (7 oz/1 cup) long-grain brown rice, cooked until tender, then drained

Dried lotus leaves are usually folded in half; don't unfold them or they will break. Lay them in the kitchen sink and pour over enough boiling water to cover. Leave for 1 hour, so they become tender and turn the colour of fresh grape vine leaves. Remove the leaves from the water. Unfold the leaves and cut in half, removing any stem. Trim each half into 30 cm (12 in) squares and set aside.

Combine the miso, soy sauce, sesame oil, salt and sugar in a jug. Pour in 125 ml (4 fl oz/½ cup) boiling water and stir well to make sure all the miso has dissolved.

Heat the rice bran oil in a frying pan or wok over high heat. Add the garlic, ginger and spring onions and stir-fry for a few seconds, or until aromatic but not burning. Add the cabbage and bok choy and stir-fry for 5 minutes, or until well wilted.

Add the rice and the miso mixture. Stir to combine, then bring to the boil. Reduce the heat to medium and cook for 5 minutes, or until almost all the liquid has been absorbed.

Lay the four lotus leaf squares on a work surface. Spoon one-quarter of the rice mixture into the centre of each. Roll the leaves up to make firm parcels.

Preheat the barbecue hotplate to medium. Sit the parcels on the hotplate, seam side down, and cook for 10 minutes, until the seam side looks dry and blistered. Turn them over and cook for another 5 minutes. Serve warm.

HOTPLATE **WEDGES**

We all love hot potato chips. Don't be tempted to constantly turn these on the hotplate. Just let them rest and sizzle letting them do their thing and get a golden skin. You can put cooked wedges in a metal mixing bowl and sit this on another part of the barbecue to keep warm while cooking your beast, bird or fish to serve them with. If you haven't already, as a simple shared snack with beer, try these dunked into a mixture of sour cream and sweet chilli sauce.

SERVES 4

6 potatoes, such as desiree
2 tablespoons light olive oil
1 tablespoon celery salt, plus extra,
    to serve

Peel the potatoes and cut each into 6–8 wedges. Put the potatoes in a saucepan of boiling water, cover the pan with a lid and turn off the heat. Allow the potatoes to sit in the water for 10 minutes. Drain well and put the potatoes on a clean tea towel (dish towel) to dry and cool.

Preheat the barbecue hotplate to high.

Put the potatoes in a bowl with 1 tablespoon of oil and the celery salt and toss to coat the wedges in the oil. Drizzle the remaining oil over the hotplate. Cook on the barbecue for 5–6 minutes, without turning or moving, until they look dark golden. Turn over and cook for another 3–4 minutes. Add the extra celery salt or spice mix and sea salt to taste.

CUBAN **BARBECUED CORN**

We all have one of these stories. I was taken to a very cool little diner in New York that specialises in Cuban barbecues and grills. The house speciality was corn on the cob, simply grilled. Just an ear of corn barbecued until dark golden and caramelised, the kernels about to burst out of their skins, then sprinkled with a Mexican cheese and some lime juice squeezed over. The cheese mostly used is cotija, or 'parmesan of Mexico'. This cheese is hard to find out of North America, so you could use a manchega, available from a good deli, and if you can't find that a good quality parmesan will do. By the way, this cheese is really good on pasta. Aye carumba!

SERVES 4

4 really fresh corn cobs
2 tablespoons softened butter
2 tablespoons whole-egg mayonnaise
50 g (1¾ oz) finely grated
    manchega cheese
2 limes, halved

Preheat the barbecue grill to high.

Put the corn on the grill and cook for about 12–15 minutes, turning often so they cook really dark golden – almost like a coffee colour around the edges. In the 1–2 minutes of cooking, brush each cob evenly all over with the butter.

Put on a serving plate. Spread some mayonnaise on each cob, sprinkle over the cheese and squeeze over the lime, to taste.

SPICED **PARSNIPS**

Barbecue parsnips in winter, when they are abundant and well priced. This vegie needs to be parboiled beforehand, otherwise it will burn before it is cooked through.

SERVES 4–6

3 tablespoons light olive oil
1 teaspoon ground turmeric
1 teaspoon fennel seeds
1 teaspoon cumin seeds
¼ teaspoon chilli powder
1 teaspoon sea salt
1 kg (2 lb 4 oz) medium-sized parsnips
3 tablespoons torn mint leaves
lemon wedges, to serve

In a large bowl, combine the olive oil, turmeric, fennel seeds, cumin seeds, chilli powder and salt.

Bring a saucepan of water to the boil. Peel the parsnips and cut in half lengthways, then add them to the boiling water and cook for 4–5 minutes, or until just starting to soften. Drain well.

Tip the warm parsnips into the bowl with the spiced oil and toss to coat. Cover and set aside at room temperature for 1 hour.

Preheat the barbecue hotplate to high.

Keeping the bowl near the barbecue, lift the parsnips out, letting the excess spiced oil drip back into the bowl, and reserving the spiced oil. Tumble the parsnips over the hotplate and spread them out so they don't overlap.

Cook the parsnips for 5 minutes on each side, or until tender and slightly charred. Drizzle the reserved spiced oil over the parsnips and cook for just a few more seconds.

Transfer to a serving plate and season with sea salt and freshly ground black pepper to taste. Scatter with the mint.

Serve warm, with lemon wedges.

LETTUCE WEDGES WITH BLUE CHEESE DRESSING

This is so easy and so tasty. Don't get all worked up about what salad to serve at your next barbecue. Just do this one.

SERVES 4

75 g (2½ oz/½ cup) crumbled
   blue cheese
60 ml (2 fl oz/¼ cup) buttermilk
60 g (2¼ fl oz/¼ cup) light sour cream
2 tablespoons good-quality
   mayonnaise
1 teaspoon white wine vinegar
½ iceberg lettuce

Place the cheese and buttermilk in a small bowl and mash with a fork until well combined but still a little lumpy. Stir in the sour cream, mayonnaise and vinegar.

To serve, cut the lettuce into four thick wedges, place on a platter and spoon the dressing over the top.

RUM AND MAPLE MASHED
SWEET POTATO

The good news is sweet potato and maple syrup are superfoods. The bad news? Rum is not. But two out of three isn't bad. This is a decadent mash to add to your barbecue feast.

SERVES 4

1 large sweet potato, peeled
125 ml (4 fl oz/½ cup) pouring
    (whipping) cream
80 g (23/4 oz) unsalted butter
½ teaspoon sea salt
¼ teaspoon freshly ground
    black pepper
2 tablespoons maple syrup
2 tablespoons dark rum

Cut the sweet potato into 3–4 cm (1¼ in–1½ in) pieces and place in a saucepan with the cream, butter, sea salt and freshly ground black pepper. Partially cover the pan and cook over low heat for 30–35 minutes, or until the sweet potatoes are very soft and falling apart.

Remove from the heat and mash until smooth. Stir through the maple syrup and rum.

SOY AND GINGER
GRILLED MUSHROOMS

Try not to use really tiny mushrooms here — or for any barbecue cooking, for that matter. Little ones are a pain to barbecue. Big, steaky mushies, on the other hand, are easy to cook, have more flesh and are tastier.

SERVES 4

250 ml (9 fl oz/1 cup) red wine
250 ml (9 fl oz/1 cup) light soy sauce
2 tablespoons rice flour
1 tablespoon sesame oil
1 tablespoon finely grated fresh ginger
6 large shiitake mushrooms
6 large Swiss brown mushrooms
6 king oyster mushrooms,
    halved lengthways
100 g (3½ oz) oyster mushrooms
sliced spring onions (scallions),
    to serve

Combine the wine, soy sauce, rice flour, sesame oil and ginger in a large bowl. Add the shiitake and Swiss brown mushrooms and toss to coat them in the marinade. Cover and set aside at room temperature for 3 hours, or refrigerate for 6 hours.

Preheat the barbecue hotplate to high. Pour rice bran oil over the hotplate to grease it.

Remove the mushrooms from the marinade and tumble them onto the hotplate. Cook for 10–15 minutes, turning them often, until dark, tender and aromatic. Add the oyster mushrooms and cook, turning, for 1–2 minutes, or until just tender. Serve hot, scattered with the spring onions.

GRILLED MOZZARELLA
WITH TOMATO, HONEY AND CINNAMON JAM

Imagine this... I go to an Italian restaurant in the middle of nowhere, run by women from Rome. A starter dish of simply grilled smoked mozzarella (but, just quietly, the cheese works just as well unsmoked) appears. It is utterly delicious. This is my version, barbecue style.

SERVES 4

500 g (1 lb 2 oz) smoked mozzarella
　　(see Note)
rice bran oil, for brushing
finely chopped parsley, to serve

TOMATO, HONEY AND CINNAMON JAM
1 tablespoon rice bran oil
1 small red onion, cut in half
　　lengthways, then cut into
　　thin wedges
1 tablespoon caster (superfine) sugar
400 g (14 oz) tin chopped tomatoes
½ teaspoon ground cinnamon
2 tablespoons honey

Cut the mozzarella into eight slices, about 1 cm (½ in) thick. Keep the cheese cold in the fridge until ready to cook.

To make the jam, heat the oil in a small saucepan over high heat. Add the onion and cook for 2–3 minutes, or until softened and starting to turn golden. Add the sugar and stir for a minute or so. The sugar will crystallise and the onion will deepen in colour.

Carefully add the tomatoes – they will bubble on contact with the hot sugar. Stir in the cinnamon, reduce the heat to medium and simmer for 5 minutes, stirring often, until the tomatoes deepen in colour. Stir in the honey and cook for a further 10 minutes, stirring often so the mixture doesn't stick to the pan.

Preheat the barbecue grill or hotplate to high and lightly brush with oil. Lay the mozzarella slices on the hotplate and cook for 1 minute, or until the edges just start to melt. Quickly turn slices over and cook for another minute. Serve hot, with a good dollop of jam and a sprinkling of parsley.

NOTE Choose the firmest brand of mozzarella available. Fresh mozzarella cannot be cooked this way. You can also serve each slice of mozzarella on a radicchio leaf and sprinkle the dolloped jam with sesame seeds.

BARBECUED CORN
WITH HOT SALSA

Corn has to be one of the best things to grill. The salsa makes sense, but you may be wondering, why the parmesan? Well, basically parmesan is amazing. It has a savoury-ness that Japanese call unami, which both enhances and complements other flavours.

SERVES 4

4 fresh corn cobs
60 ml (2 fl oz/¼ cup) butter, melted
35 g (1¼ oz/¼ cup) finely grated
   parmesan cheese

SALSA
2 tablespoons olive oil
1 tablespoon lime juice
3 tablespoons finely diced
   roasted piquillo peppers
   or red capsicum (pepper)
3 tablespoons chopped jalapeño
   chillies, in brine, drained
½ cup roughly chopped coriander
   (cilantro) leaves and stalks
2 spring onions (scallions),
   thinly sliced

For the salsa, combine all the ingredients in a large bowl and set aside.

Preheat the barbecue hotplate to high.

Brush the corn with some of the melted butter, sit them on the hotplate and cook for 8–10 minutes, turning and brushing with more melted butter every couple of minutes, until the corn is starting to char around the edges.

Transfer the corn to a plate. Season well with salt and freshly ground black pepper and sprinkle with the parmesan.

Serve warm, with the salsa on the side.

POTATOES IN THEIR JACKETS
WITH SOUR CREAM AND CHIVES

This is true to the occasion that is the barbecue. I have memories, far distant ones when fireworks were still legal, of bonfires and barbecues. Potatoes were wrapped in cooking foil, thrown into the fire and forgotten. Cooked to perfection with the addition of salt (lots of it) and sour cream.

SERVES 4

4 large desiree potatoes, about
    200 g (7 oz) each
60 g (2¼ oz/¼ cup) butter
125 g (4½ oz/½ cup) sour cream
2 tablespoons finely snipped chives

Put the potatoes in a large saucepan of boiling water. Cover and immediately turn off the heat. Leave the potatoes in the water for 20 minutes then drain. Cut the potatoes through the centre, to about 2 cm (¾ in) from the bottom. Then make another similar cut to form a cross. Put 1 tablespoon of butter on top of each potato with a little sea salt sprinkled on top. Potatoes love salt. Wrap each potato in foil, so the cut and buttered end is facing up and make sure it is well sealed. Repeat so each potato has a double layer of foil.

Preheat the barbecue hotplate to medium and then sit a cooking rack (one from your oven is ideal) on the hotplate. Sit the potatoes on the rack, keeping the sealed side up. Cook for 1 hour. Towards the end of the cooking time you should hear the potatoes sizzling away inside their foil blankets. Remove and leave the potatoes in the foil for another 15–20 minutes before unwrapping.

Combine the sour cream and chives in a bowl. Unwrap the potatoes, and then fill with the sour cream and chives.

GARLICKY **MASH**

Don't underestimate a good mash. We all love it, meat eaters and veggos alike. Make your mash, using the very tasty bits like garlic, butter and salt and put the whole lot back into the warm pan from which it came. Cover tightly and leave while you barbecue the meat.

SERVES 4

125 g (4½ oz/½ cup) butter
3 cloves garlic, crushed
750 g (1 lb 10 oz) floury potatoes, such
    as kennebec, peeled and quartered
60 ml (2 fl oz/¼ cup) warm milk
1 teaspoon sea salt

Place the butter and garlic in a small saucepan and cook over medium heat until the butter has just melted. Set aside for the garlic to soften and flavour the butter.

Bring a saucepan of lightly salted water to the boil. Add the potatoes and cook for 15–20 minutes, or until tender and almost falling apart. Drain well, then return to the warm pan. Add the garlic butter, milk and sea salt. Mash until well combined but still a little chunky. Take a large wooden spoon and beat the mixture until it is smooth and creamy.

BALINESE **GRILLED EGGPLANT** WITH TOMATO SAMBAL

Sambal is to Bali and Indonesia what harissa is to Morocco. This is an unadulterated chilli sauce – hot, spicy and with a real kick. It is added to curries and used as a condiment in its own right with grilled meats.

SERVES 4

2 eggplant (aubergines)
lime wedges, to serve

TOMATO SAMBAL
4 ripe tomatoes
4 garlic cloves, unpeeled
2 red Asian shallots, unpeeled
1 vegetable stock (bouillon) cube,
    preferably gluten free, crumbled
1 small red chilli
¼ teaspoon ground white pepper
2 tablespoons soft brown sugar

Preheat the barbecue grill to high.

To make the sambal, sit the tomatoes, garlic and shallots on the grill and cook for 8–10 minutes, turning often and removing each vegetable from the grill when it is charred all over. Remove from the heat until cool enough to handle, then peel all the vegies and discard the skins.

Put the garlic flesh in a food processor with the tomatoes, shallots, stock cube, chilli, pepper and sugar. Whiz together until smooth, then pour the mixture into a small saucepan and simmer for 10 minutes, or until slightly thickened. Transfer to a bowl and allow to cool.

Preheat the barbecue grill to medium.

Cut each eggplant in half lengthways and make several shallow, criss-crossed incisions on the cut flesh side. Brush the cut side with oil. Place on the grill, cut side down, and cook for 8–10 minutes, or until golden and charred around the edges.

Turn the eggplant over and cook for another 5 minutes, or until it has collapsed and is soft.

Serve the eggplant warm, with some sambal spooned over, and lime wedges on the side.

BAKED BEETROOT WITH HORSERADISH CRÈME

Don't be scared of beetroot. Most of us like them, very much. Some of us don't. For those who do like them, consider this: they are cheap, they are great with barbecued food, they are easy to cook and this method pays respect to this fine vegetable. Enough said.

SERVES 4

4 large beetroot (beets), about
    170 g (6 oz) each
2 tablespoons prepared horseradish
1 tablespoon finely chopped tarragon,
    plus extra leaves, to serve
125 g (4½ fl oz/½ cup) light
    sour cream

Preheat the oven to 180°C (350°F/Gas 4).

Peel the beetroot. Firmly wrap each beetroot in two layers of foil, place on an oven tray and bake for 1 hour 15 minutes, or until very tender and a skewer withdraws easily. Allow to cool in the foil for 15 minutes.

Combine the horseradish, tarragon and sour cream in a bowl. Season to taste.

Cut a deep cross in the top of each beetroot, gently prying open to make a cavity for the horseradish crème. Spoon the crème into each warm beetroot, scatter with extra tarragon leaves and a grind of black pepper and serve immediately.

D'OUGH

REAL **GARLIC BREAD**

I say 'real' garlic bread because I am using real ingredients here. Let me explain. The few times that I fine-dined as a kid in the 1970s, I vaguely remember garlic bread being special. Now it is often something made with butter substitutes and garlic flakes. When made well, garlic bread is lovely. It is so easy to prepare ahead, ready to throw on the barbecue.

MAKES 1 LOAF

1 sourdough baguette, about
   25–30 cm (10–12 in) long

GARLIC BUTTER
6 organic garlic cloves, peeled
1 teaspoon sea salt
3 tablespoons flat-leaf (Italian)
   parsley, finely chopped
125 g (4½ oz) organic unsalted butter,
   at room temperature

To make the garlic butter, put the garlic on a chopping board and sprinkle with the salt. Use a large knife to chop the garlic. Every now and then, use the flat side of the knife to press down on the chopped garlic to crush it even more. Continue until you have a very finely chopped heap of garlic. Stir the garlic and parsley through the butter.

Preheat the barbecue hotplate to medium. Sit a baking rack on the hotplate.

Cut deep slices into the bread, 2–3 cm (¾–1¼ in) apart. Spread the garlic butter into the cuts, making sure the exposed bread is evenly covered with the butter.

Completely wrap bread in foil. Sit the bread on the baking rack, flat side down, and cook for 8–10 minutes. Serve hot.

DAMPER

This bread epitomises Australian bush cookery. Like many good things, it originated out of necessity, created by stockmen on long journeys, from the most basic of ingredients. However, there's still a bit of an art to making damper – a bit like making scones. It might take a few attempts to get the damper looking 'right', but it will always taste good.

MAKES 1 LOAF

300 g (10½ oz/2 cups) plain (all-purpose) flour, plus extra for dusting
3 teaspoons baking powder
1 teaspoon sea salt
125 ml (4 fl oz/½ cup) milk

Combine the flour, baking powder and salt in a bowl, then make a deep well in the centre.

In another bowl, combine milk and 125 ml (4 fl oz/½ cup) boiling water. Pour the mixture into the flour and use a fork to quickly combine for a few seconds. Now use one hand to mix the dough – it will be a wet dough, so you may need to add just a fine sprinkling of flour.

When the mixture no longer sticks to the side of the bowl, tip it out onto a lightly floured surface and knead for 1 minute, until smooth.

Using lightly oiled hands, form the dough into a log about 10 cm (4 in) wide and 15 cm (6 in) long.

Lay a large sheet of foil on a work surface and place a similar-sized sheet of baking paper on top. Lightly brush the baking paper with olive oil. Sit the dough at one long end of the baking paper. Loosely roll the paper up, then fold the ends over to loosely enclose the dough. Set aside for 30 minutes.

Preheat the barbecue grill to medium.

Sit the bread on the grill and then cook for 10 minutes. Turn it over and cook for another 10–13 minutes, or until the bread makes a hollow sound when tapped and is lightly golden all over.

Allow the damper to cool for a few minutes. Slice and serve while still warm.

BARBARI BREAD

This intriguing bread is the one most commonly eaten in Iran. Its distinctive elements are the parallel lines made in the dough prior to cooking, and the paste of flour, bicarbonate of soda and water that is brushed on top, creating a wonderfully crisp and dry bread. It is very nice with some feta cheese and olive oil.

MAKES 2 LOAVES

½ teaspoon sugar
2 teaspoons instant dried yeast
485 g (1 lb 1 oz/3¼ cups) plain
  (all-purpose) flour
1 teaspoon sea salt
1 teaspoon bicarbonate of soda
  (baking soda)
coarse polenta, for dusting
2 tablespoons sesame seeds

BARBARI TOPPING
½ teaspoon plain (all-purpose) flour
½ teaspoon bicarbonate of soda
  (baking soda)

Combine the sugar, the yeast and 60 ml (2 fl oz/¼ cup) warm water in a small bowl. Cover and then leave somewhere warmish and draught-free for 10–15 minutes, or until frothy and spongy-looking.

Mix the flour, salt and bicarbonate of soda together in a large bowl. Add the yeast mixture and 310 ml (10¾ fl oz/ 1¼ cups) warm water and bring together into a sticky dough. Tip onto a floured board and knead for 15 minutes, or until smooth and elastic, or knead in an electric mixer with a dough hook for 10–15 minutes.

Divide dough into two equal portions. Tear off two large sheets of baking paper, about 40 cm (16 in) long, and sprinkle with polenta. Place a piece of dough on each sheet, then shape each into a rectangle no more than 1 cm (½ in) thick. Cover loosely with a cloth and set aside for 1 hour.

Put the topping ingredients in a small saucepan with 80 ml (2½ fl oz/⅓ cup) water. Cook over medium heat for 1–2 minutes, or until the mixture is thick and cloudy. Then allow to cool.

Preheat the barbecue hotplate to high. Sit a baking rack on the hotplate and close the barbecue lid.

Brush the liquid topping over each loaf. Use your fingers to run parallel divots, about 2 cm (¾ in) apart, down the length of the dough. Sprinkle the sesame seeds over each loaf. Using the baking paper, lift one of the loaves onto a baking tray, then sit the tray on the baking rack. Close the barbecue lid, reduce the heat to medium and cook for 10–15 minutes, or until the base of the bread is dark golden and the top is golden and dry.

Cook the remaining loaf in the same manner. Serve hot.

GRILLED GREEN **OLIVE BREADS**

This is a yeast-free 'bread', and the basic recipe idea hails from northern China. Although, I must admit, the real inspiration comes from Barbara Tropp, a truly passionate and inspiring food writer. This recipe has the interesting technique of using hot and cold water to make the dough, combined with the spiral 'snail' shaping of the dough – resulting in a flaky, unleavened pastry.

MAKES 4

300 g (10½ oz/2 cups) plain (all-purpose) flour, plus extra for dusting
2 teaspoons baking powder
2 tablespoons rice bran oil

GREEN OLIVE PASTE
60 ml (2 fl oz/¼ cup) olive oil
1 teaspoon sea salt
50 g (1¾ oz/⅓ cup) pitted large Sicilian green olives
1 garlic clove
½ cup flat-leaf (Italian) parsley, chopped
¼ cup sliced spring onions (scallions)

For the olive paste, put the ingredients in a food processor and whiz until a smooth paste forms. Scrape into a bowl, then clean out the food processor bowl.

Put the flour and baking powder in the food processor and whiz to combine. With the motor running, add 80 ml (2½ fl oz/⅓ cup) boiling water, then 80 ml (2½ fl oz/⅓ cup) cold water. As soon as all the water has been added, turn the food processor off and scrape the dough out onto a floured surface.

Knead briefly, until dough forms into a smooth ball. Cover and set aside at room temperature for about 30 minutes.

Divide the dough into four equal portions. Working one at a time, and leaving the others covered, roll out the dough on a lightly floured work surface, into a 20–25 cm (8–10 in) circle. Spread one-quarter of the olive paste over the dough. Roll the dough up into a long, thin cigar shape, then coil the dough from one end to make a snail shape, tucking the end in. Repeat with the remaining dough and olive paste.

Now use a floured rolling pin to roll the snails into flat circles, about 15 cm (6 in) across.

Preheat the barbecue hotplate to medium. (If you are cooking this bread on a grill, you will need to put it in the freezer until firm.)

Drizzle the oil over the hotplate, then sit one bread on top. Cook for 3–5 minutes on each side, turning every minute, until golden and slightly puffed. (If it starts to burn, reduce the temperature to low–medium.) Cook the remaining breads in the same way. Serve hot, torn or cut into wedges.

FLAVOURS OF INDIA **PIZZA**

Have you ever tried freshly made naan bread? It's pretty good, but not an easy thing to whip up at home. Well, not for most of us anyway. I wouldn't suggest that we only ever cook with ready-made items, but they do have their place. Convenience is one thing, and some of the packet naan out there are okay if they are reheated – so using them for a pizza base seems only logical. And tasty.

SERVES 4

250 ml (9 fl oz/1 cup) tomato passata
   (puréed tomatoes)
½ teaspoon fennel seeds
½ teaspoon ground cumin
½ teaspoon chilli flakes
½ teaspoon sea salt
4 naan or roti, each about 15 cm
   (6 in) long
1 zucchini (courgette), very
   thinly sliced
1 small red capsicum (pepper),
   thinly sliced
1 small red onion, very thinly sliced
100 g (3½ oz) paneer (Indian cottage
   cheese), roughly crumbled
coriander (cilantro) leaves, to garnish
lime pickle, to serve

Preheat the barbecue grill to medium.

Combine the tomato passata, fennel, cumin, chilli flakes and salt in a small bowl.

Sit each naan bread on a double-thickness sheet of baking paper – this will make it easier to lift the pizzas on and off the barbecue grill. Spread the tomato mixture over each naan. Randomly scatter the zucchini, capsicum and onion over the top, then scatter with the paneer.

Put the pizzas on the grill, then close the barbecue lid if you have one, or cover the pizzas with a baking tray. Cook for 10 minutes. Lift up the pizzas with a metal spatula to see how they are cooking underneath, just like they do with wood-fired pizzas – a toasty golden brown base is what you are looking for.

Scatter with coriander leaves and serve warm, with lime pickle on the side.

AFGHANI **FLATBREADS**

These are big, rustic, easy-to-make breads. They are really another version of naan, with the option of making them bigger and thinner than the typical naan.

MAKES 2 LOAVES

1 tablespoon instant dried yeast
750 g (1 lb 10 oz/5 cups) plain (all-purpose) flour, plus extra for dusting
75 g (2½ oz/⅓ cup) caster (superfine) sugar
1 tablespoon sea salt
60 ml (2 fl oz/¼ cup) rice bran oil or grapeseed oil, plus extra for brushing

Combine the yeast and 60 ml (2 fl oz/¼ cup) warm water in a small bowl. Cover and leave somewhere warmish and draught-free for 10–15 minutes, or until it is frothy and spongy-looking.

Put the flour, sugar and salt into the bowl of an electric mixer fitted with a dough hook. With the motor running on low, add the yeast mixture, then add 750 ml (26 fl oz/3 cups) warm water, then the oil. Knead for about 10 minutes, or until smooth and elastic. (Alternatively, mix the dough together, turn out onto a clean work surface and knead the dough by hand for 10 minutes.)

Put the dough in a large lightly oiled bowl. Cover and leave for about 1 hour, or until the dough has doubled in size and looks soft and pillow-like.

Divide the dough in half, then roll out each half on a well-floured work surface, into large, flat circles about 20 cm (8 in) in diameter. Put the dough onto a lightly greased sheet of baking paper, then use your fingers to press the dough all over, making dozens of little divots in the dough.

Preheat the barbecue hotplate to high. Put a baking rack on the hotplate. Use the baking paper to lift one round of dough onto the baking rack. Close the lid of the barbecue to create an oven effect. (If your barbecue doesn't have a lid, cover the dough with a baking tray.) Cook for 10–15 minutes, or until the dough is golden. Brush the top side of the dough with a little oil, flip it over, then cover and cook for another 5 minutes, or until golden on both sides.

Cook the remaining dough in the same manner. Serve warm.

NAAN

This Indian bread can be flavoured with a whole bunch of ingredients: nuts, dried fruit, herbs. But I like my naan unflavoured so I can really appreciate its simplicity. What I most love to do with this bread is mop up any sauce left over from a curry.

MAKES 6

1 teaspoon instant dried yeast
300 g (10½ oz/2 cups) plain
    (all-purpose) flour, plus extra
    for dusting
1 teaspoon caster (superfine) sugar
1 teaspoon sea salt
½ teaspoon baking powder
2 tablespoons rice bran oil, plus extra
    for drizzling
70 g (2½ oz/¼ cup) plain yoghurt

Pour 185 ml (6 fl oz/¾ cup) warm water into a bowl or jug and stir in the yeast. Set aside for a couple of minutes.

Combine the flour, sugar, salt and baking powder in a large bowl. Add the oil and yoghurt and combine with one hand. Add the yeast mixture and continue mixing with one hand to make a wet dough.

Lightly oil your hands, then form the dough into a ball. Place in a bowl, cover and set aside for 3–4 hours, or until the dough has doubled in size.

Lightly oil your hands again and divide the dough into six equal portions. Toss each one in flour to coat, then pull and stretch each piece on a lightly floured surface to make an oval shape about 20 cm (8 in) long.

Preheat a barbecue grill to high. Sit a large heavy-based baking tray on the grill and give it time to heat. Drizzle over some oil to lightly grease it.

Using an oven mitt, remove the tray from the grill, then carefully lay three of the naan on the hot tray. Use the flat side of a knife or the back of a spoon to press the dough into the tray. The dough will start cooking on the hot tray.

Sit the tray back on the hot grill and cook the naan for 4–5 minutes, or until crisp and golden underneath and the tops are puffing up. Turn and then cook for another 2–3 minutes, or until golden and cooked through. Keep the naan in a warm place.

Cook the remaining naan in the same manner. Serve warm.

PIADINI STUFFED WITH MANCHEGO AND PARSLEY

Piadini is a type of unleavened Italian flatbread. Its rustic nature lends itself perfectly to rustic flavours: onion, herbs and hard cheeses.

SERVES 4

450 g (1 lb/3 cups) plain (all-purpose) flour
2 teaspoons sea salt
2 tablespoons Spanish vinegar
60 ml (2 fl oz/¼ cup) extra virgin olive oil, plus extra, for brushing
2–6 tablespoons cold water
150 g (5½ oz) manchego cheese, coarsely grated
4 tablespoons flat-leaf (Italian) parsley, finely chopped
1 small red onion, finely sliced
lemon wedges, to serve

Put the flour and salt in a food processor and whiz to combine. With the motor running, add the vinegar, oil and enough cold water to bring the mixture together into large crumbs – you may need as little as 2 tablespoons cold water, or up to about 6 tablespoons.

Tip the mixture out onto a floured surface and knead for 8–10 minutes, until smooth. Wrap the dough in plastic wrap and set aside in a warmish place while you prepare all the other ingredients.

Combine the cheese, parsley and onion in a bowl.

Preheat the barbecue hotplate to high.

Cut the dough into four even portions. Roll each dough portion on a floured surface into a long oval shape, about 40 cm (16 in) long and 15 cm (6 in) wide. Brush each round with olive oil.

Sprinkle the cheese mixture over two of the rounds, then top these with one of the other bread rounds to make a sandwich. Press the edges to seal them together.

Cook the piadini on the hotplate one at a time for 4–5 minutes, or until golden and crisp underneath. Flip the bread over and cook for another 3–4 minutes, or until golden.

Cut into wedges, or whatever shapes you prefer, and then serve warm, with lemon wedges.

CORN GRIDDLE BREADS

These could be called griddle cakes or even corn fritters. When these breads are kept very flat, I like to use them as I would any soft flatbread – they are soft enough to fold around grilled vegies, or scoop up dips, sauces and mayonnaise. Or you can top them with a simple fried egg or spicy Mexican beans. Yum.

MAKES 4

150 g (5½ oz/1 cup) plain
    (all-purpose) flour
2 teaspoons baking powder
¼ teaspoon sweet paprika, plus extra
    for sprinkling
½ teaspoon sea salt
1 egg, lightly beaten
185 ml (6 fl oz/¾ cup) milk
125 g (4½ oz/½ cup) creamed corn
2 tablespoons melted butter
vegetable oil, for brushing
good-quality mayonnaise, to serve
1 spring onion (scallion), thinly sliced,
    to serve

Combine the flour, baking powder, paprika and salt in a bowl, then make a well in the centre.

In another bowl, combine the egg, milk and creamed corn.

Pour the mixture into the flour well with the melted butter and use a fork to combine.

Preheat the barbecue hotplate to medium and lightly brush with oil.

Pour or ladle the batter, using about 125 ml (4 fl oz/½ cups) for each griddle bread, onto the hotplate, leaving some room between each to expand. You should have enough batter for four griddle breads.

Use the back of the spoon to spread each one out into a circle about 12–15 cm (4½–6 in) across. Cook for 4–5 minutes, or until bubbles form around the edges.

Flip them over and cook for another 2–3 minutes, or until golden and cooked through.

Serve warm, topped with a dollop of mayonnaise, some spring onion and a sprinkling of paprika.

INDIAN BREAD WITH TRUCK-STOP POTATOES

In India, local roadside restaurants, usually located at highway truck-stops, are called dhabas. I guess the equivalent in the West would be roadside cafes. Give me the food in a dhaba any time, which is typically home-made and heavily spiced – just how I like it. The bread you find in a dhaba would be yeasted and stuffed with the potatoes. I have adapted this recipe to use ready-made, yeast-free flatbread. Quick, easy and extremely tasty.

SERVES 6–8

2 large boiling potatoes, such as desiree (about 600 g / 1 lb 5 oz), cut into quarters
1 teaspoon sea salt
½ teaspoon dried mango powder (see Note)
½ teaspoon chilli powder
1 teaspoon toasted cumin seeds
1 teaspoon garam masala
1 cup coriander (cilantro) leaves and stalks, finely chopped
1 large green chilli, finely chopped
8 ready-made, yeast-free roti
Indian fruit chutney or pickle, to serve

Peel the potatoes and place in a saucepan. Add enough cold water to just cover them and place over high heat. When the water boils, cover the pan and turn the heat off. Leave for 20 minutes, or until the potatoes are tender but not falling apart. (This is also a great way to cook potatoes for a potato salad – they always have the perfect firmness!)

Drain the potatoes and allow to cool to room temperature. When cool enough to handle, coarsely grate the potatoes into a bowl. Add the salt, spices, coriander and chilli and stir until just combined.

Preheat the barbecue hotplate to medium.

Spread half the potato mixture over a piece of roti and lay another on top. Press down gently to join the two together. Repeat to make another three potato breads.

Cook the breads on the hotplate until just golden on both sides. Cut into thick wedges and serve warm, with your favourite Indian chutney or pickle.

NOTE Also called amchur or amchoor, dried mango powder is made from ground dried green mangoes and is used in northern Indian cookery to add a tangy, sour fruit flavour to dishes. You'll find it in Indian grocery stores and good spice shops.

FLATBREADS WITH PANEER AND GREEN CHILLI

It wasn't until I began researching recipes for this book that I realised how many varieties of bread are actually made in India – breads of different grains, both leavened and unleavened, with or without egg or dairy, oil, spices and even with nuts. I wouldn't say no to any of them. This bread is a type of kulcha, the sister of naan, made with baking soda rather than yeast. Both naan and kulcha can be served plain, or filled with whatever you like.

MAKES 8

300 g (10½ oz/2 cups) plain
   (all-purpose) flour, plus extra,
   for dusting
½ teaspoon sea salt
1 teaspoon sugar
½ teaspoon bicarbonate of soda
   (baking soda)
330 g (11½ oz/1¼ cups) plain yoghurt
2 tablespoons rice bran oil
lemon wedges, to serve

**PANEER AND GREEN
CHILLI FILLING**
1 small red onion, finely chopped
2 long green chillies, finely sliced
2 tablespoons coriander (cilantro)
   leaves and stalks, finely chopped,
   plus extra leaves, to garnish
100 g (3½ oz) paneer (Indian cottage
   cheese), roughly grated

Combine the flour, salt, sugar and bicarbonate of soda in a bowl and make a well in the centre. Add the yoghurt to the well and use your hands to combine – the dough will be sticky and wet.

Make another well in the centre and add the oil. Work the oil into the dough until the dough is smooth and shiny. Cover and set aside for 30 minutes, for the yoghurt and soda to react.

Put the filling ingredients into a bowl and then combine well.

Form the dough into eight balls, about the size of golf balls. On a lightly floured surface, roll each ball into a flat circle, about 10 cm (4 in) across. Put one-eighth of the paneer mixture into the centre of each, then bring the sides of the dough together to enclose the filling.

Again, on a lightly floured surface, roll each of the dough rounds into circles no thicker than 5 mm (¼ in). Place them on a lightly greased sheet of baking paper, then cover with a cloth or plastic wrap. Set aside for about 30 minutes, or until slightly risen.

Preheat the barbecue hotplate to high. Close the lid to create an oven effect.

Using the baking paper, lift the dough rounds onto the hotplate. Close the lid and cook for 3–4 minutes on each side, or until golden and cooked through. Serve hot, with lemon wedges.

BAG OF TRICKS

JALAPEÑO JAM

If chilli is your thing, this jam is for you. Spread it over chargrilled bread and spoon over some cottage cheese to cool the heat, or smear it over grilled corn cobs and squeeze some lime juice over to tang it all up a bit. Try sandwiching a layer of the jam and some grated feta cheese between two soft burritos and cook onthe barbecue hotplate until golden and crisp. Or just keep it in the fridge and put it on anything you like.

SERVES 8–10

500 g (1 lb 2 oz) green chillies
   (about 24)
2 garlic cloves
270 g (9½ oz) jar sliced jalapeño
   chillies, in vinegar
½ teaspoon sea salt
220 g (7¾ oz/1 cup) sugar
chargrilled bread, to serve
chargrilled vegetables, to serve

Preheat the barbecue grill and hotplate to high.

Leave the ends of the chillies intact and scatter the chillies over the hotplate and grill. Cook for 10–15 minutes, using metal tongs to frequently turn the chillies, removing them from the barbecue as they start to blister and char.

When cool enough to handle, peel off as much of the charred skin as possible. (Leaving some burnt bits is fine as they will add to the final flavour of the jam.)

Pull off and discard the chilli stems. Roughly chop the chillies, then place in a food processor with the garlic. Add the whole jar of jalapeños, including the liquid, and blitz until finely chopped.

Tip the chilli paste into a saucepan and stir in the salt and sugar. Bring to the boil, then reduce the heat to a low simmer and cook for 30 minutes, stirring occasionally, until the mixture is thick and sticky-looking. You can test if the jam is ready by placing a spoonful on a cold plate. Run your finger through the middle of the jam — if the mixture stays where it is, the jam is ready. Serve with chargrilled bread and vegetables.

NOTE The jam will keep in an airtight container in the fridge for up to 10 days.

EASY **BÉARNAISE**

Does just seeing the words 'double' and 'boiler' send you running the other way? Yeah, I know we ought not dumb down cooking too much but if there is an easier way, just do it. And besides, food processors were not invented when many of the classic recipes were. Having said this, you do need a patient, steady hand when adding the hot butter to the eggs. This will keep in the fridge and is good cold. It does get tricky trying to reheat this without it doing weird things. But an old catering trick of mine is to store the sauce in a thermos and it will keep warm for a few hours.

SERVES 4

3 large egg yolks
1 tablespoon tarragon vinegar
250 g (9 oz/1 cup) unsalted butter
1 tablespoon finely chopped tarragon
2 spring onions (scallions),
   finely sliced

Put the egg yolks and vinegar in a food processor and pulse a few times.

Heat the butter in a small saucepan until it is bubbling hot and frothed, but do be careful it does not burn. While the butter is hot, and with the motor running, carefully start to pour the hot butter into the food processor in a steady stream until it is all incorporated. Put into a bowl and put plastic food wrap on top of the sauce. Cover with plastic wrap.

Refrigerate until chilled and thickened, then stir through the tarragon and spring onions.

HOME-MADE **SWEET CHILLI SAUCE**

You would see this as nam jim on a Thai menu. The ingredients are all very easy to track down and the end result really is a very authentic-tasting sweet chilli sauce that can sit on the table in a bowl and be enjoyed by the spoonful!

SERVES 4

6 coriander (cilantro) roots and
    4–5 cm (1¾–2 in) of the stem,
    washed and chopped
4 garlic cloves, chopped
2 large red chillies, chopped
375 ml (13 fl oz/1½ cups)
    white vinegar
440 g (15½ oz/2 cups) sugar

Put the coriander roots into a mortar with the garlic, chillies and a generous pinch of sea salt. Pound with a pestle until you have a murky-looking paste.

Put the vinegar and sugar in a saucepan with 375 ml (13 fl oz/1½ cups) of water and bring to the boil, stirring until the sugar has dissolved. Add the paste and reduce the heat to a steady but rapid simmer for 10 to 15 minutes, until the sauce is syrupy. Pour into jars and allow to cool.

This sauce will keep in the fridge for a couple of days.

ARABIAN **SPICE MIX**

This is my simplified version of za'atar, a Middle Eastern spice blend. Okay, so the spice mix isn't actually cooked on the barbecue, but it's such a fabulous accompaniment to barbecued foods that I just had to include it. It's particularly delicious sprinkled over chargrilled bread and sliced vine-ripened tomatoes.

MAKES ABOUT ½ CUP

2 tablespoons sesame seeds
2 tablespoons dried thyme
2 tablespoons sumac (see Notes)
1 teaspoon sea salt
grilled flatbreads, to serve
extra virgin olive oil, to serve

Put the sesame seeds in a small dry frying pan over medium heat. Cook, shaking the pan regularly, until evenly golden. Tip into a bowl and allow to cool.

Put the sesame seeds, thyme, sumac and salt in a spice mill and process into a rough powder, or grind to a rough powder using a mortar and pestle. Serve sprinkled on grilled flatbreads dipped in olive oil.

NOTES Store any unused spice mix in an airtight container in a cool, dark place. It will keep for several months, but is best used within a few weeks for maximum flavour.

Sumac is a spice ground from a purple berry, widely used in Middle Eastern cuisine. It has a pleasantly astringent lemony flavour and is available from specialty grocers.

ROASTED **GARLIC CRÈME**

Similar to an aïoli, this luscious mayo is fabulous with grilled vegetables, especially root vegies.

SERVES 6–8

2 garlic bulbs, left whole
    and unpeeled
½ teaspoon sea salt
250 ml (9 fl oz/1 cup) rice bran oil
2 egg yolks, at room temperature
1 teaspoon mustard powder
2 tablespoons lemon juice

Preheat the barbecue hotplate to medium.

Cut each garlic bulb in half horizontally through the middle. Sit each garlic half, cut side up, on a small sheet of foil. Sprinkle with the salt and drizzle with some of the oil. Loosely wrap each garlic half in the foil and sit them on the hotplate. Cook for 30 minutes, turning often with tongs, until the garlic is very soft.

Remove from the heat and allow the garlic to cool in the foil. Squeeze the softened garlic flesh out of the skins, directly into the bowl of a food processor, discarding the skins. Add the egg yolks, mustard powder and lemon juice and pulse to combine.

With the motor running, gradually add the remaining oil in a thin, steady stream and process until the mixture is emulsified and looks like thick custard. Add about 60 ml (2 fl oz/¼ cup) of warm water and blend until smooth and creamy. Serve warm, or cover and keep in the fridge for up to 3 days.

PUMPKIN, BLACK BEAN AND **FETA DIP**

This dip is a cinch. You take one really nice-looking pumpkin and cook it on the grill until the skin is blackened – for about an hour, give or take. There is no strict timing here, it depends on the size and shape of the pumpkin. The inspiration came from my Barbie Ghanoush recipe, where the eggplant (aubergine) is kept whole and simply cooked on a grill. That recipe is on page 374. Check it out.

SERVES 8–10

1 butternut pumpkin (squash), about 1.5 kg (3 lb 5 oz)
2 tablespoons olive oil
1 teaspoon ground cumin
½ teaspoon cayenne pepper
400 g (14 oz) tinned black beans, rinsed and well drained
100 g (3½ oz) feta cheese, crumbled
½ cup chopped coriander (cilantro) leaves and stalks
½ teaspoon sea salt
extra virgin olive oil, for drizzling
chargrilled bread, to serve

Preheat the barbecue grill to medium.

Sit the pumpkin on the grill and close the lid, if you have one, or cover with a metal bowl. Cook for about 1 hour, turning often until the skin of the pumpkin is blackened all over. Remove pumpkin from the grill and allow to cool slightly.

When cool enough to handle, peel the tough skin off the pumpkin and discard it. Cut the pumpkin lengthways down the middle and scoop out the seeds.

Roughly chop the flesh of the pumpkin and place in a large bowl. Add the olive oil, cumin, cayenne pepper, beans, feta, coriander and salt and use a fork to combine. Drizzle with extra virgin olive oil and serve with chargrilled bread.

NOTE This dip will keep in an airtight container in the fridge for 2–3 days.

SMOKY **TOMATO RELISH**

There isn't a better place to put food snobbery aside than at the barbecue. I was enjoying one of the best Good Friday barbecue get togethers at a friend's. As a starter to enjoy with drinks the hosts simply had plain corn chips with the best-tasting home-made dips – hummus, guacamole and a really fresh-tasting salsa. The salsa had all the usual suspects like tomatoes, coriander and red onion, but the flavour was something else. I was trying to pick what it was and was blown away when I was informed the secret ingredient was actually tomato sauce. And why not? Everyone has some.

SERVES 4

4 tomatoes, not too ripe
4 garlic cloves
1 large red chilli
6 large spring onions (scallions)
1 tablespoon tomato sauce (ketchup)
1 large handful coriander (cilantro),
   roughly chopped

Preheat the barbecue hotplate to high.

Put the tomatoes, garlic, chilli and spring onions on the barbecue and cook until the skins of each are evenly blackened, turning often. Remove them from the barbecue and set aside until cool enough to handle. You still want them to be warm, though.

Remove the charred skin from the garlic, chilli and spring onions and roughly chop. Roughly chop the tomatoes, leaving their skins on as this gives the smoky flavour you are after here. Pound the garlic, chilli, spring onion, tomatoes and a good pinch of sea salt with a mortar and pestle until you have a chunky relish, and add the tomato sauce. Stir through the coriander just before serving.

NO FRILLS **HOLLANDAISE**

No frills because you don't need a double boiler, and no frills because it saves on washing up. Dip in some potato wedges, hot off the grill.

MAKES ABOUT 250 ML (9 FL OZ/1 CUP)

2 egg yolks, at room temperature
½ teaspoon sea salt
60 ml (2 fl oz/¼ cup) rice bran oil
125 g (4½ oz) unsalted butter
2 tablespoons tarragon vinegar

Put the egg yolks and salt in a food processor and whiz to combine. With the motor running, slowly add the oil in a thin, steady stream and process until the mixture thickens slightly.

Put the butter in a small saucepan and cook over medium heat until bubbling hot, but not burnt. Pour butter into a jug.

With the motor running, slowly pour the hot butter into the egg mixture. Add the vinegar and process until the mixture resembles custard. Serve the hollandaise warm, or pour into an airtight container and keep in the fridge for up to 3 days.

TZATZIKI

This dip is best enjoyed as soon as it is made. It's great with falafel – either dip the falafel straight in, or smear the tzatziki over flatbread before wrapping up some lightly mashed falafel, fresh tomato and crisp lettuce.

SERVES 8

390 g (13¾ oz/1½ cups)
    Greek-style yoghurt
2 garlic cloves, crushed
1 teaspoon ground cumin
½ teaspoon sea salt
1 Lebanese (short) cucumber,
    coarsely grated

Combine the yoghurt, garlic, cumin and salt in a bowl. Stir the cucumber through just before serving

MUHUMARRA

There are many versions of this dip in Syria, although the combination of roasted red capsicums, walnuts and pomegranate molasses can be found in other parts of the Middle East, especially Turkey and Lebanon. Traditionally, this dip contains breadcrumbs. I have not included them here, so this version is coeliac friendly.

SERVES 6–8

3 large red capsicums (peppers)
35 g (1¼ oz/¼ cup) walnuts
1 teaspoon ground cumin
½ teaspoon cayenne pepper
2 tablespoons pomegranate molasses
2 tablespoons lemon juice

Preheat the barbecue grill to high.

Cook the capsicums on the barbecue grill for 10–15 minutes, turning often, until the skins are blistered and blackened all over. Remove from the barbecue and allow to cool.

When cool enough to handle, peel and discard the skins. Cut the capsicums in half, scoop out and discard the seeds.

Roughly chop the capsicum flesh and place in a food processor with the remaining ingredients. Process to a smooth, thick mixture. Spoon into a serving dish and serve.

NOTE This dip will keep in an airtight container in the fridge for about 1 week.

CHIMICHURRI

Chimichurri is an Argentinian salsa verde or, simply put, green sauce. But this herbaceous green sauce is more rugged than its European counterparts. Some say chimichurri should taste like it has been dragged through the herb garden, and that's a pretty good description.

SERVES 8–10

1 large, ripe tomato
4 spring onions (scallions)
4 garlic cloves, unpeeled
6 cups roughly chopped flat-leaf (Italian) parsley
2 cups chopped coriander (cilantro) leaves and stalks
½ teaspoon dried Greek oregano (see Notes)
½ teaspoon sea salt
60 ml (2 fl oz/¼ cup) olive oil
60 ml (2 fl oz/¼ cup) white wine vinegar
chargrilled potato wedges, to serve (see Notes)

Preheat the barbecue grill to high.

Place the tomato, spring onions and garlic on the grill. Use metal tongs to turn the vegies until the skins are charred – almost blackened – all over. Remove from the heat and allow to cool.

When cool enough to handle, peel the vegies and garlic and then discard the charred skins. Don't be too fussy about removing all the skins – they'll add a smoky flavour.

Place all the vegies and the garlic in a food processor and blitz until finely chopped. Add the herbs, oregano and salt and pulse to combine.

With the motor running, add the oil, then the vinegar, to make a smooth sauce.

Serve with chargrilled potato wedges as a dip, or spoon over chargrilled eggplant (aubergine).

NOTES The chimichurri will keep in an airtight container in the fridge for 2–3 days.

For this recipe I prefer to use Greek oregano, sold in bunches with the leaves and stems still intact. It is sweeter and somehow less medicinal tasting than the pre-packaged stuff.

To chargrill potato wedges, first parboil them until nearly tender, then drain well and allow to cool completely on a tray. Chargrill them on a hot barbecue grill for a few minutes on each side before serving.

BARBIE **GHANOUSH**

This one is made for the barbecue. Actually, I don't believe you can achieve the same flavour without cooking the eggplant over a naked flame. The smokiness of the charred skin somehow gets into the flesh of the eggplant with really very little cooking time.

SERVES 6–8

2 large eggplant (aubergines)
2 teaspoons sea salt
60 ml (2 fl oz/¼ cup) lemon juice
3 garlic cloves, crushed
2 tablespoons extra virgin olive oil,
    plus extra for drizzling
chargrilled Middle Eastern
    flatbread, to serve

Preheat the barbecue grill to high.

Prick each eggplant several times with a fork. Cook them on the barbecue grill for 10–15 minutes, turning often, until collapsed and tender. Remove from the barbecue and allow to cool on a tray.

When cool enough to handle, strip off and discard the skin of each eggplant. Place the flesh in a sieve over a bowl and set aside for 15 minutes to drain.

Put the eggplant flesh in a food processor with the salt, lemon juice, garlic and olive oil. Whiz to a purée, then pour the mixture into a bowl and drizzle with a little more olive oil.

Serve at room temperature, with chargrilled flatbread.

NOTE The barbie ghanoush will keep in an airtight container in the fridge for 2–3 days.

GREEN TOMATO AND **CAPERBERRY SALSA**

This salsa, or sauce, is great spooned over barbecued haloumi, tofu or firm mozzarella cheese. Try tumbling corn chips onto a serving plate and simply topping them with this salsa and some light sour cream. Very nice.

SERVES 6–8

4 green tomatoes, cores removed, flesh finely diced
80 g (2¾ oz/½ cup) caperberries, chopped
1 red onion, finely diced
60 ml (2 fl oz/¼ cup) white vinegar
½ teaspoon sea salt
½ teaspoon caster (superfine) sugar
½ cup finely chopped coriander (cilantro) leaves and stalks
½ cup finely chopped mint
grilled haloumi, to serve

Combine all the ingredients in a serving bowl. Cover and set aside for 30 minutes for the flavours to develop.

Serve at room temperature, spooned over the haloumi.

NOTE The salsa will keep in an airtight container in the fridge for 2–3 days.

GRILLED SWEETCORN AND
SOUR CREAM DIP

I have a café in the grounds of an art gallery. We made this dip to be photographed and afterwards I served it up to the staff at the gallery. Wow, what a positive response this one received. I served the dip with a crusty baked baguette and it was devoured in no time.

SERVES 6–8

4 whole fresh corn cobs,
   preferably unpeeled
1 tablespoon rice bran oil
2 teaspoons dijon mustard
1 red onion, sliced into thick rings
½ cup finely chopped coriander
   (cilantro) leaves and stalks, plus
   extra leaves to garnish
3 tablespoons chopped flat-leaf
   (Italian) parsley
1 tablespoon white wine vinegar
½ teaspoon hot pepper sauce, plus
   extra for drizzling
1 teaspoon sea salt
370 g (12¾ oz/1½ cups) sour cream
warm flatbread, to serve

Preheat the barbecue grill to high.

Peel the corn and discard the husks. Brush the corn with the oil and the mustard. Brush the onion rings on both sides with the oil. Grill the corn and onion for 10–12 minutes, or until golden, turning often. Remove from the barbecue and allow to cool.

Cut the kernels from the cobs and place in a food processor. Roughly chop the onions and add them with the coriander, parsley, vinegar, pepper sauce and salt. Whiz until well combined but not too finely chopped – you want some texture in the dip. Just before serving, combine the corn mixture and the sour cream in a bowl. Drizzle with extra pepper sauce, garnish with extra coriander and serve with warm flatbread.

SMOKY TOMATO, GARLIC AND LIME **SALSA**

Thai food was one of my first cuisine crushes, and this recipe is one of the oldest in my repertoire. The Thai version of this salsa would include fish sauce and lime juice. You can just imagine how good that would be, too.

SERVES 4–6

4 vine-ripened tomatoes
2 large green chillies, finely sliced
2 garlic cloves, roughly chopped
2 tablespoons lime juice
½ teaspoon sea salt
1 teaspoon caster (superfine) sugar
30 g (1 oz/½ cup) thinly sliced spring
  onions (scallions)
1 cup roughly chopped coriander
  (cilantro) leaves and stalks
organic corn chips, to serve

Preheat the barbecue grill and hotplate to high.

Put the tomatoes on the grill and cook, turning often, so the skin blisters and blackens. Remove from the heat and leave until cool enough to handle.

Cut out and discard the core of each tomato. Cut the tomatoes in half and then gently squeeze out some of the liquid and seeds.

Put the tomatoes, including any bits of burnt skin, in a food processor with the chilli and garlic. Blitz until finely chopped, then spoon into a bowl. Stir in the the lime juice, the salt, the sugar, the spring onion and the coriander. Check the taste and add more salt if needed.

Loosely wrap the corn chips in foil. Sit the foil parcel on the barbecue hotplate for a couple of minutes to heat through. Serve the dip with the warm corn chips on the side.

INDEX

INDEX

Published in 2014 by Murdoch Books, an imprint of Allen & Unwin

Murdoch Books Australia
83 Alexander Street
Crows Nest NSW 2065
Phone: +61 (0) 2 8425 0100
Fax: +61 (0) 2 9906 2218
www.murdochbooks.com.au
info@murdochbooks.com.au

Murdoch Books UK
Erico House, 6th Floor
93–99 Upper Richmond Road
Putney, London SW15 2TG
Phone: +44 (0) 20 8785 5995
www.murdochbooks.co.uk
info@murdochbooks.co.uk

For Corporate Orders & Custom Publishing contact
Noel Hammond, National Business Development Manager, Murdoch Books Australia

Publisher: Diana Hill
Design Manager: Hugh Ford
Designer: Katy Wall
Stylists: Lynsey Fryers, Sarah O'Brien and Matt Page
Editors: Liz Malcolm and Shan Wolody
Editorial Manager: Barbara McClenahan
Production Manager: Mary Bjelobrk

Text © Ross Dobson 2014
The moral rights of the author have been asserted.
Design © Murdoch Books 2014
Photography © Nicky Ryan and Brett Stephens 2014

Photographic credits
Nicky Ryan 3, 11, 16, 19, 24, 28, 31, 42, 50, 55, 56, 59, 63, 68, 72, 75, 78, 83, 88, 91, 92, 95, 99, 108, 119, 120, 126, 130, 144, 148, 158, 164, 169, 174, 176, 187, 191, 195, 199, 200, 203, 217, 218, 221, 235, 236, 242, 245, 251, 255, 263, 267, 272, 279, 286, 300, 305, 309, 312, 321, 327, 331, 335, 375, 380, 390, 391.
Brett Stephens cover, 6, 9, 15, 20, 23, 27, 32, 35, 36, 41, 47, 60, 64, 67, 71, 81, 82, 87, 96, 100, 103, 104, 107, 111, 112, 115, 123, 133, 134, 137, 138, 141, 147, 151, 154, 157, 163, 175, 178, 179, 183, 184, 188, 192, 204, 209, 210, 213, 214, 224, 227, 228, 231, 241, 246, 247, 252, 259, 260, 264, 268, 271, 275, 276, 278, 283, 291, 294, 297, 306, 315, 316, 322, 322, 338, 341, 345, 348, 351, 354, 359, 363, 368, 376, 381.

Recipes in this book have been previously published in *Fired Up*, *More Fired Up*, *Fired Up Vegetarian* and *Grillhouse*.

A cataloguing-in-publication entry is available from the catalogue of the National Library of Australia at www.nla.gov.au.

ISBN 978 1 74336 468 0 Australia
ISBN 978 1 74336 474 1 UK

A catalogue record for this book is available from the British Library.

Colour reproduction by Splitting Image Colour Studio Pty Ltd, Clayton, Victoria
Printed by 1010 Printing International Limited, China

IMPORTANT: Those who might be at risk from the effects of salmonella poisoning (the elderly, pregnant women, young children and those suffering from immune deficiency diseases) should consult their doctor with any concerns about eating raw eggs.

OVEN GUIDE: You may find cooking times vary depending on the oven you are using. For fan-forced ovens, as a general rule, set the oven temperature to 20°C (35°F) lower than indicated in the recipe.

MEASURES GUIDE: We have used 20 ml (4 teaspoon) tablespoon measures. If you are using a 15 ml (3 teaspoon) tablespoon add an extra teaspoon of the ingredient for each tablespoon specified.